SHIRLEY
AND
PIPSI...

IN THEIR OWN WORDS

BY

SHIRLEY J. HALL

Enjoy!

Shirley Hall.

DEDICATED TO ALL LOVERS, YOUNG AND OLD

Co-authored by: Sylvia L. Paymer
Edited by: Judith G. Cope
Cover Design by: Shirley J. Hall
Back Cover Photography by: Valerie A. Kelly Top Photo - 2007
                           Cathy Conheim Bottom Photo - 2008

Note for Librarians: A cataloguing record for this book is available from Library
and Archives Canada at www.collectionscanada.ca/amicus/index-e.html

Printed in Victoria, BC, Canada.

ISBN: 978-1-4251-6518-5

*We at Trafford believe that it is the responsibility of us all, as both individuals
and corporations, to make choices that are environmentally and socially sound.
You, in turn, are supporting this responsible conduct each time you purchase a
Trafford book, or make use of our publishing services. To find out how you are
helping, please visit www.trafford.com/responsiblepublishing.html*

*Our mission is to efficiently provide the world's finest, most comprehensive
book publishing service, enabling every author to experience success.
To find out how to publish your book, your way, and have it available
worldwide, visit us online at www.trafford.com/10510*

 www.trafford.com

North America & international
toll-free: 1 888 232 4444 (USA & Canada)
phone: 250 383 6864 ♦ fax: 250 383 6804 ♦ email: info@trafford.com

The United Kingdom & Europe
phone: +44 (0)1865 722 113 ♦ local rate: 0845 230 9601
facsimile: +44 (0)1865 722 868 ♦ email: info.uk@trafford.com

10 9 8 7 6 5 4 3

Contents

Acknowledgements

My grateful thanks to:

Gerald Gaucher and Jane Renniger, who responded immediately to my calls for help relating to computer problems.

Valerie Kelley, who supplied the original photo and the digital file for the back cover.

Judith Cope, who condensed the many original letters and tape transcripts to the selections contained in this book. She graciously gave of her time (away from her rowing activities in Ashland) to work here with me.

Our respective families and friends, who have always accepted our relationship by showing us much love and caring. You all *know* who you are.

To my darling Pipsi for her love, encouragement and patience shown to me, not only through this process, but throughout our wonderful life-partnership!

Perhaps I would never have undertaken the task of organizing these letters and compiling this book had I not been diagnosed with breast cancer in 2005 and become convinced that such a project would significantly contribute to the healing process. And surely it did. Rereading our own words has brought back many memories and rekindled, for both Pipsi and myself, the intense emotional and sensual excitement we experienced so many years ago. Thirty-six years after I sent the first note, we remain as happily in love as ever.

In April 2007 Pipsi was diagnosed with colon cancer. We continue to treasure each day together as a gift.

Shirley Hall
La Jolla, California, 2008

Introduction

EVENTS WHICH LED TO SHIRLEY'S MOVE TO SPAIN IN 1969

My ambition after growing up in the suburbs of Birmingham, England, was to see as much of the world as possible. After leaving college and having gained some teaching experience, I was successful in obtaining a contract with the Shell Oil Company to teach in their schools in Venezuela for the children of the company's expatriate employees. I arrived in Maracaibo in August 1958. I was twenty-four years old and I could not have been happier! (Upon reflection, I realize that the disintegration of my affair with my French girlfriend Desiree was the catalyst which prompted me to make that application. She married a doctor and I moved to South America.)

I found oil company life to be idyllic. Christmas and Easter vacations afforded the teachers an opportunity to explore the Caribbean and South American countries as well as areas of Venezuela. I had realized my dream. The company's contract stipulations, however, did not allow British teachers to continue their tenure, unlike the Dutch teachers whose contracts allowed them to stay indefinitely. I left Venezuela in June 1964 and accepted a post with the Iranian International Oil Company, arriving there in August. After an orientation session I was sent to the company school in Ahwaz, Khuzistan.

Social activities in oil camp life consisted of events organized at the various clubs provided by the companies in both Venezuela and Iran. These were usually a Social/Swimming Club, a Golf Club, Tennis & Squash Club and a Boat Club, to name a few. There was no television in these areas at this time. Entertainment consisted of attending cocktail or dinner parties where everyone watched home movies or slide shows or played cards. Single women outnumbered single men. As the teachers, secretaries and nurses were all in search of future husbands, it was an ideal place to be. However, for those women who were Lesbian, it was not easy, we led closeted lives.

It was while living in Ahwaz that I met Irene. She was married to a retired Army Brigadier General who worked for an American company. Irene was born in Belgium and had met her husband, who was much older than she, whilst working in Paris. It was she who initiated the more intimate friendship with me and we began spending a lot of time together She owned a horse and before long I bought one too and we spent many happy hours galloping across the desert. We became close friends and closeted lovers.

Some months had passed and it began to dawn on me that despite the fact that Irene thought that she was bisexual and had enjoyed other affairs with women, she would not consider leaving her husband and commit to a life-long Lesbian relationship. She was financially secure and comfortable with her married existence, whilst I was ready for a more permanent relationship.

That was when Delyn entered the picture. She had recently been sent to the Ahwaz school to replace the Dutch teacher who had been repatriated for medical reasons. Within a few weeks of her arrival, Delyn told me that she had also had affairs with women and that she found herself very attracted to me. (This coincided with Irene's and Peter's move to Teheran where Peter had been offered another job.) Thus began my relationship with Delyn. I had every hope that this would be a longstanding, committed relationship, despite the fact that I was to be transferred to a one-teacher school in Banda Mashah. Fortunately, I was allowed to fly by company commuter plane each week-end to Masjid-i-Sulieman where Delyn had been transferred. Then in 1968 I was also transferred to the same school in Masjid-i-Sulieman.

In 1969 our relationship began to change. One of the bachelors was ardently pursuing Delyn. What I had envisioned as a permanent relationship began to unravel. Terry was persistent in courting Delyn and I was left feeling emotionally battered. The situation took its toll on me and I felt that I could no longer remain in the close confines of the oil camp, nor give full-time attention to my teaching. I asked to be released from my contract, which was granted.

I knew that Peter and Irene were to leave Teheran for good in June and were planning to drive overland to Spain, so I asked if I could join them and then drive in convoy to Spain. They graciously agreed. To be honest, I was devastated by the fact that my relationship with Delyn was over and that I was now unemployed. I left the oil camp and spent the next two months with Irene and Peter in Teheran where we were kept busy preparing for the overland trip. (Both Irene and I had driven from Ahwaz to Paris together previously. I had also done that trip before, including driving to Holland with Delyn to meet her parents.)

Peter and Irene had decided to retire in Spain and had already purchased land there. Furthermore, we all had friends who had retired on the Costa del Sol. We arrived in August 1969 and settled into a rented house. I did not want to go to England at that time because I was still emotionally upset.

My sister was in the middle of a marital break-up with her husband and my parents were trying to help their two young grandchildren cope with the situation.

Irene and I resumed our intimate relationship. A few weeks after our arrival on the Costa del Sol, I saw a house under construction in Fuengirola, in an urbanization built in typical Andalucian-style called "Pueblo Lopez." On the spur of the moment I decided to buy it! I told myself that it would be a good investment whether I remained in Spain or not. I arranged for my personal effects in Iran to be shipped to my new home. I soon made friends with Gays and Lesbians as well as with many expatriates who had worked overseas. However, I was still without a financially rewarding job.

In 1971 Gino Hollander, an American artist, approached me and offered me the post of tutor to his three children for the forthcoming school year in September. (He had seen a show which I had written and directed, in which Lew and Jenny Hoad's children had acted, and he told me he was impressed.) I explained my financial situation and he immediately offered me the job of Manager at the gallery in the Hilton Hotel in Marbella where he exhibited his paintings. It was there that I first met Marc Neukorn, Pipsi's father, and my life changed.

HOW SHIRLEY MET MARC NEUKORN, PIPSI'S FATHER

In April, 1971 I began my job at Gino Hollander's Art Gallery at the Marbella Hilton. Gino's paintings adorned the walls of a ground-floor corridor. One afternoon, I noticed an elderly gentleman emerging from the elevator. He was dressed in a bathrobe and slippers—not quite the usual attire for that area of the hotel. Furthermore, he appeared to be somewhat disoriented and confused. Prompted by the "Good Samaritan" side of my character (which others might describe as being meddlesome), I walked over to the gentleman and asked if I could be of any assistance. He explained that he had been down in the pool area and upon returning had taken the wrong elevator and that he felt rather embarrassed to be seen near the Reception Area dressed as he was. I assured him that even in his bathrobe he looked far more elegant than most of the people standing around in the lobby. I suggested he pretend that he was Conrad Hilton himself, point his nose in the air and march down the corridor and across the Reception Area acting as if he truly owned the place! He laughed and I directed him to the elevators to take to the floor where his room was located. He thanked me profusely and marched away with his head held high.

A day later I met the gentleman again at which time he formally introduced himself as Marc Neukorn and asked if he could repay my kindness by inviting me to dinner. He assured me that I would be well chaperoned because his cousins would also be present. And so our serendipitous encounter led to a week of cocktails, dinners, laughter and great conversation.

Marc Neukorn became a father-figure whom I found to be intellectual, amusing and generous. I told him how I had ended up living in Spain and that I was a Lesbian. I learned that he lived in New York City and that ten years earlier his beloved wife, Regine, had died from congestive heart failure at the age of fifty-five. It was obvious that he still missed her dreadfully. He talked of his son Andre and his daughter Sylvia—whom he always referred to as "Pips"—and their respective families. He was proud of the fact that he was in good health at the age of seventy-five and that he walked daily from his apartment on Riverside Drive at 72nd St. to the Diamond Dealers' Club in mid-town where he still conducted his business. Over these dinners and lunches, Marc described how he and his family, including his elderly mother, had escaped from Antwerp when the Nazis invaded Belgium in May 1940. The family had left everything they owned behind in the apartment and took only what each person could carry in suitcases. Their circuitous journey took them by way of France, Spain, Morocco, back to Spain and to Portugal. In Lisbon the Neukorn family found passage aboard a ship, the *Nyassa*, bound for New York. Finally, in August 1941, some fifteen months after fleeing Antwerp, they landed safely in Manhattan and began their new lives as refugees.

I knew that I wanted to maintain the friendship with Marc. Realizing that he was a lonely man, I made the decision to write to him and mail the letters off before his vacation in Spain had ended. In this way the letters would probably arrive before he did. We corresponded regularly and our friendship continued to blossom. In May, only a few weeks later, Marc wrote that he planned to return to Spain in July and invited me to join him on a car trip through Andalucia. I eagerly awaited our sojourn, as he had already proved to be an excellent tour guide, and I was not disappointed. His breadth of knowledge and enthusiasm made European history come alive.

My parents and other family members, whose long-arranged visit overlapped with Marc's, also enjoyed his company. Our vacation was wonderful and I knew that this deepening friendship had given this lonely man a new lease on life.

When the trip was over, I thought that it was time for me to contact his daughter Pipsi. I wanted to assure her that her father (whom she addressed as "Poppy") was not running around Spain with a floozy or being taken advantage of in any way. I sent her a couple of souvenirs, together with a recording of

Joaquin Rodrigo's "Concierto de Aranjuez" and "Fantasia para un Gentilhombre" for guitar and orchestra. Marc told me that Pipsi enjoyed strumming the guitar, as did I. I explained to her in a short note enclosed in the package, which Marc would deliver on my behalf, that the "Fantasia para un Gentilhombre" was an appropriate musical description of her father, that he was not only a gentle man but also a gentleman. I could not have known that this note was the springboard for the ensuing correspondence and our future life together.

THE TIMING WAS RIGHT!
SOME OF PIPSI'S BACKGROUND PRIOR
TO AUGUST 1971

A hasty decision made by Pipsi at the age of eighteen led to her marriage to Marvin in March 1949. However, within three months she realized that she had made a mistake. Pipsi spoke to her father about her concerns but he was of little help. At his urging, she returned to Marvin. Their son Steve was born in September 1951 and David was born in August 1954. They moved to Oceanside, Long Island, NY. where their life in suburbia began. Pipsi's energy was centered upon nurturing and raising their children.

Although they lived amicably as a family, she managed to hide her marital unhappiness. Pipsi had two extramarital affairs with men, each of which proved to be totally unrewarding both emotionally and physically. It also became evident to her that her interest in women was more than superficial. She was attracted to them.

In 1958 she began a relationship with Deborah which lasted

for at least ten years. It was during this time that Pipsi decided that she would stay with Marvin (who knew nothing of these affairs) until both boys were in college. Pipsi believed that during their formative years the boys should have the close presence of their father. However, she had definitely decided that once David left for college, she would make plans to leave. In August, 1971, when Pipsi began her correspondence with me, she had been married for twenty-two years. Steve was attending college in Boston and David was a senior in high school.

Pipsi had a close relationship with her father, Marc, who visited the family regularly. He had married her mother Regine when she was eighteen and he was thirty-two. He absolutely adored Regine and was devastated when she died at the age of fifty-five, in 1961. He kept himself occupied with his work in the diamond business and he traveled often and extensively, visiting family and friends.

In April, 1971 Marc decided to take a trip to Andalucia in southern Spain. He made arrangements to stay in Marbella, knowing that his cousins, Jos and Julia, were staying close by at the Club Med. It was while staying at the Hilton there that he first met me. He returned from this holiday very excited, exhilarated and full of enthusiasm for this young woman whom he described as "a dear, sweet child." He also informed Pipsi that I was a Lesbian and explained how we had first encountered each other. Pipsi was somewhat taken aback when he told her that he had made plans to return to Spain in July for another vacation with me!

Upon his return from THAT trip, Marc went to Pipsi's for lunch and presented her with my note and the Rodrigo recording. That is how OUR correspondence began—the rest is "our story."

NOTE: Other than those of the immediate family and a few close friends, names have been changed to protect privacy.

August-September

New York   August 23, 1971

Dear Shirley,

Forgive the delay in writing you, but I didn't have your address and only saw "Poppy" (Marc) two days ago, at which time he gave it to me, together with your record and lovely note. *Tambien* (one year of Spanish in school allows me to show off once in a while), many thanks for the postcard. I had never heard of Rodrigo. I liked the "Fantasia para un Gentilhombre" very much, especially the first and last movements.

You must let me reciprocate. Do you know "Jacques Brel"? Let me know as I would like to send you that or another of my favorites.

I don't recall ever hearing so much about someone without being able to form a clear picture as to what they look like? So...I'm enclosing a photograph and am hoping that you'll do the same soon! You'll notice how clever I was in choosing it! My thighs (which are fat) and legs (which are peasant-like) and feet (pigeon-toed, alas) are hidden, while my face (the nose is not quite in the middle of the face) is hidden in the shadows, but at least you have an idea.

You ask me how I've managed Marc during all these past years? I haven't! He is still colored by the shadings of my childhood, when I used to view him as a kind but impatient man, apt to be somewhat brusque and not too interested in small children. He likes toughness. (You and I fit into this category.) He doesn't realize that this is usually a cover-up. As a child I was a tomboy, taking the greatest pleasure in giving and receiving a bloody nose and bruises!

I decapitated dolls that people would give me. Come to think of it, I used to feed them candy pills first, after which I would cut off their heads! Truly a charming child! End result? Today I despise violence, though when I lose my temper, people lock themselves in and barricade their doors. But I think that I've bored you enough for one day.

I'll be waiting to hear from you and this may turn out to be a "Madame de Sévigné" interchange[1], except that her letters were damn dull and full of idiotic advice.

And how British of you to sign your letters "Sincerest Greetings" or "Yours sincerely" etc.

Love,   Pipsi.

Spain   August 28, 1971

My Dearest Pips,

From one "tomboy" to another, please find enclosed three photographs as requested! The one with the Arab was taken in March 1968. I was crossing the desert (and I mean real desert) from Kuwait to Doha, Qatar in the Persian Gulf, and would never have made it, had it not been for the Arab in the photo. The other two photos were taken last month. One shows me holding a friend's baby. (I'm very maternal, believe it or not!) The other shows me setting up our stall of leather goods at the Hilton hotel. As you're interested in descriptions, I'm five feet, four inches, and fat, size 36C bra (very well endowed). I take size six in shoes (UK size but I have no

---

[1]   Marie de Sévigné was a prolific seventeenth-century writer whose 1700 letters shed light on the times of Louis XIV.

idea of US size). I have short brown hair and blue eyes. I have a scar on the left side of my face running down from the lower lip towards the jaw, which I got in 1947 when tobogganing.

Thank you very much for your letter. I like your sense of humor. I'm very pleased that you liked the record. I really like the Rodrigo concerto. No, I have never heard of Jacques Brel.

Oh, before I forget, I know exactly what you look like because I asked Marc to bring photos with him and he obliged.

Marc, of course, is the ideal father figure for me. I see everything in him that I have always wanted in a father, although I doubt that I would have seen these attributes if I had met him much earlier. We get on very well indeed and I love him dearly. I have a pretty good idea how his relationship has been with you. He and I discussed this earlier. I told him that I thought that perhaps due to the fact that he was so fond of his wife, and was absolutely wrapped up in her emotionally, he probably had little time for his children at a time when they needed him most? Ah well, we find these things out too late, when the damage has been done. He thinks the world of you now, of course, and is full of praise for you and yours. He thinks that you're a wonderful person and that the whole family revolves around you. I am sure that it does. I liked the look of you the first time I saw your photo.

I have never enjoyed a man's company as much as I have your father's. We walked hand in hand and arm in arm through the streets of Seville, Cordova and Granada. We joked, laughed, wined and dined, and I was sorry when it came to an end. He has spoiled me.

Yes, I saw his impatience with shopkeepers. Sometimes I rebuked him by quoting from an old Native American prayer which goes something like "Oh Great Spirit, grant that I may not criticize my neighbor until I have walked a mile in his moccasins." He agreed that I was quite right and that, indeed, I was very much like you!

And all this because I saw, and helped, a lost, bewildered man standing at the end of the corridor in the Hilton, someone who looked like a mixture of Igor Stravinsky and Mahatma Gandhi, with his white spindly legs! (He was returning from the swimming pool.)

I take up the tutoring post on Wednesday of the coming week. I will commute at first until I have managed to rent my house. I'm off to England with the Hollander children around 20 September, so I'll include various addresses where I can be reached, including that of my parents.

As for being "terribly British," you must be joking! I'm far from formal. But how the hell did I know that you are SO much like me? I suppose that I wanted to be correct. Now that I am one of the family, so to speak, and I would also like to please you, here, you can take your pick!

> *Affectionately,*
> *Fondest love,*
> *Much love,   Shirley.*

P.S. Yes, you really were a ghastly child, how did your governesses cope with you I wonder?

New York   September 3, 1971
Dear Shirley,

Curses! You have pulled the rug from under my clumpy toes. Here I am, as pleased as Punch because I graduated from a 34A to a 34B! Then you come along, blissfully bragging of your 36C bra. No wonder you are maternal!

So...tobogganing, horseback riding, cleaning pools, car racing...tell me, do you wrestle bears for relaxation? I am convinced that were I to spend one week with you and try to keep up with all this activity, an untimely end would be my destiny! Yes, we have much in common, and, yes, I do want to continue the correspondence, but don't spend your *pesetas* on express letters. I'm here, and not going anywhere.

Back to "Poppy" or Marc. I am very touched about the way you feel about him. He is, of course, quite extraordinary. He has a terrific intellect, is generous to a fault, terribly kind to those he loves. He is very impatient and not too understanding of human frailties, at least, not in the world at large. He had the unbelievable good fortune of having loved the same woman for some 37 years or more. Mind you, this, to me, is the crux of the matter—the fact that from the minute he fell in love, his love continued to grow and became stronger even during the latter years when she was no longer here. To me, this is the rare thing, because, after all, we all have been cherished at one time or another by someone, but unless one can reciprocate those feelings, it doesn't mean too much. I'm sure you know the old saying "There is always one who loves and one who lets himself be loved." But I like this one better: A well-known French writer had been involved in a deep love affair with a lady and it broke up. A friend came to him and said "But I thought you loved each other so much?" "Yes," said the writer, "but at different times."

Am I expressing myself badly? The subject of LOVE, in capitals, I think will always remain for me, slightly out of the realm of reason and reality. It's like strawberries, a whiff of them at certain times (very, very seldom) brings back a day of childhood which I taste, and then it's gone and that's it.

At any rate, I consider Marc to be very, very lucky, one of the chosen few, to really have loved.

As for my mother, I will regret to my dying day that I didn't really try harder to understand or know her better. And that, my love, is the folly of youth.

My governesses did not cope with me, I coped with them, and if I was ghastly, at least it was done with all the panache of Cyrano. (In profile I do resemble him.)

I know how busy you are, so don't worry about writing back immediately. I have your different addresses, and thank you for the choice of sweet endearments. Don't run yourself ragged. This is Tweedledee over to Tweedledum. (God, we do look a bit alike!)

With much love,   Pipsi

Spain   September 4, 1971
My Dear Pips,

Things are moving fast around here inasmuch as I'm taking the children on a trip to England as from September 20. Gino has decided that he and his wife Barbie should take the opportunity of going to New York. Hence I have to move up here sooner than I had originally planned.

I think that I'm going to enjoy this coming school year teaching these children. They are interesting kids. I'll have to brush up on my French because Lise has to study it this year.

How did you enjoy your holiday? I seem to recall that you went to Yugoslavia? I have never been on the Adriatic coast but have been right down the middle of the country quite frequently as I used to drive to Iran regularly. Teachers in oil company schools had rather long summer vacations, so I drove instead of flying to London. It was far more interesting. I have been to Rumania and Bulgaria but I was not impressed. You know, "Bread shop #45 will open between 9:00 and 10:00 am." I'm not really very politically minded. Most people seem to be making a mess of it these days. However I feel strongly about freedom of speech and the press, and England seems to give its people that if nothing else.

I presume that you know that Gino Hollander is the American artist for whom I work? He has a gallery on Madison Avenue. He will be staying there while he's in New York so if you happen to be in the city, do drop in and take a look at his work and meet them.

How old were you when you first read Kahlil Gibran? What did you write that you had published? Was it music or what?

I have decided I will visit the States next summer so I hope that you will be there and not gadding around communist countries!

Trust that you and yours are well?

Love, Shirley

Spain September 6, 1971
My Dear Pips,

As Gibran would say: "You cannot have wealth and knowledge of it at the same time; For youth is too busy living to know, and knowledge is too busy seeking itself to live."

In answer to your comments about your parents, it was quite the reverse for me as I always adored my mother and tolerated my father. My parents are very young, and to me, my mother has played the role of mother, sister and friend, whereas my father always seemed like a tiresome older brother. He was, and sometimes still is, jealous of my relationship with my mother. It is small wonder, then, that I have turned out to be as I am, a very "normal" example, a straight-out-of-the-textbook type!

As you say, Marc is one of the few people on this earth who has experienced an almost perfect relationship, who has loved and was loved. But this has also brought its problems inasmuch as I think that they, Marc and Regine, were so much aware of each other, that you two children missed out somewhere along the line. That's my thought on the matter. The great love which Marc had/has for Regine is one of the things which endeared me to him. I noticed this rare thing about him almost immediately.

I'd like to tell you that you could do far worse than to spend a week with me. I'm not sure what your destiny would be but it would not be an untimely end! And no, I do not wrestle bears for relaxation! And what do you do for relaxation? What do you DO period? Of course I realize that you have a house to run and three men to look after but what do you do other than sit by a pool and have your picture taken? Yes, I wear sunglasses all the time, otherwise I cannot see in this bright sunlight. The eyes, when seen, are fairly large, friendly and blue.

Right now the house is very quiet because Gino and Barbie have left for New York and the children went to the airport with their older brother. I'm taking advantage and writing letters, so you're in luck.

I feel that you would love it here. There is absolute quiet, disturbed only by the sound of bees. There's a comb on the roof, or rather, the remains of a comb because the other part of it has been put in the pantry to drip. I have never tasted honey collected right from the comb.

Actually you express yourself very well, and I understand but do not agree with you that "LOVE" will always remain for you slightly out of the "realm of reason and reality." You never can tell. One thing I'm sure about though, and I haven't even met you or observed, and that is you are the one who is loved. Do I make myself clear? And I wonder, if you were not the responsible sort of person you are, would you be living in Oceanside? That is not a question and it doesn't need answering, it's just me thinking out loud.

With fondest love, Shirley

New York   September 11, 1971

Pipsi's Day!

2:00 a.m.   Get up and have coffee and a cigarette preparatory to waking the boys because Marvin is taking David and Steve to Boston for the weekend. David has a college interview and Steve moves into his dorm tomorrow. He is starting his second year in college.

3:30 a.m.   They depart. Pipsi dances madly through the house. Sheer joy at the thought of being by myself for two days!

5:00 a.m.   Took a bath, did laundry, then back to bed and sleep until 7:00 a.m. I'm expecting Poppy for lunch.

8:45 a.m.   Poppy calls, he begs for a light lunch as he had dinner and drinks with Gino and Barbie and he's tired!

10:30 a.m. The mail arrives and I have time to read Shirley's pink letter, and ain't we glad that I can read it quietly and alone, by myself!

11:30 a.m. Pick up Poppy, have drinks, feast on sturgeon and smoked salmon. Talk about you. (Not your letter!) Take him back to the train early because he's tired.

4:00 p.m. A visit from my friend and ex-lyricist, Deborah. She's now a teacher and used exactly your expression ten years ago: "What I want, I want NOW!"

6:30 p.m. Write to Shirley

Dear Shirley,

If you will insist on quoting Gibran, here are a few of Oscar Wilde's epigrams in return:

"One should always be in love: that is the reason one should never marry."

"Life is a *mauvais quart d'heure* made up of exquisite moments."

"Conscience and cowardice are really the same things. Conscience is the trade name of the firm."

Untimely end or not, a week does not a destiny make. And I do detect an aggressive bite in your nasty remark about sitting by a pool to be photographed. That I do once a year on vacation. But certainly you should know some more about me. To begin with, my biggest sin is that I'm lazy! I really am. I read a lot. I think a lot. I'm a great cook. (Voila, already we are at odds, each wanting to rule the kitchen!) Smoke too much, drink a great amount of coffee and vodka, bite my nails, and in moments of great stress, I kiss my knees (true). Of course I must start thinking about doing something constructive and have just about decided to take a course for travel agents. I feel very strongly about just being home until David goes off to college. Perhaps as a reaction to my own childhood, I think it very important that when a kid gets home from school, there should be someone to chat with, discuss things, to share a laugh, to feed them and all that. But I'm not a "Yiddishe Mama" and not at all possessive. I just think, especially in this day and age, that it is important. I'm very good with teenagers though I don't think that I would have made a good job of it if I had had a daughter.

You are a goose! What is a "normal" example or type? I think that it's simplifying to keep going back to parents. It may be the original cause, perhaps, but surely other people, and events, even genetics play a part in all of this?

Yes, I have tasted the strawberries, but as far as being a "responsible" person, it is, a little bit more than that of course. How to explain? It's very hard because even though you have heard about me, and vice-versa, and even though we are (I think) delighting in each other with this correspondence, you really don't KNOW me. You do but you don't really know too much about my life, or rather, the life I lead, or much about Marvin! I shall now use an English phrase, "This is a sticky wicket."

Portrait of Marvin:

He is fifty years of age, very talented, intelligent, with the emotions of a child. For instance:

He gets upset when my Father addresses his letters to "Dear Pipsi" instead of "Dear Pips and Marvin". And I simply cannot bring myself to tell my father this, it's too infantile.

He was very upset that your letter was addressed only to me. I'm speaking of your first letter. (Not the pink letter which is hidden away!) As to the reasons for all this, it goes back to childhood. He has two older sisters. His mother was in full bloom of menopause while he was very young. He was the only Jewish boy in a predominantly Irish neighborhood. He had few friends as a kid and was not good at sports. He was also shy and who knows what else?

He was an uninterested father until a few years ago. If I take pride in anything at all that I have accomplished, it's that today, the relationship between Marvin and the boys is an excellent one and I worked to make it so. They joke and tease each other and the boys are really fond of him.

You see, your life and mine are very different. You are responsible only to yourself, and though I may feel the same about many things, I am quite a sham artist at heart and though it may be despicable, I think way ahead. Par example: If you want to continue this correspondence (by now you must be wondering just what kind of a nut I am?), then send the letters off on a Thursday or Friday. Then, hopefully, they should reach me on a Tuesday or Wednesday when I'm alone. I simply can't tolerate the idea that Marvin would want to see your letters when they came, or the resulting scenes if I refused to let him see them. A very occasional postcard addressed to Mr. and Mrs. M. Paymer every three months or so would probably endear you to Marvin forever. Whatever you do, don't think of him as beastly.

Your father was/is jealous of your relationship to your mother. Marvin is jealous of my relationship with anyone.

As for Poppy, unless I'm mistaken, he thinks of me as ruling the roost with cheerful competence, which I do. You have, to a great extent, given him a new lease on life and I don't want ANYTHING to ruin that relationship. It means as much to him as I'm sure it does to you.

I realize with horror how serious this letter has become. Having listed my sins somewhere in the mishmash above, do let me acquaint you with my virtues:

I have big feet (a size 10 in the U.S.) which is always a sign of tremendous intelligence.

Great daring—if you'll get me a Shetland pony I'll go riding with you when we finally meet.

I am a person of great gentleness. Beneath this rugged exterior lies the soul of a lamb.

My height? I'm two inches taller than you.

Jacques Brel is Belgian. (All Belgians are greatly gifted and nice people too!) He will explain himself to you when he arrives shortly at this address. The idea of you toting the damned album along on your travels, seeking to find a record player, fills me with delight!

Much love, Pipsi

Spain September 12, 1971

My Dear Pips

I'm mightily pleased with myself today because Irene Hardenbergh and I rode our horse from Mijas, all the way to Pizarra, a distance of some 46 kilometers! (Irene is a very dear friend of mine, married to a retired U.S. army general).

I rode the horse up to Mijas from Fuengirola yesterday and we left him in the village stable. Then Peter drove Irene to Mijas this morning and she began her journey on horseback following the road to Coin. I drove from Pizarra and met her. We took it in turns, riding or driving and made excellent time. Irene left the stable at 9:30 a.m. and we arrived at the Hollander stables at 4:30 p.m. The horse seemed to have enjoyed the experience and he obviously likes his new home, and so he should with eleven other horses for company. I can go on my forthcoming trip to England now without having to worry about him.

In haste, love and all that, Shirley.

New York   September 13, 1971

Dear Shirley,

What a treat! Two letters in as many days! Have you re-
covered from my last one? I hope that it didn't upset you? All
this correspondence will forever be crisscrossing each other
over the Atlantic. I don't express myself well at all very often,
however, when you come here next summer (wonderful, wonderful, wonderful!) we'll talk, talk, talk, etc.

I loved Dubrovnik. I had been there before in 1964 with
Marc. (It was a ghastly trip, which I'll tell you about some
time.) I think it one of the most beautiful places in the world
and we stayed there for one week. I go to Europe every summer, in June usually. During the past two years, pleasure
has been combined with research on Marvin's part, for his
Ph.D. on the subject of Pergolesi. (Did Poppy tell you about
THAT?)

I hope you understand the occasional French words and
sentences in my letters? For some reason I took it for granted
that you spoke it fluently?

I AM politically minded and am forever working for Peace
candidates. They never win and my friends tell me that my
getting involved means "The Kiss of Death" for whoever is
running! Still, the situation in the U.S. is appalling and one
has to try and do something.

It's one of those ghastly, fantastic, tornado-like days,
great gusts of wind, driving rain and thunder. I love it.

I first read Gibran about ten years ago. I think perhaps
that you are closer to him having lived in Arabian countries?
He's not too well known here. At any rate, I have no great
patience for poets. This is one of my lacks and a strange one
because, I have, buried deeply within me, a very poetic soul,
though very few people would know it. My favorite poet is
Edna St. Vincent Millay. Do you know her works?

No, I'm not published, and yes, I wrote music. I was nearly published but somehow did not make it, not quite good enough, and it's difficult to break into this field.

I wrote my last song about eighteen months ago, this time, both the words and the music. It is my protest song, since the world seems to be blowing itself to bits.

SPINNING[2]

Children don't play with the games they were bought
Hoops are not tossed and hoops are not caught.
Jack-In-The-Boxes lie idle and still
Kites do not fly up high on the hill.
Pink chalk and white chalk have all turned to dust,
Miniature trains are the color of rust,
Raggedy-Anne with a hole in her head
All the world is dead.

Chorus: And it's spinning, always spinning
in an endless starlit sky,
Yes it's spinning, always spinning,
Goodbye World Goodbye.

Prophets are silent and bells do not ring
Where is the beggar and where is the King?
Makers of music and schemers of schemes,
Gone are the weavers of yesterday's dreams.
Where are the lovers who walked hand-in-hand?
Where are the castles we built in the sand?
Wheatfield and pasture have all turned to lead.
All the world is dead.

Chorus: And it's spinning......

---

2   Music and lyrics composed by Sylvia Paymer, 1970.

No marble buildings with eighteen room flats
No dirty slum streets infested with rats.
No one is happy and no one is sad,
Who now is sane and who now is mad?
Countries of power and nations of poor,
None has a skyline and none has a shore.
God of our Fathers and Satan in red,
All the world is dead.

Chorus: And it's spinning.......

I have a recording of it but last week I decided that it needs work. Since I'm lazy, as I told you in my last letter, it will take time, but eventually I'll cut another record and send it to you, though my voice is none too good.

Bon Voyage. Drive carefully, much love,   Pipsi

New York   September 15, 1971
Dear Shirley,

I can't even keep up with your letter writing efforts, bless you. Your missives keep heaping upon my pointy head and I love it. Your good wishes reached me in three days so I'm taking a chance on sending this to the Hollander Hacienda.

Primo: I'm a nonbeliever, but thank you for the Jewish New Year card. However, I do go to Temple for the Holy Days, where, between gentle snores, I kick the rest of the family who are giggling. Actually the boys had a bit of a religious education and both had a Bar Mitzvah, etc.

Segundo: by now you must have received my last two letters in answer to yours and after your tale of a 46-kilometer horse ride, do you understand my request for a pony? Which part of the horse do you own, head or rear? The horse, you say, stood up to the trip very well. How about you?

As for my "anticipated" bad behavior in Temple five days hence, I'll give you another of Wilde's epigrams: "If one hears bad music, it is one's duty to drown it by one's conversation."

Love, and all that stuff, right back to you,   Pipsi

Spain   September 18, 1971
Dearest Pips,

Merçi beaucoup pour les deux letters que j'ai reçue hier, and although I understand French, I'm pretty useless when it comes to writing in the language. I'm a great mimic, so people tend to think that I speak it with fluency, so they're misled because it ain't that good. Do the boys and Marvin speak French?

No, Marc did not tell me that Marvin was writing a thesis on Pergolesi. Tell me more. The only thing that I remember about Pergolesi is that he wrote a piece called "Stabat Mater" which our choral society did at college and we sang it in about three different churches. The religious ceremonies meant nothing to me, I'm afraid, but I loved the music. I love listening to Gregorian chant, and I enjoy organ music too.

Yes, you tease, but not too much, and I laugh out loud. Actually you express yourself very well and I quite understand. What I don't understand, maybe I'll find between the lines?

I enjoyed the quotations, there was no nasty bite, just my warped sense of humor when I made a crack about your "lounging around the pool all day."

Do you think that you could possibly cut out the nail-biting and, more importantly, the smoking? I gave up smoking in January. It is Poppy's dearest wish that you would do the same...no other changes are necessary.

(Don't you think that this girl has a damned cheek?)

I'm delighted to learn that you think staying home (whenever it's at all possible) is important when raising children. Agree with you one hundred per cent. Many a time, as a teacher, I have said "It's the parents I need here in class, not the children!" I'm a responsible person and I like to see it in others and I get very impatient when I see irresponsibility.

Hope that David had a successful interview. How did it go? I must send a birthday card to Marc. I have been thinking about him most of the day, et toi aussi, and I don't know what to say...

We had a great drama on Wednesday. I found our dear little puppy drowning in the swimming pool. Well, I gave it the kiss of life and artificial respiration. I dried it and poured brandy down its throat (incidentally, I drink vodka too), wrapped it in a blanket together with a hot-water bottle and nursed it all night, yes, in my bed! I almost crushed its rib cage earlier by squeezing out endless amounts of water and, in fact, I learned the next day that its lung had collapsed. I had arranged to spend that day with Irene and Peter, because it was my birthday, so Jimmy, the elder Hollander son, took the puppy to the vet. When I returned on Friday, it was very much alive and thoroughly spoiled!

I seem to have clammed up.

I only write to people who write to me but give my love to Marvin and the boys.

Must away. I'm very tired and the thought of all that packing to be done tomorrow fills me with horror!

Greetings and love to you and yours, Shirley.

Shirley's Day:

7:45 a.m. *Rise, write letters, then type out an invento-*
ry of my household effects. Wash, dress, and
eat a bowl of cereal.

9:30 a.m. *Arrive at Irene's house. Return her keys.*
Drink a cup of coffee, discuss last-minute de-
tails concerning domestic affairs, etc. Give
her my English address. She departs for the
beauty salon.

10:30 a.m. *Call at the post office and mail letters. Call in*
at the hairdresser's to surprise Irene and say
"goodbye" once more.

11:00 a.m. *Arrive at Pueblo Lopez and visit my tenant.*
Buy and deliver flowers to an elderly friend
and neighbor who has just returned from
England and arrange to lunch with her. Pay
outstanding bills at the Pueblo Lopez office.

11:30 a.m. *Drive to Marbella to collect money from a*
shop to send to a friend in the U.S.

12:30 p.m. *Call into the Hilton to look at Gino's paint-*
ings to see if there's one I prefer to the one I
had chosen previously from another gallery.

1:15 p.m. *Lunch with Christine Tyndall.*

3:00 p.m. *Call at LaVeta and Margaret's house to beg a*
bed on which to rest while LaVeta finishes the
suede vest which she's making for me.

6:00 p.m. *Make and drink tea, try on vest and wait*
for LaVeta to make a small alteration. Write
birthday card and pack Irene's birthday pres-
ent which I'll leave at their house as I know
that she'll be visiting.

7:00 p.m. *Drive to Torremolinos to Pez Espada Hotel to*
collect three of Gino's paintings.

7:30 p.m.   *Deliver my old bicycle to some French Cana-dian woman who is interested in buying it.*

7:45 p.m.   *Drive back to Pizarra and arrive at 8:30 p.m. Greeted by delighted children. Have supper. Chat with kids. Try to fix a broken door han-dle in my room. Write letters.*

12:15 a.m.   *Go to bed with a book, perchance to dream...?*

At the end of September, I set off with Lise, Siri, and Scott Hollander on our overland journey to England. This special 'Field Trip', I promised them, would be fun as well as educational. I knew that it would be a wonderful opportunity for us all to get to know each other. They kept daily journals which included historical and geographical information which they gleaned as we drove through Spain, France and England. There we stayed with my parents in their home in the Midlands. We visited numerous places of interest including Kenilworth Castle, Warwick, Stratford, and various Warwickshire villages. My parents were happy to have a full house and surprised and delighted when the children gave them one of Gino's paintings. We then left for Surrey where we stayed with Celia Crossley. I had taught two of her sons when they were at school in Ahwaz, Iran. John, her husband, was away overseas at this time working for the Shell Oil Company, and all three boys, Graham, Trevor and David, were also away at boarding school. The Crossley's house was large, comfortable and within easy train connection or driving distance from Central London.

Spain, North of Madrid   September 20, 1971
Dear Pips,

    Sorry about using this flimsy, pink paper again. I should have used it for "loo" paper as it's much softer than what we have here! Well you CAN laugh. This morning we passed the post office and they had a package for me. It was your record album from New York! Here I am driving to England and so frustrated because I can't play it! Thank you so very much. Did Poppy tell you that it was my birthday? When is yours?

    The children and I have had a most enjoyable trip so far and I feel as if I'm their mother! We have learned many songs. Their repertoire was somewhat limited and we have laughed a good deal.

    Am too tired to write more, and anyway, this damned pen has run dry and I loathe using a ballpoint. Sitting up in bed is not conducive to good script.

            Love, and all that,   Shirley

New York   September 24, 1971
Dear Shirley,

    MERDE!—Having disposed of THAT heartfelt cry, many thanks for your letter. By now I'm convinced that when we meet, it should be in some innocuous place like a village square or in the courtyard of a church. This way, if we don't like each other (and don't smile, this could happen, I strongly believe in chemical reactions), we could pass each other by and mutter a quiet "ugh" or "yuck" to oneself. Once and for all, I beg you (and I never beg anyone for anything!), forget about my responding letter to your pink one. Anyway, make believe that it never was written and certainly never was read. I should have known you would have a temper, and do you clam up very often? By the way, I'm very good at fixing doors that don't close! I hope you don't imagine me as spending my time reclining on a sofa eating Turkish gumdrops?

I will not give your love to "You and Yours." You've made your point and sound very pedantic when you state "I only write to people who write to me." How beautifully arrogant of you! Has anyone ever tried to cut you down to size? I thought at first of writing between the lines with lemon juice since you seem to consider yourself a real "pro" but I decided against it. However, should this letter smell of onions, it's because I have just sliced half-a-dozen.

Don't clam up!

Yes, I'm very funny, I've always been like this, it drives Steve and David wild. Of course David's interview went well, he's got a 93% average, is 22 in a class of 867 and with all that, and with the educational state of this country, it's not certain that he'll make the university of his choice! Steve, who was the worst student in the world, ended his first year of college with a B+ average (88%) which is fantastic. (The way I used to get down on my knees, just before report cards were due, and pray to good old Jehovah, is a riot.) He is extremely lucky, as he knows, to be in his college of choice. He has always wanted to be in the field of Communications, mainly Film and Television. Both Marvin and David speak a little French. David reads and writes it admirably but is shy about speaking.

It's funny, I love Gregorian chant, always sending flowers to elderly ladies, and shall certainly do so for your next birth-day. (I don't mean that you're elderly.) Many happy returns, tell me the date. I'm sorry that Jacques Brel didn't reach you in time for it and where the hell is it?

How does it feel to give the kiss of life to a dog? Mine has very bad breath. (He's old and dying, but comfortable.) Have you heard about my animals? (They are all males, and

I blush to admit it, all castrated!) The dog, "Mr. K," named for Khrushchev but the initial stands for Kosygin. Then there are Ralph and Norton, the two cats. There used to be Oscar 1 and then Oscar 2, hamsters, but they died a blissful death.

My friends tell me that I killed them with kindness.

How nice to know that you spent a day thinking of Marc and myself and never mind "I don't know what to say"—sometimes there's no need to say anything. He really enjoys your letters and marvels at your energy. Because of this, I think I'll start doing exercises (a little shadow boxing and such). This time of year is difficult for him because of the Jewish Holy Days. Somehow he reverts, if you can call it that; he has bad dreams about my mother, etc.

I do promise to stop biting my fingernails (I'll hold on to the thumbs for a while). But forget the cigarettes. Those and vodka are important to me. What made you give it up? Were you 35 or 36? How did you end up in Fuengirola? And do please remember that I am a few years older than you, or have I mentioned this in my list of assets before?

Samedi passer je suis aller chez les amis sans Marvin, he was playing a "club date" that night. I looked great, felt marvelous, and ended up by slapping my hostess's face! I'll tell you all about it next time. (Poor thing, she was an innocent bystander, but she was THERE!) This happened, I'm sure, because in a previous letter I told you that I abhor violence.

All my love, Pipsi

New York   September 25, 1971
Dear Shirley,

We must have letters flying all over by now. By the way, you're still missing one of mine sent to Pizarra and containing some of my unforgettable prose. I'm addressing this one, as I did the last one, to Woking. Did you follow the road through Blois, Amboise, Tours, etc.? I did once and even stopped at Chinon. I'm a great one for castles, moats and such. You'll be happy to know that I'm following your trip on a map.

I'm glad that the record reached you with such great timing. Occasionally, my plans come out just right.

I play your record VERY often.

Of course I have birthdays! I'm 41 and the infamous date is June 16 which makes me a Gemini baby, which figures. You are Virgo (forgive a gentle smile) and Marc is Libra, so is Steve, as I presented Poppy with his first grandson on his birthday twenty years ago. I'm meeting Poppy for lunch on the 28th, and I'll take him books (the best present for that man). We'll drink, joke and talk about you...

It took me an hour to decipher "loo" paper; I thought you meant 100! This is something that they do well in the U.S., soft and in all colors, including polka dots, pink elephants hearts, etc. Well, be careful and don't incur any permanent injuries! Why are you always sorry about the pink paper, and why do you "loathe" ballpoint pens? I mean, how can anyone LOATHE anything like that?

Have you heard about my 17-inch scar? I love to throw these things at you. I mean, there you are, saying "What scar and where is it?" Ah well, I'll tell you about it in some other letter.

I'm driving David and four of his wild-eyed friends to a party. Their expectations are high; there will be girls there. I always give them great advice as to how to handle the fair sex but since one of them listened to me and then got his face slapped for his pains, no one listens to me anymore!

C'est ça pour le moment. Amuse toi, ne sois pas trop severe avec les gosses and let me know if I'm writing too much nonsense?

Much love,   Pipsi

October

Woking, England October 1, 1971
My Dear Pips,

Now it's my turn to swear (I can do it very well in Dutch but only verbally), so merde—which, as you can see, I can spell. In your last three letters you have dangled a carrot in front of my nose. In each letter you begin telling me something which arouses (watch it!) my curiosity and then you say, "Well, I'll tell you more about that in a future letter."

1. Why did you slap your hostess's face? Actually I've never slapped anyone's face, though I have certainly had cause on some occasions, but then, I don't preach anti-violence.

2. How did you get, why did you get it and just WHERE is that 17-inch scar?

Yes, I suppose that you could say that I'm pedantic on occasions. (Many people would say all the time!) And yes, I have often been cut down to size. I have a strong feeling that it would not be very long after we meet and you would be doing it, or slapping my face of course!

I don't know much about chemical reactions but do you think that you could stay in the kitchen while I fix the screws in the door? (I'm kidding, like you, I think that I'm quite proficient at both.)

Last week was hectic. We saw Much Ado About Nothing at Stratford and it was hilarious. It was an excel-

lent production and the kids roared with laughter. We visited places of historical interest such as Kenilworth Castle and Aston Hall. Now we are back in Woking, all ready to begin our London visits next week.

Which leads me to the Jacques Brel record. My mother has an excellent record player so I was able to listen to it. Well, you know that I'm honest, so I have to admit that I'm not at all sure that I like it. I must admit that I've been unable to listen to it in peace and quiet so I will play it again at the first opportunity.

...Thought of you when I was in Aston Parish Churchyard yesterday and I smiled.... I love vodka and have come to loathe cigarettes, so I would ask you then to keep the nail biting and the vodka but quit smoking!

No, not 35 or 36 but 37! You see the age difference is negligible. And what made me give up smoking? I could not think of one good thing about it except that I enjoyed it. More than one good friend had died from cancer of the lungs and they were all heavy smokers. Then my dear friend, Irene Hardenbergh, who used to be a heavy smoker, gave it up. Eventually I thought, "Damn it! If she can do it, so can I!" It was really difficult for the first couple of days or so. Now I hate the smell and feel nauseated when...oh you know.

Today I'm going off and leaving the children with Celia Crossley. I knew Celia and her husband John in Iran. He works for Shell Oil and I used to teach for the Shell Oil Company in Venezuela, and I taught two of their three boys. Then I'm off to the silver wedding anniversary of my aunt. It will be a fine opportunity to see many members of the family whom I've not seen in years.

Looking forward to your next letter,
Much love,   Shirley

New York   October 8, 1971

Querida,   (Just to show off again.)

Just when I despaired of ever hearing from you again, because it took six days for your letter to reach me, it arrived and once again, you guessed it, found me in the kitchen. Actually I'm cooking for tomorrow as Poppy is coming for lunch and since he comes early, I usually fix something the day before. However, so that you should not have a self-satisfied smile all over your face, I'll go off for a few minutes and sand down a drawer that hasn't closed for the past three years.

(...13 minutes later) I'm not only competent but quick too, and this is only to show you that I will NOT stay in the kitchen. We could have an alternate day schedule. Mondays, Wednesdays, Fridays for you, the rest for me and Sundays we'll just drink vodka.

Now for some of the carrots. I slapped my hostess's face (Deborah) because, oi, oi! There was a small gathering of people at her place, all of whom I know well. An argument starts. I disagree with one of the girls (Jewel—she isn't!), who sports the most fantastic "décolleté." (I think she's got you beat.) I tell her she's wrong in her point of view. She tells me I've got a big mouth. I get up, start to leave through the kitchen. Deborah stands in my way, incoherent with rage, (How dare I act like this, etc.) I calmly tell her she's hysterical and to MOVE IT! She snarls, so I slapped her and walked out. Of course, as I told you, I was very ashamed and I did apologize, both to her and to Jewel.

The 17-inch scar... Did that really intrigue you? Let me assure you, it's barely noticeable, though I don't wear bikinis. That's an excuse. I don't wear them because I don't have the figure for it. I'm also a bit past the age. Four years age difference may be negligible, but just right. That, together with my grey hair, should certainly inspire you with the proper veneration. ...Yes, yes, the scar...a kidney was removed when I was twenty-five. All very dull really, it extends from the top of the appendix upwards and it curves around towards the waist and ends in the back somewhere. The relatives who came to see me in the hospital, with saddened faces, were appalled to find the place in an uproar as I spent my time telling the other patients dirty jokes and trying to bribe the nurses into sneaking me some extra rations of morphine, and lacking that, vodka.

...It's funny, I can't think of you as being lonely, you seem so damned busy all the time, which of course has nothing at all to do with being lonely. I am, quite often, but not enough to seek out many people. I think that I'm a loner by nature though no one would think of me that way.

...Damned glad that you smile when you think of me, and well you should, I do the same thing when thinking about you, or when Poppy speaks of you. ... And...I'm sorry about the record, however I'm sure that our tastes are different in many things. (What do you like to eat? I LOATHE vegetables.)

Also, there's no reason why a 75-year-old (I'm looking at my future) shouldn't have intimate relationships. You see how narrow, pedantic and British you are?

Enough for today! Don't let me rush you about revelations as to how you came to Fuengirola, I don't mean to pry. Here's another carrot, remind yourself to ask me someday about Marlene Dietrich! All my love, Pipsi

P.S. I'm not giving up cigarettes! I WILL shower, bathe, brush my teeth before giving you a kiss since the smell bothers you, but I'm NOT giving up!

All my love,   Pipsi.

New York   October 10, 1971

Dear Shirley,

A letter for no reason except that Marc was over for lunch yesterday and we had a hilarious conversation when he told me about your travel plans with the kiddies, showing them the sights but foregoing Coventry Cathedral for a horse show, and feeding the pigeons instead of admiring the architectural splendors of Nelson's Column or The Houses of Parliament! Then in a Greek chorus together, "It reminded me of you and Dolgoruki in Moscow." When I was there with him, we used to sightsee from morning til cocktail hour, at which time he would test me to see what I had remembered, if anything, of what I had seen. Well, the first thing that particular morning was a statue of a man on horseback, the founder of Moscow, a certain Prince Dolgoruki, magnificently carved in bronze and surrounded by pigeons which I was feeding while my father was relating his whole life story. (Dolgoruki's not Marc's!) Needless to say, as we were sitting over our drinks, Poppy smiled and with a lifted eyebrow said, "And tell me, dear child, what was the name of the man on horseback, at the corner of such-and-such street?"

"Ah oui, l'homme à cheval?" "Yes." *"Celui en bronze?"* "Yes." *"Le fondeur de Moscou?"* "Do you, or don't you know?" *"C'est, c'est, c'etait Tropotkin?"*

"Idiot!" he yelled. "It was Dolgoruki!" So we, or rather, he, decided yesterday that we are, you and I, two of a kind in intellect and perfectly apt to pass up possession of facts for the sheer pleasure of sitting on the grass and relaxing. His knowledge is, of course, formidable and his memory outstanding. We do have some great, lively conversations on many subjects. As a child I resisted learning in an almost fanatic way, but of course, some of it seeped through and by the time I was twenty, I set out on my own to fill in the holes. The end result is that I can tell you what Marie-Antoinette did during the few hours before she stepped in front of the guillotine but remember with difficulty that Choiseul was Prime Minister (I think) at the time. I cannot ever recall the succession of the various "Carlos's" but can name Henry VIII's wives in order and give you priceless nuggets of their private lives.

It is raining very hard and the house is divinely quiet. I love this time of morning, there's a special feeling to it and really I could think of no better way of enjoying it than to write to you these few lines.

Much love,   Pipsi

Woking, England   October 12, 1971
My Dear Pips,

When people ask me which end of the horse is mine, I reply that the ass end is mine because I can sell the shit for profit, the feeding end is Irene's.

Did the two girls in question accept your apology gracefully? Thank God you don't have a name like "Jewel."

...I should not bother about the cleaning if I were you, I would like to arrive at your house unannounced and take you quite by surprise but I doubt very much if I will be able to achieve this! You know, we are very much alike in many ways, maybe too much so? Time will tell I suppose.

Now it's your turn to be "British" (conservative). Judging by the photo you sent me, I'm sure that you would look good in a bikini, you look thin enough. I don't wear them because I bulge all over. I keep kidding myself that it is all the more for someone to love, but I am going to make an effort to slim a little when I return. ...I promise to have due respect for your grey hairs.

We plan on leaving here around the 20th. We have not done half the things we had hoped to, but we have been very busy. All the children wish to return at some time.

...I'm reminding me, to remind you, that I'm to ask you about Marlene Dietrich sometime, and it might as well be now, so tell me please. About three years ago, she was performing in Birmingham and I met her! Unfortunately I did not know then what I know now, so I had my hair done at the hairdresser's and was wearing a dress and high-heeled shoes, looking rather elegant and not like me at all. I was told later that I should have turned up in a shirt and pants...ah well. (I must say that I do not take to all this facelifting. I shuddered inwardly when I met her.)

I LOVE vegetables cooked and raw in salads. I like vodka with lime and ice or neat when eating caviar but haven't had any caviar since leaving Iran. I like most things but LOATHE Brussels sprouts, and don't care for macaroni and cheese. I don't eat food that I don't like, even if it's someone's special recipe.

God, where do I start and how DID I get to Fuengirola? Well...in 1964 I got a post with an oil company in Iran, after having taught with the Shell Oil Company in Venezuela for six years. So I was sent to a small town called Ahwaz. The other two single females were terribly boring and I was rather miserable at first until I met Irene. She taught me to ride and then I had a raison d'etre, but she was married and not free to spend all her time with me. When an attractive Dutch teacher turned up, I saw that we had many interests in common. She wanted to learn to ride, so I taught her.

Delyn and I lived and worked together until 1969 when she decided to get married, but all that is a story in itself, and if you are interested I will tell you. I'm over it all now, and am quite my gay old self. At a critical stage, when I needed help, Irene came down to Ahwaz to collect me and escort me back to Tehran to stay with her and her husband Peter. That was in April of 1969. They planned on leaving Iran in June, by road. I stayed with them in Tehran, helped them pack and then we drove out in convoy. I had a Volkswagon which had to be taken out of Iran, so we traveled together. At that time I was in no emotional state to travel alone, so we eventually arrived in Spain. I enjoyed it there and decided to buy a little house in Pueblo Lopez. The next two years were rather difficult.

There are quite a few ex-Shell company people who have retired to Spain. I like living in small communities and I like it here. I must admit that I was really pleasantly surprised to learn just how many REAL friends I had in a time of trouble. There were offers of help, including financial and emotional support, and offers of hospitality poured in for which I will be eternally grateful. The funny thing is that last year I flew to England twice for job interviews and was offered posts teaching, one in Brussels, and one in Sierra Leone and refused them, and despite the time, effort and expense to attend those trips to London, I'm glad now that I refused the posts. It all happens for the best.

(I will interrupt here while I begin fixing supper for the children and Celia.)

They soon demolished the meal, and again, seemed to have enjoyed it. Yes, I have self-satisfied smile on my face. I'm feeling quite happy today for some reason. Probably because Marc is there and because you are there and I would love to call you right now...

At this point, at Celia's urging, I went upstairs and telephoned Pipsi for the first time. It was approximately three p.m. in Long Island. I have never forgotten the opening part of that conversation, which went something like this:

Pipsi   "Hello."

Shirley: "Hello, is that you, Pipsi?"

Pipsi: "Yes. Who is this?"

Shirley: "It's Shirley!"

Pipsi: "Shirley? Shirley who?"

         Silence.

Shirley: "Well how many Shirleys do you know for God's sake?"

         Silence.

Pipsi: "You mean it's MY Shirley? Oh my God!"

Shirley: "Yes, it's your Shirley! "

         Silence.

Pipsi: "You do realize that I've fallen in love with you, don't you?"

I cannot recall any more of that conversation! I danced down the stairs, head over heels with joy! I only remember that upon hearing that soft, wonderful voice with the slight European accent, I was completely captivated! I could not have been happier. Excitedly I recounted the first part of the conversation to Celia, then, in a daze, continued with the letter I had already begun. Slowly, it began to sink in that our relationship was suddenly heading in a new direction and we had not even met.

So! Now I know what you sound like! Much nicer than I EVER imagined! I am now left speechless, I honestly don't know what to say except that I'm SO pleased that I called. I'm all at sixes and sevens and cannot write another word, just wait for your next letter. Did you go and play the guitar or did you write? I wonder just when and where, we'll meet? The thought makes me nervous and that is putting it mildly. As you would say, that's enough for today, hope you will teach me to play the guitar?

I'm going upstairs right now to tune the one that's here, and I'll sing a couplet or two.

With fondest love, Shirley.

P.S. And you think I'M mad!?

New York   October 12, 1971   3:45 p.m.

Bébé,

AM IN A STATE OF SHOCK! I'm seldom stunned but you win the first hand! Damn it, I usually have the upper one… Do you know that I have such a reputation for cool behavior that I've been told that if someone took a shot at me and missed, I'd probably say "bad show!" and walk on. Well, you know better. My shaking left hand alternates between a very STIFF vodka and a soft cosh with which I'm hitting myself, none too gently, over the head. Forgive my outburst and don't let it frighten you away. I quite blush at it and will probably climb the walls in utter mortification later on. But all I said is, without doubt, partially true. I say "partially" because, as I mentioned in an earlier letter, it could be that when we're nose to nose (we're getting closer all the time), we might be facing something different than expected. Par example, our voices, didn't you EXPECT an accent? Yours is lower than I thought and you do giggle a lot, probably nervous hiccups! In the meantime, your letters delight me. Of course we're working in reverse. Relationships usually start from an outer surface and turn inwards, while we're doing exactly the opposite.

Now, to be serious for a minute, I know that you've had a bad experience, as far as love is concerned, and that's all I know, nor do I particularly want to know more. The only reason I mention it is that YOU might think of me as a flirt who's amusing herself by playing upon your emotions. I've had a few affairs in the past ten years and though I prefer to say nothing of them until we meet, whatever my faults, and there's a stream of them, I am very conscious of the frailties of human emotions. I mean "frail" as being easily shattered and hurt. I have found myself most at odds in this world for being far too romantic, being much too gentle (even though I slap people on occasion), and refusing to accept that love's place is only in bed! (Don't misunderstand, I love it, but that's not all there is to it.) Also, you might as well know that I'm a fantastic lover! DON'T LAUGH, it's true! And, of course, knowing IN FACT what I had guessed and realized for a long time was that I was quite indifferent to men, but not so at all to women.

Since I'm probably not expressing myself too well, as usual, I'm telling you all this because I would not ever want you to think that I started this correspondence for ulterior motives. What intrigued me was what I heard about you, your reaction to Marc, and also the fact that he thought so highly of you. So, believe me, both my letters, and for that matter, what I told you on the phone are, to use one of your favorite words, "sincere"! I'm quite smitten (what a nice old-fashioned word), and though Marc keeps saying how alike we are, listen, maybe we've been chasing the wrong girls all these years. I blush to admit that though I would have liked to have been the "seducer," I ended up the seduced! Are we each other's types? Well, mentally yes, I would say so, for the rest, we'll see.

I'm rushing a bit now, but I want to get this off before the post office closes. Of course the phone call will not be mentioned to Poppy. Do you have any idea what it would do to him if he knew what I was really like? I may be over-protective of him, but be wise, don't mention me too much in your letters. He's very possessive of you and it may be my imagination but I think that I have been bringing your name into the conversations I have with him too much and I think that he resents it a bit.

For the call, there are NO words to tell you what it meant. I hope that you were good and nervous before you picked up the phone and not too disappointed when I answered?

Je t'embrasse,   Pipsi

Woking, England   October 13, 1971
My Dearest Pips,

That beautiful voice! It rings in my ears and I keep hearing you say, "But you're mad, absolutely mad!"

The rain has caught up with us and it's pouring down. Everyone else is in bed and I would hope so too because it's 1:00 a.m., which makes it 9:00 p.m. in your part of the world? Who, in their right minds, would get up at 5:30 a.m.? Do you then go back to bed later in the day?

Today we shopped, after which we visited the dentist. Tomorrow we hope to go up to London for more sightseeing. As I explained to Marc, it is just as important to get the "feel" of a country by visiting its inhabitants in their natural environment, playing in the park, feeding the pigeons, etc., as seeing historical sights. After all, Scott is only ten and I don't want them to get bored with visits to too many buildings. So we space it out, but I have to admit that we're unable to do all that I had in mind, there simply isn't time.

Today, I was told that I have a South African accent, and the other day, someone said that my accent was distinctly American. It's rather mixed up but with a hard, very definite "R"—peculiar to me and no other member of my family. Anyway...I can hear it now, that voice, "But I do, I really do!" with that distinct European accent!

I'm tired, the heating is off and I have thin blood, so I'm off to bed.

With fondest love, Shirley

New York   October 18, 1971

Dearest Shirley,

Never, NOT ONCE in all my letters did I ever say you were mad! But...how marvelous that you are quite as insane as I am. You're also slightly vulgar (I'm speaking of the horse's ass), which comes as a relief as I am too. I don't want to go into too many details as to my reaction to your call, some of them you've read about in my last letter. However from the time that I mailed it to you until Thursday night, in other words, for a full forty-eight hours, my symptoms were as follows:

A pounding heart

Chills

Hot flashes (OK. don't get cute.)

Mind you, I've been chastising myself, not so much for the way I spoke to you, but for not waiting until I was quite calmed down before writing back. You may very well be stuck with a side of me no one has ever seen—"HONEST PIPSI."

Now for your letter, and why do I keep thinking of the feel of your hand on the back of my neck? I can, in fact, make out your questions. Jewel is no jewel, she also is NOT. I'm taking into consideration how alike we are! But have you thought that we are perhaps, outgrowing our visions of ourselves as young Greek boys, which is damned hard to do if you have a chubby figure or sport Pillars of Hercules for thighs, like I do. That's why I said what I did about chasing the "wrong" type of girls. As far as taking me by surprise, you'll never duplicate what you did with the call.

Talk about *"cri de coeur"*—and as far as the dashing up and down the stairs...

You should be warned that I'm not only doing that but also the Marine Corps Exercises to get into condition, I mean, so that I can tackle you when we meet. Truly, don't be deceived by the photos. From neck to waist, pure aristocrat, then something goes wrong and I expand. This is what is known in French as a *"fausse maigre."*[3] It just ain't so. And because I'm kind, sweet and good, I bought a roll of film and under various explanations, am having David take pictures of me. The ones that are good—I take a ghastly picture—I'll send you. I WILL make a record and send it to you, but be patient.

For me, it's a terrible experience to record, microphones scare me to death. I have no voice and I can never play in the right key as I don't know the chords. But I promise that by Christmas you'll have a record.

What the hell did you imagine that I would sound like, some nasal American voice? I don't know how I retained the accent, I think that it's more pronounced than Marc's.

And speaking of dear Poppy, my darling girl, don't ever, ever, not even if you're dead drunk on your vodka, lime juice and ice, let HIM know that I now know that he brought you your breakfast in bed.

He and I are alike in some ways. He and I differ mostly,

---

3   "Fausse maigre" refers to a woman who appears thin because she manages to hide the fact that she is actually fat.

I think, not in intellect—though I can't quote Nietzche (have you been subjected to this yet?)—but in two things: In the way in which I regard humanity, which he rather despises, also because I'm rather a sensualist, which he is not, not at all! It's not a question of "age"—it's just the way he is. By the way, I mean, having already bragged about being a great lover (don't be stupid, I mean with women), I'm a sensualist insofar as I love making love more than being made love to. Here we go again with another hot flash!...

I'm impressed by the luncheon menu but how barbaric can you be? I mean boiled onions? That's terrible! I feel that you should know that I detest stews, love steak, rare or raw, adore cooked kidneys, BUT NOT AS MUCH AS I ADORE YOU! I'm wild about cheese, and how do you feel about ice cold, very dry champagne? Also, do you, by any chance, sleep in black transparent nightgowns? (I did not think so.)

As far as Dietrich is concerned, I can see that you feel the same way about dresses, etc., as I do. Yes, you are quite right about her, but I've never met her. About ten years ago, maybe a little more, I was entertaining Deborah. At that time, we didn't know each other too well. She had confided in me that she had a lover, male, that she was insane about. There's one thing to be said about American women, they talk a lot! I used to give her lunch, being quite aware that she was mystified by me, the accent, blah, blah and of course, she started to flirt. Not too much, but flirt, nevertheless. Well, on that particular day, while she was here, I received a call from Lucy, who used to be Marvin's boss years ago when he worked as a pianist in night clubs. (Are you getting confused?) Well, Lucy's Viennese and I've known her since I was eighteen. For some reason she always speaks to me in German, which I can barely understand. She tells me this whole story about Marlene coming to her club and how they reminisced about the good old days, and goes on to ask me to have lunch with her in the City. (Yes, she IS, but pas avec moi, and she's about 63 years old.)

On my end, the conversation goes something like this: "Ach, ja, ja, ya ya, Marlene? Naturlich, ya wohl, gut, gut, danke. Aufwidersein. OK." Then I hung up. Just to make conversation, I tell Deborah that I'm going into the City the next day, at which point, she says that she is too, to meet her lover, and why don't we go in together on the same train? The next day, we're on the train, she's strangely quiet. (I figure that she's thinking about her lover.) And suddenly she says

"Holy Jesus, YOU and Marlene Dietrich?" Not being too bright, I gaped at her until the implication hit me and I calmly answered, "Well, yes. Didn't you know?"

Need I say that I got myself so involved in that lie and with Deborah, who calmly walked into my house five days later and simply said, "Let's go to bed!" Our relationship lasted for at least five years, during which time she kept her lover and during which time I own up to having another affair, which ended in 1964. This must all sound terribly messy and it was. There were so many complications. The two girls were neighbors, to begin with. (If you're laughing I don't blame you.)

Deborah thought nothing of telling "numero 2" (Alexis) of my affair with Dietrich (which is the reason she came panting after me). And when I finally decided that I couldn't keep that up, I told them the truth, separately of course. They were both so enraged with me, not because I had made up this fantastic story, but because I had NOT gone to bed with Marlene! The ramifications of this whole story are rather complex and would take pages to explain. Our experiences, yours and mine, are different inasmuch as I'm the one who broke it off in both cases. With Deborah, it has been very difficult because we were very close, and we always worked together. However, different circumstances forced her to take a full-time job as an English teacher. Also, basically, it is men that she likes, and she would reproach me at the ODDEST moments for not being one. Still, I don't negate what was, nor do I regret it in any way. We remain good friends. I would do anything for her. Don't think me dissolute. I'm not...

I'm very glad to know that you're your "gay old self" again because so am I. ALSO, don't try to draw any similarities between "you and me" and "them and me" etc. There aren't any, so don't be afraid of that. Like you, I believe in fate (your decline of the job offer in Brussels; Poppy coming from the pool area at the Hilton in Marbella). I vowed to myself back in 1967 or so, that if I ever fell in love again, that would be IT, so let's hope it all works out sometime in the not-too-distant future. No silly, you don't have to wait until I'm 75!

All my love, Pipsi

Woking   October 18–19, 1971

I have been wanting to write to you all day but was committed to taking the kids up to London by train and then traveling on the Underground as they had never done it before. We went to Madame Toussaud's and to the Planetarium, then on to Oxford and Regent Streets where we shopped for some riding boots and a new hard hat (a protective riding hat) for me.

... I enjoy this correspondence; it sets the adrenaline flowing and I feel more and more that we are very much alike. Furthermore, I just KNEW from the beginning, from the very first letter in fact, just intuition, of course! I'm sure that when faced nose to nose there will be disappointment. Mainly from your side I would think. Incidentally, I'm not easily frightened by such

things, and do you blush? The voice was marvelous, I hear it still, soft and musical and quite unlike what I had expected and while we find this correspondence delightful, let us continue...with no promises. ...Rest assured, never for one moment did I imagine you to be amusing yourself. I know that you're sincere! I think that you express yourself quite clearly, particularly to someone as discerning as myself! (What a cocky little brat I am!)

Have you read Violette Leduc's La Batarde?[4] (My train of thought of course.) I enjoyed it and right now I'm reading, oh blast, I can't remember the title, but it's the sequel to the first part of the autobiography and I'm enjoying it very much.

We plan on leaving England either this coming Saturday or Sunday. My mother arrives at Southampton on Friday at 8:00 a.m. and I plan on driving down to meet her before she goes up to Birmingham. I should be able to see her for about an hour at least.

...Oh Lord, it's quite late and I could go on and on. ...I feel torn apart. I like your letters but I'm scared of the eventual meeting. Je t'embrasse très fort, mon français est terrible. J'ai oublié tout, mais, avec "le practice" j'espére que ça reviendra...anyway, what do you expect from me at this hour of the morning? (No, don't say it!)

Much, much love, Shirley

---

4   Violette Leduc (1907-1972) was an acclaimed master of words who wrote nine books, the most famous of which is *La Batarde*. The passionate affairs Leduc describes with both men and women reflect her search for her own identity.

Woking   October 19, 1971   11:00 p.m.
My Dearest Pips,

Perhaps that is the most expensive seven minutes[5] I have ever spent, on communication anyway, and the most ghastly! This time I was TERRIBLY nervous—Why I wonder? I'm frustrated, jealous, and annoyed. I spent over an hour trying beforehand, and then to become speechless—quite unknown for me! I'm restless, very restless, a little dashed, I can't even write in a decent hand.

Just as well that I'm returning at the end of this week, and will get back to a routine, work and play hard. I'm in such a state of nerves I can hardly understand English, let alone French.

I feel it would be better if the number of letters you receive from this direction were reduced somewhat— what do you think?

I am enjoying Mad in Pursuit.

This has been written but I wonder if I'll post it? There are many unanswered questions. Oh foul, foul day! (Too much Shakespeare.)

Querida mia, hasta la luego. -   Shirley

New York   October 19, 1971   4:45 pm.

Dear Pudgy, Dear NOTHING! Thank your lucky stars that you're not here, I think that I would make you wish that you had never been born. I am SO furious with you! With myself, for not handling the call better and simply saying, "Call me tomorrow or Friday or whatever." The worst of it is that I KNEW that if you got my letter you would call me! OK—you

---

5   Refers to a telephone call to Pipsi.

can try for four hours and not get a line through and I did NOT go out after 10:00 am this morning, just in case you did call...So Deborah walked in twenty minutes before because her daughter came in for the weekend from college and told her that she's tried drugs and had had her first sexual experience and all the rest... it's her first year. Granted, I probably should have told Deborah "Forgive me, go away, this is private." My mistake and you should know that I just rushed to the nearest telegraph office to send you a cable but it was closed and I'll try again tomorrow. By now, hopefully, you will have received my previous letter explaining a little of my life in the past ten years. Now I'm going to say this once, and I'm not going to say this again:

1. The ONLY one in my life is you.
2. The ONLY one I write to or receive letters from is you.
3. The ONLY time I ever MILDLY pay a woman a compliment is when I'm very high at a party and the extent of that is "That's a pretty dress you're wearing tonight."
4. Yes, I'm busy because my friends do listen to me when they have problems with their kids. They call and ask what should they do? And because I did have a pretty rough time of it when I was young, I remember how it was and work by instinct. The advice I give is usually right.
5. Right now, there are four people whose welfare is as important as life itself: David, Stevie, Marc and you. And you're in the last place of the four.
6. Whomsoever I love are under my protection. This is my D'Artagnan complex. The fact that I always end up as Don Quixote has nothing to do with it.
7. Would you please believe that when you called me the first time, that THAT was ME talking? You can't be such a goose as to not realize truth when you hear it?

I was tempted to write in that first letter, after your call, that our "fun" time might be half over. Perhaps I should have. Bébé, we haven't even met yet! Maybe I'll be much too boyish for you for you or you won't like the way I stand, or dress, or make love!

8. We haven't got a past, you and I, and I don't know if we have a future. I beg of you, don't let your imagination run away with you. There's no one else in my life. If you can't believe that, we haven't got a chance in the world.

All my love,   Pipsi

Woking   *October 20, 1971*
My Dearest Pips,

No one has ever used the term "Bébé" before, I like that! I can assure you that I have been called ALL kinds of things before, some of them unmentionable! I just had to write a note to you before I leave. The weather has brightened since yesterday when we experienced the most awful storms and when everything seemed so foul! I have decided to post these and hope that they arrive after Monday!

Today we went to Windsor, the sun shone and we all enjoyed it. Tomorrow will be our last day for visits so we'll probably go into town to the Victoria and Albert Museum. On Friday I want to see my mother. She thinks that I've left already, so this will be a surprise. She has been on a cruise around the Mediterranean with a couple of friends. She is a good sort and I love her dearly. She is 55 this month. We are often mistaken for sisters, more so these days as age seems to have caught up with me and I sport a lined and wrinkled face! So I will leave the kids in Celia's capable hands and dash off to South-ampton early on Friday morning and try to see Mom.

We are leaving early on Sunday morning and, God willing, should arrive in Pizarra Tuesday or Wednes-day, probably about the same time you receive this.

How does one explain this deluge of letters from Eu-rope?

Continued: Thursday, October 21

We have so much to talk about. When we do meet I hope that you'll do all the talking. On rare occasions, I'm known to have bouts of shyness and I have a feeling that this will happen when I meet you.

I'm mentally calculating if I could count my affairs on two hands! Yes, I have loved, I love, and I hope to love. I also count myself lucky inasmuch as I've sunk to the depths of despair and have enjoyed the heights of happiness. Some people go through love experienc-ing neither of course. I am sure that I have mentioned before that I'm a great believer in the cause and effect of early childhood relationships. When I say "early," I mean before the first seven years. I'm not sure that ho-mosexuals are born that way but think that it's pos-sibly a more psychological thing. Well, enough of that. I've lost my train of thought because some twenty-four hours has elapsed since I wrote the above. Yes, it's Fri-day, October 22. I got up at 5:00 a.m. (I can when it's necessary.) and drove down to Southampton and met my mother. She was quite taken by surprise and was absolutely thrilled to see me.

...Have asked numerous friends and not one of them thought that I was in any way typically "British." In fact, quite the reverse, Celia said, and I'm inclined to agree with her. I've never thought of myself as "narrow" *either—bigoted, perhaps. ...*

Pleasant thought, there will be mail waiting for me in Pizarra !

Much love—remove your cigarette while I...
Shirley

New York   October 20, 1971   3:00 a.m.

Dearest Pudge,

I've just read over what I wrote after the call. I misunderstood, you sounded a bit wild but I will send it along with this. I'm hoping against hope that you'll call either today or Friday. Tomorrow I must pick up Steve at the airport sometime in the afternoon as he's coming in for a long weekend. I wish you'd call so I could tell you to PLEASE drive carefully. I wish that you were safely back in Pizarra and I'm glad that there's no phone there. The damned thing rings at the wrong time or doesn't ring at all. I'm sorry, I feel I let you down badly yesterday. I think it's the first time, I know it's not the last and I hope that "Snoopy" helped?

Do you like the name "Pudge"? I prefer it to "Pudgy" but if you're terribly attached to "Shirley," I'll go back to that.

This is what's left of my face, a long nose, crowned with a curly grey mop. When emotionally disturbed, I stop eating, so I have lost 6 pounds in the past week. This would be great if those six pounds were removed from my thighs or my rear end, but of course, no such luck, the face gets it, and my wrinkles are getting wrinkles! The eyes are huge, and right now, very sad.

Don't be upset by the 3:00 a.m. I got into bed at 8:00 p.m. last night with the announcement "We do not wish to be disturbed." And that's the royal "We" of course. I fell asleep around ten, woke up at 1:30 .a.m., tossed for twenty minutes, got up, had a cup of coffee. I took a boiling hot bath, put on panties, a gray shirt with white stripes, a navy linen skirt and my blue, furry slippers. I wear furry blue slippers even when it's very hot. I'm wearing the skirt because I saw a red spider on the wall and then I didn't see it and if it's crawling around, I didn't want it going up my pants leg. In this way, I can feel it and brush it off.

Yesterday morning, before I mailed you the letter, my instinct was to wait to do so until today. What with all those confessions included, plus your call, I think that I would have torn it up and started all over. Are you very upset that you are not the first for me? Does it give you comfort to know that, if it comes to that, you are the last and final one? Think about it!

I read *La Batarde* a few years ago when it first came out, and read *Mad in Pursuit* about two months ago. The thought had crossed my mind to send you the second one a few weeks ago but felt, not knowing you all that well, that it might offend you. I think LeDuc is a fantastic writer and an unbearable person. Her attitude, as far as love is concerned, is beyond my comprehension. Do you know Genet at all? I don't think too much of his work but her attitude is so ridiculous. Here is a man, who is not only a homosexual, this is not so important, but he has spent at least twenty years in prison with the worst elements of society, and LeDuc is stupid enough to make this fantastic fuss about his not wearing a jacket or sweater or whatever it was. I don't know if you've reached that part yet? Her idolatry of de Beauvoir (having just finished her *Memoirs*, it's not for me) is infantile and besides, she's a far better writer than de Beauvoir. LeDuc's characteristics, her rapacity, lust and the eternal moaning about her big nose, drives me up a wall! However, she is so human and so honest about herself that I love it. I find her very clinical, not at all erotic. Like her or not, and I don't, she has all my admiration as a writer. The period of the twenties in Paris fascinates me. Artaud, Misia Sert, Maritain[6], that very *"raffiné"* group, all very interesting and my God, how creative!

Things which I have found out about you, you'll correct me if I'm wrong:

You're terrible at arithmetic. If it's 1:00 a.m. in Woking, it's either 7:00 or 8:00 p.m. here, not 9:00 p.m.

You need a LOT of loving care!

You don't think highly enough of yourself.

You are very emotional and very possessive.

You don't accept the fact that if you send a letter to me on a Monday or Tuesday, I may well get it on a Saturday, and since that is the day when everyone is here, including Papa, and there's no assurance that I can get to the mailbox first, would you bear in mind my dormant ulcer, take pity, and if possible, send off your letters on Wednesdays or Thursdays?

Despite all the letters and all my explanations, you don't really trust me and deep down, you're not sure that I love you. Believe me, I do!

Je t'embrasse, Pipsi

New York   October 20, 1971   10:20 a.m.

By now you've received the two letters I hope, including the one I wrote at 3:00 a.m. this morning? I will not mail you this today or even tomorrow, perhaps Friday, but I will note down whatever is running through my mind at odd moments and then send it off. I'm thinking that it's 3:20 or 4:20 in Woking?

---

6   Antonin Artaud (1896-1948), a French playwright, poet, actor and director. Misia Sert (1872-1950), an accomplished pianist who hosted an influential literary-artistic salon in Paris. Jacques Maritain (1882-1973), a French philosopher and political writer.

I hope that you're not too unhappy? The call yesterday had a bad effect on me. Perhaps it's all my imagination...I'm not really here, my eyes feel so sunk into my head and I looked in the mirror—Lord, what a sight! I'm waiting for Margaret, who comes to me every second Wednesday, stays six hours, and makes a pretense of cleaning the house. Sometimes she doesn't show up and I hope that today is one of those days. It will do me good to get down on hands and knees and do some scrubbing! If she isn't here by 10:45, I'll start in.

10:45 a.m. Not here, bless her, she must have known I needed the therapy. Fresh coffee is brewing. I drink too much of it and I loathe tea. I'm yawning. I'll never make it through the day, but for your question, no, I seldom go back to bed but I think that today I will.

12:30 p.m. It's afternoon. I just woke up and feel much better but my nose is stuffed. Now I'll drink coffee, have a bite and get to work.

2:10 p.m. *Et me voila*! Of course I'm bragging, but just call me "speeds" for short. Ate some toast, cold pot roast and coffee and cleaned half the house, not too well, I admit. ... I also took another hot bath and am now sitting here writing and writhing with mild cramps. Maybe I had pre-menstrual tension this morning? Do you have that sometimes? I wonder where that red spider is? I think what upset me is something you either said or I imagined you said about me being very busy and having admirers and some hogwash about getting many letters! If it was not my imagination, you are building up a completely false image in your mind and are going to be greatly disappointed. And if this was so, you must have had a very bad day and I don't like that at all.

Papa is going to walk in here on Saturday, pass a bony finger along a piece of furniture, stare at me with lifted eyebrow and say "Pips, my dear, have you dusted this month?"

And since Steve was more than hirsute when he left six weeks ago, I shudder to think what he looks like. Ah well, another charming Saturday!

...I'm putting this away now, I'm on car-pool duty and had better get some clothes on.

October 21, 7:00 a.m.

Went to bed around eleven and slept like a lump until 4:30 a.m. this morning. Gently rubbed chicken fat (how lewd!) over the turkey, poured orange juice over the beast, sprinkled salt and paprika over it, wished it luck and popped it into the oven. And who, sez you, roasts turkeys at 4:30 in the morning? Me, sez I, when you have the kind of day this is going to be!

You know, for us, this may well be the best way to communicate. Since we are both *"très emotioné"* and liable to pour our hearts out, perhaps we should adopt this form of daily notes? It's very soothing and quite sane. By the way, should you have any particular questions on any subjects that you want to ask me, and which you feel can't wait until we meet, don't be shy, and ask away. I promise to answer.

9:00 a.m. Alone at last! Shopping's done, washing machine's going, beds made, cleaning picked up, and I think that my dog may have broken his leg! He's very old but he forgets that he is and loves to go sliding around on rugs. He is now lying on the couch. (I'm a very bad disciplinarian) The vet is closed today. He doesn't seem to be in pain.

Poppy was terribly depressed yesterday. With him, it's always a combination of business not going quite the way he would wish it to be, the stock market going down, and worrying about Andre. He said that his carpeting was getting frayed and so it was high time he went on his merry way so that he wouldn't have to replace it.

So I called him a goose, told him I have some good books

for him and suggested that we take a slow boat to China and thumb our noses at the world. He perked up and of course he'll be here on Saturday. I can always make him laugh but I really wish I could be by myself for a few days. Instead, I pick up Steve and his friend from the airport at 2:30 this afternoon, and besides, it's a long weekend because Monday is Veteran's Day or something. Ah well, the fridge is loaded with beer, and I do enjoy it when the boys bring their friends home, and if I mention them, here and there, in my letters, it's probably my incompetent way of acquainting them to you in a gentle manner. I'm off to Fanelli's.

10:10 a.m. Back! Now into the shower and I'll allow myself one lapse from the general decorum of this missive. I WISH YOU WERE GOING INTO THE SHOWER WITH ME! SO THERE!

10:30 A.M. WONDERFUL! I just poured myself a very short drink. I don't usually this early, though I'm a pre-lunch drinker, very seldom have any during the day except when there's company or I go out.

...Did you know that from the age of 13 until I was 16 I was very fat and apt to go through doors sideways? I trimmed down to about 140 lbs. when I was 17, but it was not until my mother died that I lost the rest. I came back from the Russian trip weighing 113 lbs.—you can imagine what I looked like! My usual weight now is about 126–128 lbs. but now I'm down to 121 lbs. (your fault!) so I'm taking a break for lunch.

11:30 a.m. Lunch is a turkey wing, (not bad at all) a chunk of Swiss cheese, coffee and a cookie. I'm holding "*La fameuse lettre rose*" and I'll quote your words back to you: "But what I want, I want NOW! Oh well, it always comes to him who waits...I wonder." It does you know! I wonder if you have the vaguest idea as to why I'm writing to you like this? I'm going to sit on my bed, re-read your beautiful last two letters, and go to the bakery.

I'll stop at the draft office for some information (I detest the military, Vietnam and all that. Steve is quite OK—he's got a high number.) and pick up the boys. I'll be back around 4:00 p.m. I love you.

3:35 p.m. Well, it could be worse, the hair, I mean. It isn't that it's too long, it's just so messy. We stopped along the way, they had had no breakfast or lunch, and while they gulped hamburgers, French fries and fried onions, told me of their doings in Boston. Plenty of girls and plenty of booze! However, the work seems to get done. We got back at 3:25 and they left five minutes later, bless their pointy little heads. Steve is well on his way to being well able to take care of himself in every aspect, which pleases me no end!

I shall do whatever I must between eight and nine and will remain quietly at home for the rest of the day, playing the guitar and learning my new arpeggios, doing my push-ups (don't make a face), reading my *New York Times*, which I haven't done in five days, and wondering what you ate for lunch and whether you'll call?

...It seems to me that I have told you many more things about myself than I know about you and that seems grossly unfair. Par example, what are some of your REALLY nasty habits? Give me a chance, at least, to prepare for the worst. And thinking of Violette LeDuc, since we both have been reading *La Batarde*, here's a happy remembrance of my classic remark to Steve some sixteen years ago as he sat eating his bowl of cereal with one hand, while the other was busy elsewhere, "Yes, my darling, but not at the table."

I'm going off to write a few lines at the back of the card, and will add a few to this in the morning...*à demain*...

October 22, 8:10 a.m.

I was up at 5:00a.m. I thought I'd get rid of minor, puny, details before settling down and finishing this off. So I will finish with these thoughts: I hope that the two letters which awaited you in Pizarra did not make you too unhappy and that, as you read this one, you are again sporting a smug little smile all over your face! .

Have you read *One Day in the Life of Ivan Denisovich*?
You have just spent two in mine.
All my love. Pipsi.

The children and I left England on October 24th, and retraced our route back to the Costa del Sol. We were all greeted most happily by Gino and Barbie on our return to the Cortijo. Gino proudly showed us the newly remodeled schoolroom and so our regular school routine began. Whilst In England we had purchased school uniforms which I thought would set the tone and give some formality to those hours which were scheduled for schoolwork— normally 9:00 a.m.–2:00 p.m. However we always had some flexibility depending upon our needs. I often spent time with the children horseback riding or cycling (my choice). I really enjoyed working together with these youngsters and watching their academic growth. I, in turn, learned much from them. My time alone was spent in corresponding with Marc, Pipsi, my parents, other family members and my friends. I often drove down to the coast to visit friends or attend to personal business.

France, The Relais de Poitiers   *October 24, 1971*
My Dearest Pips,

We left at 7:30 a.m. and caught the 10:30 a.m. ferry. (Nearly missed, it owing to the spell of carsickness

that one of the children suffered.) Wonderful cross-
ing, a perfect autumn day and much too warm and
sunny for Europe at the end of October! We arrived
here at 9:00 p.m. and this motel is really superb and
absolutely deluxe. There are many changes since I
was in Poitiers some twenty years ago. I won a travel
scholarship at school and spent a month here with a
family—there were two boys—I think they found me
somewhat disappointing.

Have just finished half a bottle of wine and am feel-
ing no pain.... But all this luxury and only three chil-
dren with whom to share it. Actually it's an ideal hon-
eymoon/seduction place. Merde!

Love, Shirley

New York   October 24, 1971
Darling Pudge

I received your beautiful letter yesterday, the one without
your signature and though I won't be able to settle down and
write to you until Tuesday, everyone is still sleeping, so *me
voila*! I'm thinking of you of driving along, singing perhaps,
and wish you were already in Pizarra where my letters are
kept (I hope), waiting for you.

I realize that so far I have told you that I'm gentle and
promptly slapped someone's face, claim to be cool and collected and proved to be anything but, assumed a sophisticated style in my letters which is immediately disproved by a
bumbling phone call, so I'm beginning to think that when I
say "fantastic" and someday you say to me "OK, show me. Be
fantastic." I'll probably hide under the bed and carry on like
a raving maniac. So that's what it is, adrenaline! Ah, ha, ha,
oh, oh, oh, fantastic!

Some hours later.

What is a "hard hat"? Here a hard hat is a reactionary man, usually very bigoted who drinks a lot of beer, has a pot belly and hates college kids. Have I told you of my riding lessons when I was fifteen? And speaking of horses and categorically related subjects like boots (I approach all of them by stating, "me Tarzan, you Jane!"), I trust you're not too peculiar about whips!? Better we should know all about these little things!

I couldn't write back to you in Woking as I didn't think that it would reach you in time. I do hope that your smug little smile is back, you cocky little bitch, or bastard, or bunny? Or...never mind. Also, after all these letters, and I am sorry if I was nasty in the one written—God knows—at what time in the morning, I was very angry with myself and of course, took it out on you. I think that I must be more romantic than you. I visualize hysterical situations between us. Par example, when alone in a room (pas encore!), nice music playing, then we'll go into "Do you care to dance?" "Yes, I'd love to, I'll lead." "What do you mean, you'll lead? I'll lead." "Not on your life, I always lead." "Really?" Well that's what you think!" etc. HOWEVER, I have figured this one out, taking into consideration height, weight, build, etc. If I put both arms around your waist, you can encircle me a little lower and rest your hands on my Popo (derriere in French), and this way we'll both be left with our masterful feelings. Lord...I'm so good to you!

Later. Oh yes, in case I forgot to mention it, thanks a whole lot for invading my every moment throughout the day! You have quickly disposed of my great love of literature and it was only with superhuman effort that I managed to do my *New York Times* Sunday crossword puzzle. This, by the way, is one of the great pleasures of my life (*on s'amuse comme on peut*) and since I'm not modest either, I especially enjoy doing the damned thing in ink at the beach during the summer, which prompts fair maidens (of 65 or so) to approach me wide-eyed and open-mouthed and say "Do you always do them in ink?" To which I answer in those cool, sophisticated tones you know so well, "Oh, doesn't everyone?"

Well, Thursday did come and I've just gone through my five minutes of paranoia for the week. Someone has swiped my pen. THE pen with which I write to you, and I can get carried away by trifles like that. Which is why, dear Hall, this paper, which I started to use after the first few letters, is used only for you and since we're fast reaching the bottom of the box and if I can't get more of the same, we'll probably, like Picasso, go through our pink, blue and green periods!

No need to be scared of our first meeting! There may be icky moments but if we can meet alone for an hour or two, after ten minutes of being tongue-tied, fifteen of giggling, we'll simply hold each other's hand and talk quietly and all will be well. And as far as being a disappointment, of course I worry that I will be to you. But what are we really concerned about? Here we are, picking each other's minds, and you seem to enjoy it as much as I do, so mentally we're OK. Physical attributes? I REALLY do like Renoir's nudes and as long as you don't wear false eyelashes, wear heavy make-up, (somehow I'm not too concerned) you don't have too much to worry about. In reverse, since you like it so much, I have my voice going for me; the face, once you get used to it being somewhat stark, is really not too bad. Of course, if you're fixated on large bosoms, you've got a problem. Blondes? Brunettes? YOU have nothing to worry about as my hair is a lovely shade of grey (only on my head!) and anyway, I'm quite convinced that I'll be bald by the time I'm fifty.

So we are left with that indefinable word, sex appeal! I simply don't believe that when two people write to each other, the way we do, and set adrenaline going, that we will come face to face and feel nothing. Not possible and quite ridiculous! However, you say "No promises" and "If nothing else, we'll be great friends." Great, but do you mind if, until then, I continue to woo you with my letters? I should like to feel that I'm not the only one being slowly turned to mush by this correspondence. So much for your worries!.

...I think that you should know that I love Bach, raw chestnuts, Piaf, (not your type of voice at all, much too raspy!) most of what the Beatles have written, Simone Signoret, cold lobster with mayonnaise, seeing movies by myself, though I'll gladly hold hands and smooch with YOU, and seeing one of your letters in the post!

I have a theory of AWARENESS, which has nothing to do with intellect and probably not even too much with intelligence. I simply feel that the diameter of people's awareness of each other (also nothing to do with love or great friendship)—as far as the innermost capabilities of relating to others—is completely limited by a circle which one cannot transcend. And of course, these circles have different sizes ranging, let us say, from the size of a button, to the size of a barrel, or a moon, or a satellite, etc. Of course I rate myself very highly and as a result do not see things as black and white but only in various shades of grey.

Je t'embrasse,   Pipsi

P.S. I think you must have been badly hurt with Delyn.

Spain October 27, 1971
My Dearest Pips,

   Although I'm writing this on the 27th, I might well not post it until Sunday as per instructions. The missing letter, and two more very thick ones, were waiting for me on my arrival at the Hollanders. I'm going to begin school "proper" on Monday morning. I'm very much looking forward to that as Gino and Barbie have fixed up a perfect schoolroom for me. It resembles a private library.

   You ask me what I do. I am a schoolteacher, for my sins, this you know anyway, and I'll be teaching Lise, Siri and Scott, supplementing their American correspondence courses with a lot of extra stuff that these courses fail to provide. For example, their written expression has improved tremendously already. There are gaps in history and geography and appreciation of music. I love folk songs, always have, and had a vast repertoire, long before it became the "in thing." I believe a great deal in "learning through experience" and am somewhat of a follower of Froebel and Piaget. I can give them virtually nothing in the way of arithmetic, as you have noticed! And physics and chemistry are foreign languages to me—Gino will fill in the gaps.

   Now for the letter written October 18th:

   ...No, never once, in all your letters did you say I was mad, but the first words you uttered over the phone were "You're mad, absolutely MAD!" and I said "Yes, and that makes two of us!" ...I think that I expected you to sound more masculine somehow. You really have a beautiful speaking voice.

   I NEVER get dead drunk. Marc does not know that we correspond as frequently as this. I love him dearly, in a way that I find difficult to explain and would do any-thing for him, and the last thing I would EVER want is that he be hurt in any way by me, rest assured.

I love anchovies, kidneys, raw vegetables, steak, cooked and rare. Irene makes an excellent steak tartare! And what is all this about being so modest and pecu-liar when undressing? Sounds as if you were raised in a convent to beat all convents! No one has a chance to be shy in that way with me. Thank God, we were brought up with no hang-ups about being seen without clothes. Irene used to be a bit like you, until she met me, must be something about you Belgians!

Me, in black transparent, underwear? You must be joking! Mine, my sleeping attire I mean, is very plain and practical, the sort of thing one can wear to open the door to the milkman.

And as for being dissolute, my dear girl, you are a mere novice. I have told you that Delyn was not the first, but I will admit that our affair was the longest because we lived together from 1965–1969, and I mean together like a regular couple. I had had affairs before this, and I've had affairs since and I'm not married and am living a "gay" bachelor/bitchelor existence!

Now what I want to know is:

How CAN you possibly think that you love me when you have not MET me?

No, I don't like the nickname "Pudge" or "Pudgy!" Thanks, but I prefer "Shirley."

Continued: ...Which leads me to the last letters of Oc-tober 19th and 20th. I'm sorry about the second phone call, I really am, and thank God I had the sense to ask you if you were alone! I do not understand why you

were so angry with me. Except that I was speechless...
and it seemed a waste of money. I dreamt about the
whole thing again last night, damn it. So why should
you wish to make ME wish that I had never been born?
Your letter of the 19th is quite an onslaught and I fail
to understand why? Of course I believe that it was you
talking the first time that I phoned. What do you mean
about "The fun time being half over?" What I do not
understand is what makes you think that you can care
for me when you have not met me, and how can one
have feelings that deep for someone you have not met
and do not know? There are many reasons I know as to
WHY I should like you, but I have no idea as to whether
I would ever LOVE you!

The correspondence I enjoy, it is exciting and I appreciate your letters and I would be a liar if I did not
admit that it turns on the adrenaline fast and furious...

Yes I know about Genet, and no, I do not like or enjoy what I have read about him, just too vulgar for me.
Like Henry Miller, one has to read through so much filth
for one sentence of sheer beauty, forget it. Yes, I liked
Leduc's Mad in Pursuit. I think that masturbation is a
great thing, it's better than frustration and definitely
better than nothing.

Yes, you're right, I need a lot of love and care, and I
need to KNOW, there are always feelings of great insecurity. Yes, I'm very emotional and very possessive.

Don't put me on a pedestal, so no more talk of loving
me when you don't know me...Fondest love and many
thoughts...S.H.

Spain October 27   midnight
Dearest Pips,

It was Irene's birthday today. You know what we had for lunch? Stew!

I was going to tell you about Irene, perhaps I might be able to send a photo. She's 49 today, I think, anyway she doesn't look it. She's a dyed blonde, has very blue eyes, is slightly taller than me, has put on some weight but still has a good figure on the whole. She has a British mother and a Belgian father who died just after the war. She used to work for S.H.A.P.E. in Paris. She is very intelligent, adores difficult crosswords and mathematical problems, is an excellent cook, a good horsewoman, a good dancer. She paints and sings out of tune! She has the most beautiful hands I have ever seen on any woman. Her teeth are as good as perfect, white, even and strong looking and she has beautiful lips. She's extremely hospitable and is very generous. She met and married Peter, in Paris, when she was 36. I have known her since 1964 and I love her dearly, she has been very good to me, don't know where I would have been without her when I left Masjid-i-Suliman (Iran). She drives almost as well as I do and she's patient with me. She's a dear friend...she never liked Delyn, neither did my mother!

My parents know how I am....Marc was telling me that when he told you about me, you said that it didn't interest you as to what people did in bed...there's my girl! (All right, you are not my girl!) Am off to my virginal couch, together with a book...for want of something better!

With love,   Shirley

New York   October 28

Dear Bébé, (since you like it.)

I wish that my hot flashes would stop. Perhaps, after all, it's not you, but the change of life! *C'est possible après tout!* I mailed you a letter yesterday wondering all the time whether I wasn't flooding you with too many words, too much this, too much that and your blue letter tells me that you want to reduce the number from your side. Do you really, or was it the nerves, the jealousy, or whatever? ...You have once again thrown me into a state of shock! Count your affairs on two hands! Sweet Jesus, don't tell me you're a loose woman? I vaguely remember begging YOU not to think of ME as dissolute...and anyway, how in your young life could you have had the time? Also, what is your definition of an affair? I mean, jumping into the "kip" (I know all the proper English expressions) does not an affair make unless you continue it steadily for a year at least. God help me, I've fallen in love with a lecher! Unless, of course, you've had dealings with the wrong types! ...*Yo tambien*, if in the back of your mind, you are hoping to make me just another conquest so you can take off your sandals and start counting on your toes, forget the whole thing! Unless we both faint dead away when we come nose to nose (and I'm rubbing yours with mine) if and when we do meet and decide THAT'S IT, then perhaps, in a few years (*allevei*, an old Jewish expression), we could try things out on a permanent basis and since I'm terrific in the kitchen and other places too, you'll do well to remember that I swing a mean frying pan and will certainly go into a towering rage at the first sign of any hanky-panky.

Basically and seriously for one moment, I think that the relationship between two women is the most difficult thing in the world. However much one is masculine in attitude, and the way one deals with people, dressing, walking, etc, the glands and the emotions remain totally female, governed by the phases of the moon one might say. I don't think too many women make it. HOWEVER, with my unfailing good humor, splendid intelligence, and clarity of purpose, we shall overcome!

Your letters make me very happy. Mine are supposed to do the same. They ARE NOT (and that's an order) to make you annoyed, jealous or nervous! Restless, yes, it can't be helped, and frustrated? Why should I be the only one?

Will you please believe that I love you dearly and should you have some tiny freckle or beauty spot in a private sort of place, I'll kiss it now and say

All my love,   Pipsi

Spain October 29, 1971
My Dearest Pips,

Somewhere along the line there has been a misunderstanding I feel...but how and why, I'm not sure.

I made a special trip to the Cortijo yesterday because I heard that there was mail for me. Sure enough, there were letters from you and one from Marc. I was very sorry to learn that he had been depressed but I hope that after he had lunched with you and the family, he was much better and more his usual self? As for "sitting down and writing Poppy a cheerful letter," I write to him EVERY day! Mind you, they are not nearly as interesting as the ones I write to you! But then, he doesn't give me any leads!. I think that there is every possibility that we will meet for Christmas and then I have asked him to come back here and enjoy some sunshine before dashing back to New York.

I have a strong feeling that you will have been disappointed with my last few letters. I enjoy this correspon-

dence (by now you will have realized that I'm repetitive) and I do not want to terminate it. This flirtation by mail is most stimulating but I'm a little concerned by your idea that you love me very much. YOU are the one who will be disappointed and that is the last thing that I would want. I hate hurting people in any way and I have the feeling that you, like me, are easily hurt.

I'm most concerned that you have lost so much weight, and why blame me? Please, please take care! How has the stop-nail-biting progressed? I suppose that the cigarette smoking has increased?

And thinking about taking a shower, do you take your shower with your panties on? Well you did say that you would like to take me into the shower and I certainly have no objection, but then, what happens to false modesty? I bet that your hair is the type that tempts one to run one's fingers through it...?

There has been some misunderstanding about "many letters" and "admirers." I'm the dissolute one, not you.

Explain to me why you are on car pool duty? I thought that was only done by mothers of young children, to and from school?

As for nasty habits—I asked Irene about that this morning. We can think of quite a few faults, like being pedantic, intolerant of those nearest and dearest, possessive, expecting other people to do what I say, not what I do, (it's alright for me to flirt but not my girl!) and argumentative—but nasty habits? Well, I gave up smoking.

Where did you meet Marvin? I know that you went into your parents' bedroom at about one or two in the morning and announced your engagement! Sounds like rebellion to me.

...I know that I'm going to be scared silly when we meet because of the ideas we will have built up about each other. I'll possibly do something silly like get sloshed, when in actual fact I am not a great drinker. Oh Lord, I don't want to think about it!

You disturb me, you know. I should really say, "Enough of this, no more of this type of correspondence, but I can't! And I think that you should destroy the letters, although I must admit that I have all yours!

I really must make a move. Fondest love, Shirley.

New York   October 29, 1971

Chère Madamoiselle, I'm back in my mood of utter decorum. This is a virgin piece of paper from a brand new box. As you can see, I was unable to get the same type. Yesterday was two month's since you wrote me your first letter in answer to mine in which I know you were SO clever as to discern the "inner me." I feel as if I'm damned if I write and damned if I don't, so back to the keeping of notes for a few days and then I'll send it off. Does it strike you as odd that both of us, after that call, resorted to this keeping of notes? That I accuse you of being possessive and you admit to jealousy (same thing), and that you went through a tortuous time, as I'm sure you have gathered since reading my letters, so did I. That you wanted to call and I was waiting for the phone to ring, etc. I find all this very frightening and—your last two letters from Woking upset me, I don't know why, except for the feeling I've missed out on something, somewhere, along the line. The transition from divine and gentle, beautiful teasing between us to this outpouring of emotion (and I'm much more guilty than you are, but then I did tell you I thought myself more romantic than you) was so sudden and abrupt that I'm still trying to catch my breath—and every time I do, or think I do, you write something like "Take the cigarette out!" and that, Bébé, drives me up the wall—and that, Pudge, I'm not used to!

You see, I was not joking when I told you I'm used to having the upper hand. I'm the one who drives people up a wall. I'M the one who says "*Querida mia*." I'M the one who holds the reins—but now, I just don't know and believe me, this is not a love letter, so to speak, though I do love you so much, I'm trying to explain myself to you, and perhaps, even more to me. So of course, being two fairly bright girls (and by the way, DO you know that you're a girl? I do.), the most obvious thing comes right up, which I've mentioned in a joking way as "chasing the wrong types." "Aha!" I say, "Wow! You've been looking at all the wrong ones, unknown to you, all along you've been looking for a male counterpart of yourself!" I'm convinced that this is not so! I really think of relationships as one party being male, the other being female, dominant yes, but only to an extent. (All this, by the way, are just thoughts and you, my sounding board.)

For instance, I know American women well. I speak now of friends, circles of acquaintances, a milieu in which I find myself. They are ALL, without exception, the toughest, most dominant, most ball-breaking bunch, that you could ever wish to meet! (Forgive the expression.) Feminine to distraction, fantastic at what they can do with eye shadow and rouge, but womanly? Forget it! As I've said before, American women talk a lot and for some strange reason, they always fill my ears with details I'm not interested in. but I have found out this: they look sexy but are not, look soft but are tougher than you or I could ever hope to be. They adore adulation and don't know what to do with it once they've got it! They are hopelessly unromantic but want the car door opened and the cigarette lit for them, and, with few exceptions, seem to have no fun in bed.

This is only to explain that these women, who are purely "normal" as far as society is concerned, would faint dead away at the thought of a Lesbian relationship, but they are men! And me? I am not! O yes, I'm the dominant one, I have to a great degree, boyish features, occasionally stand like one, hold my cigarette like one, throw a ball the way a man would but I'M NOT A MAN! But also—I'm not a soft piece of fluff, and baby, if that's what you're looking for, oi, is you gonna be disappointed! I told you that you might well be the first to know the "honest" side of me and so you are! I told you not to be shy and to ask questions and I would answer and I will! By the way, in relationship to Marvin, I do NOT count myself as an American woman, I always think of myself as European. I could not conceive of doing anything so degrading to any human being as what my friends do to their husbands.

...Why am I talking so much, and believe me, Bébé, none of this is written here in anyway to make you suffer, or wonder, or worry, I'm only trying to dig in as much as one can within oneself and TRY to explain me to you, and of course, ask you to do the same. You are so open on the surface, and yet, since yesterday, I feel I'm reading you wrong.

Your facetious remark of "Love affairs being counted on two hands"—my answer to that in yesterday's letter was typical of me, the one I like the world to accept, easy, funny, very sophisticated, glib, and it is true what I wrote yesterday, but also, it is true that I'm so at sea, so bewildered. I think that I'm so upset at the thought that you have gone to bed with a dozen odd females—I'm not saying it's wrong—just that I can't conceive of it!

I just don't believe that you thought yourself, or that anyone could think of themselves, in LOVE that often? THAT is alien to me, but I should know the truth soon because I'm not sending this out for a few days and may well tear it up instead. And you will, hopefully, answer yesterday's letter and tell me the truth. Whatever you do, DON'T LIE! I CAN stand the idea of living with a Casanova, though I should hope (I know) that a few days in my arms should tame you down. No one, Pudge, has looked after you properly, that's the problem!

Also, you might wonder if I'm being a hypocrite as far as Marvin is concerned, and might well think that being unfaithful is degrading enough. *Naturellement*, I don't look at things like that at all. I think that acting towards people, be they lovers, husbands or friends, and treating them like dirt, is the most awful thing one can do. That's what I was referring to in connection with the married women I know. ...

...It's unbelievable how young your parents are! Poppy says your mother is a "lady" and he seems to have found your father very nice. I think it must have been difficult to have become one at the age of nineteen. Tell me about you as a child, small, medium size and about you as a teenager?

I went to a private school, wore a navy jumper, white shirt, navy coat, navy hat with red lettering, grey smock over the uniform during class hours and mine was always covered with ink spots, gloves were lost, shoe laces trailed, homework never done, fantastic in reading and composition and quite hopeless at everything else. Every afternoon we had knitting for an hour while one student read aloud. The project was a scarf during my third year. By May, mine amounted to six inches, an uneven, ratty looking thing, which was finally hung on my back, while a sign on my chest read *"Neukorn est paresseuse!"* I had to parade with it for a week in school, and I loved every minute of it! I was a tough little kid. It came in handy later on. I also remember being carried on a big girl's shoulder and getting a funny feeling down below and liking it. Other memories include being excused early from school once a week and being taken by chauffeured limousine to the ice-skating rink where I had lessons. I wore a burgundy short dress, trimmed with white angora wool which my mother had knitted for me. I was very good and still am. I also had dancing lessons, the Isadora Duncan type, with Issa Vos. Twice a week and I was a star pupil, very graceful, and as supple as a snake. We wore short black silk Greek tunics. Issa Voss died in 1938 but I continued my classes with a star pupil of hers, I don't remember her name, only that I adored her. She looked like Loretta Young.

When my mother died, I stayed with Poppy for a few days where we had an endless stream of visitors coming by. Two little old ladies, sisters, came and I was chatting with them and they said *"Vous, vous souvenez de...?"* The young dancing teacher had been their niece and was killed in God knows which concentration camp! They had pictures of her in their handbags and we looked at them and when they left, I went into the loo, turned on the faucet so that I shouldn't be heard and cried bitterly. And those were the only tears shed since I was about five and I haven't cried since.

October 30

I have come to the conclusion that while in Iran, you kept a harem of lovely young things and that is why you have to count on your fingers. I must stop harping on this subject or I might well slap your face when we meet.

We are in agreement on the psychological bit. What I was trying to say was that you had a good relationship with your mother, a tolerable one with Ernie *et te voila*! I had an un-caring one with my mother and probably a non-existent one with Marc, *et me voila*! Same result, different causes—but you know, we're too old to feel any resentment, or at least, so it seems to me. Since you're so fond of "The Bard"—"What's done is done and cannot be undone!"—and I say, enough of all this. Think I'll remove my cigarette again—Tell me about you. Why do you wear shirts buttoned to the top? Do you not like your throat? What is the ring which you wear on the pinky of your left hand? Why are you bigoted and what are you bigoted about? Where were you during the war? Did you stay in Birmingham? Tell me!

Your letter of October 27th just came. BITCH!

Thanks a lot for what you say! Do forget all the nonsense I have written, better still tear them up! You have quite succeeded in making me feel an absolute, complete, moronic idiot. Am sending this off AS IS so you might well know that I will always romanticize where there is nothing to romance about, love, where there is possibly no desire, and to think that I said that we were two sides of the same coin! The only thing that I was right about was saying, "I don't think I'm reading you right."!

> Je t'embrasse, Bébé,   Pipsi

New York   October 30, 1971

Having posted the letter with the nasty lines at the end of it, and feeling quite like "Charlie Brown" having been punched with a left to the stomach and a right to the chin, just a few words of apology for my breach of good manners in imposing on you all the romantic hogwash, and for God's sake, tear it up and throw it out! And by the way, it won't happen again, so not to worry. All's well, friends if you like, *et pour le reste on vas voir* and let's keep it at that!

As far as Marc and hurting him, I was not speaking of

our correspondence. There is reticence between he and I and he would not like me to know that he served you breakfast in bed, ditto with your love life, he's very fond of you, as you are of him, so do leave him his illusions. I certainly don't see any harm in it since you've added so much to his outlook on life, leave well enough alone. Nowhere in your letters did you say that Delyn was not your first. It's unimportant but just to set the record straight, you didn't. The black transparent nightie (if you'll re-read that passage) was my way of teasing you and I'm not terribly impressed with your sleeping attire as I've worn the same for the past five years or so. "Pudge" has been wiped out. I hope you allow an occasional "Bébé"? I am fully aware that we haven't met and the question had arisen from me to me as to how I could possibly think I loved you? I had decided that I was quite insane! However, you will note that in the letter sent off this morning, I was uneasy in some vague way I could not understand. So there probably is ESP and all is OK, etc. The onslaught of the letter of the 19th after the phone call, was due to the fact that I had that morning sent you a letter with my "confessions" and I was very upset about Deborah being here and concerned that you might be imagining all kinds of things. Your letters after that, did not exactly denote tranquil peace of mind, and my mistake has been in NOT reading between the lines. As far as putting you on a pedestal, the thought would never occur to me. Having occupied that niche, I know how uncomfortable it is! I agree with you, *naturellement*, that there are many reasons why you should, and will, like me. Let me give you fair warning though, and do not fall in love with me. I never make the same mistake twice.

At least I read you right on the love and care and insecurity and being possessive. About the emotional, well, I'm getting the full brunt of it and your need to "KNOW." I obviously told you the wrong way. I would remind you that I'm not possessive, neither with love, children or anything else. Romantic, yes, possessive, no!

And other than saying sorry for calling you "bitch," when you really are a bastard, and taking perhaps a nasty dig at Irene, let's let it go at that, and say that's all for today.

Je t'embrasse, Pipsi

P.S. I shouldn't really tell you but I'm grinning from ear to ear!

Spain October 31, 1971   10:30 p.m.
My Dearest, Delightful Pips,

Thank goodness that all the household have gone to their respective beds and I can write to you. Tomorrow is my first day of school in the new schoolroom!

So—I have just read your letter. The first three pages of your letter made me smile, and then roar with laughter, not giggle. I don't giggle really, I simply laugh and you make me do that quite a lot.

I am familiar with the other interpretation of "hard hat." Mine is to protect my pretty little head against damage in the eventuality of a fall from my horse, whose name, by the way, is Cancionero.

Of course I have a whip, but not for what you think, I just carry it sometimes when out riding. It depends on the gee-gee. I haven't carried it in ages. I might be peculiar, but not that much!

Cocky little bastard sounds better, don't you think? Wonder who'll grab who first?

...On the subject of romanticism, I think that you and I are pretty much the same as far as that goes. And I am an "aware" person. I know exactly what you mean

and agree with what you say that it has nothing to do with intelligence, or intellect, or love. I can name those whom I know who have this awareness.

I might have known! Crosswords! And done in ink! Who is "cocky" now? Ah well, we can't be good at everything, and someone has to walk the dog!

And it is precisely that, that when we meet face to face there will be an explosion! I have decided that I am going to continue this delightful correspondence, and to hell with what might happen, we'll cross those bridges when we come to them.

I love Bach, Vivaldi, goat's cheese, lobster mayonnaise, crab in any way, adore Piaf—so there! And I have her records! I DO NOT ENJOY SEEING MOVIES BY MYSELF!

And I LOVE receiving your letters, and dislike "PUDGE"—but that you know by now. I ADORE Marc, and love driving fast, riding a horse that is difficult to handle—and when we meet, I'll tell you all about the Delyn episode. Yes, I was hurt but I got over it. I like caviar (Iranian) and enjoy fishing (but haven't done any in an age). I like water-skiing and sailing too, but again, haven't done either in years.

I really am very outspoken and dramatic. You disturb me, I am torn apart, oh Hell, it's midnight and I'm going to bed!

Your circles remind me of that song which I like, "The Windmills of Your Mind." Do you know it? Rex Harrison's son sings it, and so does a girl called Dusty Springfield. (She is!)

A bientôt,   Je t'embrasse très fort,
Much love,   Shirley

November

During the first week in November, Pipsi (who had never held a paying job, except as a sales assistant at Gimbel's in Manhattan for approximately four months), was accepted as a trainee at a local privately owned travel agency. This was her first and a most important step on her way to independence. (And I don't mean in Missouri!)

To our mutual delight, our correspondence increased. By this time, we were each writing two or three letters daily. At the end of the month Pipsi went to a recording studio and made a recording especially for me. She sang both in French and English, while accompanying herself on the guitar and included songs for which she had composed both the music and the lyrics.

Spain   November 1, 1971

Pips, What the Hell did you expect? Do you honestly think that I have spent all my life in a convent?

(Wow, hold me back!) I was not married at nineteen and I have been free and roving around from place to place. Real affairs? Sure I've had some, four real ones and no, I'm not one to go for wrong types. It isn't as bad as it sounds, believe me. When we meet I'll explain and tell all. I promise to give you my life story, and no, I don't want to start counting on my toes!

I LOVE your letters and you damned well know it!.

...Today we had our first day of school here and I

enjoyed it very much and so did the kids. In fact, later, I had to return to the schoolroom and order them out into the sunshine! We have arranged an excellent display of posters of all the children's work, their pictures and descriptions of what we saw on the trip to England, etc. Gino and Barbie were most impressed and I'm pleased.

Oh, I do something very well. I'm very good at whistling! I whistle in perfect tune and with little trills. It comes in very useful when one wants to hail a taxi in the middle of cities like London, New York or Teheran!

...Of course I BELIEVE you, but I do not understand how it is possible? I do not want to analyze my feelings towards you. It frightens me!

Continued. November 2, 1971

Do you like artichokes and avocados, Brie and smoked salmon? Oh, of course I know that you like THAT!

... I'm mush too. As Gibran said, "Half of what I say is meaningless but I say it so that the other half may reach you!"

I am very musical but I don't read music. You will have to be patient! I learn songs quickly. It will be fun to sing together. How about that?

Fondest love, Shirley

New York   November 2, 1971
Bébé,

...You've had my apologies by now and they will have to suffice. We have our vanities, all of us, yours, perhaps, are to send photos which are not too flattering. And mine? Never to apologize and say "I'm sorry." But of course, I am! Like hot milk, I boil up quickly and simmer down just as fast.

Having a ghastly memory, by now I've quite forgotten some of the things I wrote! Much, however, I have not forgotten. And I think I will never understand your obvious delight in hearing me say that I love you and your anger at seeing it written down? And Marc was right—no, I'm not interested in what "people" do in bed. And I'm not petulant so skip the "Alright...you are not my girl!" I am perfectly delighted and capable and more than willing...as long as you'll be mine! And here we go again. Since, willy-nilly, we have, like it or not, become an important part of one another's life, I'm sending you a lyric. It reads like a poem, but it is a lyric, inspired I admit by your letter but not written FOR you. I like it and would like your opinion. It wrote itself in ten minutes, very early last Sunday morning and I'm now working on the music. This, as usual, is damned difficult and words are being changed as I go along. As it is untitled, the date of October 31 will have to do.

Song of No Title[7]

You like it when I play the games of make-believe

and link for you a chain of myriad lies,

And spin a web of all the stars and moons that ever were,

for you to gaze at with your indifferent eyes.

And you like it when I make you laugh with glee

at hearing me whisper words that have been said before,

Or see me, clumsy, pick an apple off a tree,

---

7   Music and lyrics composed by Sylvia Paymer, 1971.

Or listen to my foolish jokes as we walk some sandy shore.

So I put on my jester's hat and strike a funny pose.

Weave rhymes into couplets to make a funny song.

And walk into a store and buy you a single rose

And whistle a tune when you are gone.

So you think me cynical and believe that I don't care?

You will never know that all the lies are true.

And my sophisticated sayings are the illusions of my despair.

For you love no one at all and I love only you!

Ride your horse. (WHAT'S HIS NAME?) Or play tennis and I'll go to my guitar...the outlets are all different and yet all the same.

All my love, Pipsi

New York   November 3. 1971
Dear Shirley,

Was it only two weeks ago that I was hoping that Margaret would not show up and that the therapy would be good for me? The dirty rat has done it again! Therapy is no longer needed and here I am with all the cleaning to be done. Well, it will get done sooner or later. I should have hoped, dear heart, (with levity, luv, with levity) that you would have been smart enough to ignore the avalanche of sentiment that has been pouring over you little head. I am not at all disappointed by your last few letters.

By now you will have received the "Charlie Brown" Schultz card? Another one of his favorite expressions is: "Good Grief." Yes, I am very much like him, so have no fears, I'm not easily hurt. As a matter of fact, I've been told often enough that I don't have deep enough feelings to feel much at all. I simply stepped out of character for a few days and when one has been "in character" for some forty odd years, it's a stupid thing to do!

Jewel has just returned from Florida, so Deborah tells me, where it seems that my name is being bandied about as someone whom a lot of people would love to meet, for obvious reasons. This means that Alexis # 2 (I call her Alioushka, I have a great fondness for pet names.) must have been there recently and, once again, opened her big mouth. I say "once again" because she told her husband about us and THAT'S a funny story which I'll tell you some other time. It involves my career as a producer, director and actor (a year in Greenwich Village) working with amateurs, etc.

You asked about the car pool? Well, the high school is quite far away and David, until last week, did not have his driver's license.

We have one thing in common and that is: it's perfectly OK for me to flirt but I get annoyed if my girlfriend does, or rather, did, while trying all the time damned hard not to show it!

Yep, I like having fingers running through my hair. I know you have a lovely little nose and I still don't understand why you should be scared silly about our meeting? I should think that you would realize that we're going to have a tremendous amount of fun, in and out of ...and I fully expect to teach you all kinds of lovely things, but not the guitar! I'm not good enough. ...

Je t'embrasse, Pipsi

Spain   November 4, 1971   2:30 p.m.
My Darling, Delightful, Terribly Difficult Pips.

First of all please believe me when I say that I tried hard with the mail so that it should not arrive on a Saturday. I suppose that it goes quicker from some places than others. Yours to me never get here quickly enough!

I NEVER LIE! I have been told too many lies and the one thing that I do not appreciate from anyone, least of all someone that I love, care for and respect, is lying. Maybe I might not be too forthcoming about some things and therefore not mention them until requested to do so, but I do not tell untruths.

You have never asked me if I was involved in any way with anyone, you just PRESUMED that I wasn't.

First of all, let me clear up the story about Delyn. I told Marc about my relationship with Delyn and being the honest sort of person that I am, I never led him to believe, in any way at all that I was seduced by her. He thinks that it was all a mistake and that I'm "as normal" as the next girl! That is because he DOES NOT want to accept it in any other way. He is into denial. I told him that I was a Lesbian before I met her, and that she had indulged in Lesbian relationships before becoming involved with me.

I do not understand your remark about me looking for "more male counterparts of myself." This is not true at all. On the whole I have always enjoyed chasing, conquering and seducing, etc.—surely the more male roles? The more I learn about you the more alike we are it seems to me. It's that which makes me think that I'll be a disappointment to you. I'm very boyishly/masculine but do admit to being very soft, very romantic, very sentimental and easily hurt, etc. I'm probably more feminine than you, but not too much so.

Perhaps you will understand and be a little patient and realize why I wrote "I'm being torn apart!" and "I'll cross those bridges when I come to them." I am "mush" and bad tempered these days when I don't receive a letter.

You are dominant, and so am I—very! I drive like a man, sometimes walk and stand like one, ride like one, throw a ball like one. I used to win prizes at "throwing the cricket ball" which I could do better than anyone, boy or girl, of my age. AND I AM GLAD THAT YOU ARE NOT A MAN! If I wanted a man, I would damned well go out and get one! I have tried, by the way, I'm just not interested and I have never felt emotionally towards men in the same way that I have felt towards women.

I suppose that you must be rather Victorian to a degree, as far as the removal of clothes is concerned, we'll have to change that! I have been fortunate inasmuch as I have young parents. There was a war on, air raid shelters which were shared etc. and ever since I can remember, we have all seen each other in various states of undress and naked. I have never felt shy about the removal of clothes or of being seen with or without!

I'm not going to mail this because it's far from finished but will you excuse me while I go off to ride?

Continued: 9:00 p.m.

We saddled up the horses and Gino, Scott, Siri and I rode over to Pizarra. There was no mail for me but then I did get a letter from you this morning and one from Poppy too.

...You say on page one of your letter that you shed

tears easily and on another page you say that you hadn't shed tears since you were five and also when you learned that the dancing teacher had been killed.

I do not feel any resentment towards my parents, it's just that Ernie and I do not really enjoy each other's company for too long. Actually it's better now and we're really quite friendly. As for my mother being a "Lady"—she is a dear girl and I have been very close to her, as you know. They began their life together when I was six months old and they lived with my Nan.

We stayed in Birmingham throughout the war. My mother had to go out to work in a factory as part of the War Effort and Ernie was not allowed to enlist (he tried to, as a rear gunner in the RAF!) because his work at the Joseph Lucas factory was too important. Components for armored vehicles and aircraft were made there and he had to help train women factory workers. I used to collect shrapnel and found some in the garden quite often.

There are many things about World War II I remember: the air raids, food rationing, the sirens' warning and "all-clear" sounds, Vera Lynne singing "The White Cliffs of Dover," all types of military uniforms, crowded railway stations, the "blackout," cooked, mashed parsnips flavored with banana essence spread on bread and rancid margarine (yuck)! Canned corned beef prepared in every possible manner, as well as Spam. We had a map of Europe on the wall into which we stuck flags to show advances and retreats of the Allies or the Nazis. I remember gas masks, which we had to carry to and from school, the air-raid shelters built at the top of each garden in the neighborhood, the air-raid shelters built at school and sandbags. I remember the arrival of the American soldiers who were always referred to as "the Yanks"! They seemed to have an endless supply of candies, chewing gum and wore very smart uniforms and we kids would burst into "Over There, Over There, Oh the Yanks are coming, the Yanks are coming... ." I could go on and on, those early years are entrenched in my memory. I saw the first newsreel pictures of the opening of Bergen-Belsen Concentration Camp. It was vivid and horrifying.

At the end of the primary school years, I passed the entrance exam for the King Edward VIth Grammar School for Girls, in Birmingham. It was a great school and I enjoyed every minute of it. I was a member of the school's hockey team at its various levels and had a crush on one of the "Prefects" but my adoration changed when a new young geography mistress appeared on the scene!

...I went away to college which was situated in Exmouth, Devon, as far away from the Midlands as I could go! I enjoyed the communal life. It was there that I discovered that some women were attracted to me and I was attracted to women also. I was attracted to one in particular and I experienced my first affair which was not shared with anyone else, either her family or mine. Enough about the past for now.

...Oh Lord, I hate being called a "Bitch." I've just re-read your letter and it makes me sad. You sound jealous and you're not supposed to be the jealous type, and I'm feeling sick and I have a sore throat and I'm sneezing so I suppose I've caught the family's cold after all.

Why will you be ready for a job next fall? Would you ever leave him?

I would embrasse you too but you might catch my cold and anyway, I'm not too sure that you're receptive?

Bébé

Spain   November 5, 1971.   11:30 p.m.
My Dearest Pipsi,

I spent most of yesterday, after school, in bed, having dosed myself with anti-cold pills and tablets to soothe my raging sore throat, plus vitamin C tablets. I'm still not sure who is winning the battle as my head aches and my throat is very sore and I have a general feeling of malaise. Of course I blame you somewhat. They are probably your cold germs and anyway, my morale is low because of the letter I received on Friday in which you called me a "Bitch." I also received a letter from Marc, as you know, and he sounds depressed and quite unlike himself. There has been talk of spending Christmas together with Irene and Peter. Apparently he wrote to Irene but now he's not sure and doesn't feel like it.

Continued: Sunday a.m.!

I find myself wondering what you might be doing on a day like today, a Sunday, for example? WHAT is your routine on a Sunday—if you have one?

You might like to know that I love wearing trousers, shorts, shirts, sweaters, my leather waistcoat, a leather jerkin—all casual clothes. I love wearing my jeans and my riding clothes. I do quite enjoy dressing up sometimes when the occasion warrants it and looking feminine but it's not REALLY me. I do not like, nor do I look good in, "frilly" things. ...You know, you would look good in a black velvet smoking jacket. I have always wanted to wear one but I'm too plump! I have a couple of gorgeous kaftans and two Benares silk saris, so you see, I'm a girl in quite a few ways!

I have just finished reading the biography of Hildegarde Kneff and I enjoyed it. It seems that Marlene was always very good to her. Marlene is well known for her *great culinary efforts. Did I tell you that Marlene and Garbo stayed together, for a short time, when they first met in Hollywood?*

Watch it!   You'll catch my germs, Shirley

New York   November 5, 1971
Bébé,

A few words only as it's Friday night and really impossible to do more until Monday morning. I began my seven-year indenture with the Travel Bureau this morning! I rushed home during the lunch hour to find David sitting on the front step and holding your two letters, two beautiful letters! I must admit that by now I feel like a yo-yo! Your moods do change, Cheri. (I'm leaving the "e" off, which should flatter you!) I dashed to the office for two hours and then did the routine of dinner and dishes, etc.

Marie-Marikasha, my boss and a voluptuous brunette of Italian ancestry (actually she's more dumpy than voluptuous), left me alone in the office for ten minutes, though I begged her on bended knees not to do this. "What if a client walked in?" I asked. She smiled kindly, told me not to be an idiot and left!

Thirty seconds later, a strange man wearing strange clothes walked in. I thought of hiding under the phone and kissing my knees. Instead, with chin held up high and without giving him a chance to open his dry, cracked lips, I offered him Miami and Puerto Rico for eight days and seven nights for $225, two meals a day, one free cocktail and an evening at the Dog Races included. All this was said without pausing for breath and with the fluttering of eyelashes and wringing of hands! He looked at me coolly and answered that he was the plumber and that he had come to fix the toilet! I didn't even know there was one!

Hardly a few words, but that's IT!

Caresses and Baisés, Pipsi

New York   November 6, 1971

Dear, Dear Shirley,

I find it frightening that our letters cross with the same thoughts, writing about how long we have been corresponding with each other, the mentioning of acting, producing, doing crosswords and so on! And I think that, quite illogically, what threw me, WAS the fact that you had been presented to me as someone who was rather innocent and that it had been a one-time thing with Delyn. You were described as being quite emotional and yet, at the back of my mind were vague thoughts of "No, not possible, she's a certain type, she's 37 years of age, she's independent, very independent and hides nothing, the presence of Irene" etc. It didn't bother me until the second phone call when I reacted. Then, the letter, yours, which left me in a daze for the weekend, finally consoling myself by writing the lyric. The lyric, by the way, I hope you realize, is not "me to you" but an entity of thought of you and me as one unit! In other words, who is saying what to whom in those lines? And they did write themselves.

After that weekend I got horribly drunk, disgustingly sick too of course, after which I went to the guitar and spent every minute of the following days, until yesterday, working on the music. I'm not happy with it and I must stay away from it for a while so that I can be objective about what's right and what's wrong with the damned thing. The end result of all this turmoil is complex: My left hand has a mass of calluses, there's a renewed "boyishness" in the way I walk and talk and in the way I dress. My new pants are tight and not baggy and my new turtlenecks are sleek and dramatic. So now, my love, the problem is different, somewhat the same, but different. Fact: I love you! Not possible? There are many things in this world which are not possible, but are! Is it illusion on my part? Possibly and it's not too important, we'll certainly find out soon enough. Will WE, each of us, be soft enough, girl enough for one another? I don't know. I would have said, ten days ago, that you would be. Now? I don't know. *Quien sabe?* And since I hear stirring footsteps overhead, I'll see you later.

(I LOVE your Spanish and *tambien, tengo amor para ti!*)

Continued: 12:15 p.m.

O.K. So back to the above. I am aware and damned well know that it might be a terrific let-down when we meet, on one part or another or even for both of us. What has that got to do with my LOVING you NOW? Or you telling me that you're torn apart? You have done far more for me (so far) than I for you. I make you laugh, perhaps I'm funnier on paper than in real life? I disturb and interest you? I also manage to make you angry, and if this letter does, *zut et flute.*

You have managed to rid me of inhibitions! I will never have qualms again about taking off clothes and jumping into bed. I've never felt shy about getting undressed in front of men, just bored. There have been, long, long ago, three affairs with that species.

And of course, I'll never know HOW you raised me off my ass and kicked me into getting a job, something that old friends have been trying to do for a long time. And that's it! So, have your flings, perhaps I'll have mine, though I admit to not being too interested. Stop trying to make me jealous of Irene by putting two exclamation marks each time you mention her. DO tell me if, besides singing off key, she is flat-footed too, somehow it would please me no end if she were.

Continued: 6:30 p.m.

I had decided that this coming summer, I might go to a school for Travel Agents. Then I met Francine for lunch and she told me that a friend of hers, Marie-Marikasha, had just opened an office and wanted to train someone as an agent.

I went over to the office yesterday and we discussed things and both agreed to try it out. There will not be a salary but there will be commission. My hours are of my own choosing, the office is just five minutes away and it's actually a storefront type with a large window, showing large posters. There are three desks—Marie's, Adele's and "Speedy Gonzales'." (Natch. They stuck me in the back, but now and then I climb on my desk and dance a mad jig just to let everyone know I'm here.)

It was quiet in the office with not too much going on. Around 4:00 p.m. Marie walked over and sat on my desk (thank god we wear pants!), stares into my eyes and says very calmly, "I'm now going to teach you about "OPEN LEGS!" Now I bet you think that I panicked and turned purple? No! Quietly I got up, hitched up my pants and started for the back room. "No," said Marie, we can do it right here." (I said to myself, "Oi, Gevalt! An exhibitionist!") I remained calm and noticed that people were looking in at us as they passed the office window as if we were in a movie. I turned to her and said, "Of course, YOUR DESK OR MINE?" I did NOT faint with relief when I found out that "OPEN LEGS" refers to parts of flights, but just sank back, gracefully, into my chair and spilled my coco-cola all over the new carpet!

I'm going out tonight together with the same group who were there the night I slapped Deborah!!!

(The amount of exclamations you use after Irene's name!!!) I shall continue tomorrow. I am off to my guitar and lovely thoughts of you.

Continued: November 7, 1971   2 a.m.

A delicious thought, you are probably sleeping still, with all your hot water bottles and bricks and God knows what else!

We had a pleasant evening and we're all going off on December 11th. I'll have to have my ice skates sharpened so that I can dazzle everyone with pirouettes!...

I was not 19 but 18 when I married Marvin. He was the pianist at the hotel in New Hampshire where I was staying with my mother. My aunt Sonia, who was there too, entered me into the "Amateur Night" contest, which of course I won, singing an Edith Piaf song. Marvin is 50, has an IQ of 159, if you believe in these things, which I don't, drinks a lot without ever getting nasty, is a great asset at a party, lives in a world all his own, is very wary of strangers, is liked by many and understood by none, except perhaps by me.

Yes, David is still at home and finishing his last year at high school and he'll be off to college in September. He is a delight, a fantastic human being, hasn't the vaguest idea of what he wants to do. He adores Marc who, in turn, is wild about him. David looks very much like his grandmother, Regine, and like me.

Steve is in his second year at college and he's studying mass communications. He is talented in music and film making, a terrific actor and a fantastic "ideas" man. His idea of heaven is Las Vegas. I get along extremely well with both of them and they have always come to me with their problems, etc. Neither is, thank God, involved with drugs, and in this country the problem is rampant and ghastly. I seldom lose patience with either of them, but when I do, they retreat—wisely! All their friends think I'm the greatest thing on earth but I think that my boys would prefer it if I were more like other mothers. Also, for some reason, they are a little frightened of me. ...

Now I'm tired and am off to bed. Good night. Je t'embrasse très fort!

Continued: November 8, 1971   8:00 a.m.

Who knows about me? There must be many people who have heard about me of whom I am unaware as I don't know who they are. It does happen that when I meet strangers and when they are introduced, they get a certain look and say: "Oh, you're Sylvia! You know Alexis Blumberg." (Her husband, Michael, knows.)

Yes, many people do wonder about me, I mean, I go to a party and come in, bend down to kiss someone on the cheek (women) and quite often some have offered their lips, maybe not quite realizing what they are doing and then look either horror-stricken or giggle nervously. Then again, there are those, you know, who show an interest or curiosity and I get the odd phone calls: "You never call me, why don't you come over, we have so much to talk about." I just don't have the patience for it, I'm bored by the thought of even starting...but with your guidelines, *quien sabe*? And should I let you know if I seduce anyone? I AM TEASING NOW!

...Your flattery about my cooking is an obvious ploy to get me back into the kitchen and keep me there and I ain't falling for it! I refer a lot to cookbooks and my kitchen is ALWAYS a total mess when I have finished. But we do seem to have the same tastes, which is important. I mean, if one is eventually looking ahead to living together and all that.

Do you mean that you can stick two fingers in your mouth and whistle? That's fantastic! I have always wanted to and never have managed to do it.

Et ç'est tout pour aujourdhui. I send you—all my love, my thoughts, my adoring glances, and my brilliant mind. I'd much rather send myself, preferably unclad, airmail or even parcel post! However, don't be greedy and be happy with what you get.

Je t'embrasse, Your friend, Pipsi

Continued: November 8, 1971   3:15 p.m.

Cheri,

I mailed you a thick envelope this morning and I'll wait until tomorrow's post before sending this off, just in case. Of course, it's enough that I'm asking, "Are you Catholic?" and your letter, which has crossed mine, says: "And if I were Catholic..." For sure that's an omen and no mistake so take notice of it!

Answer me Querida, what do you mean by "I'm mush too"? Is it an expression?

I was at the office for four hours and learned a lot of new expressions. My God, what dirty mouths! Marikasha says that my accent and my grey hair add a certain tone to the place. I don't know about that but I am having fun and the boss and Adele seem to be spending half their time rolling on the floor, quite hysterical at my stories. Oh, I BOOKED my first flight! Two from New York to Albuquerque and did such a great job that the couple will get there at 3:15 a.m. after making five stops!

Have I told you that I love you? Recently, I mean? Yes, I too was very dramatic by writing "Fair Warning, never make the same mistake twice, don't fall in love with me" blah blah, which comes from being an old time actress....

Don't worry about Poppy. He's fine you know (knock on wood!) and we have our own private means of communication if anything goes wrong. So rest easy, the man will be around for quite a while, Inshallah.

And now for more confessions: I love Brie but make sure it's out of the fridge at least an hour before we eat it. I love artichokes boiled, drained and eaten with mayonnaise rather than with melted butter. I love avocados and I'll gladly send you a recipe for guacamole, however, they do not agree with me!

November 9 10:00 a.m.

...I must admit that you're right about Marc having the tendency of being in denial. So I am sorry for jumping to conclusions. I was very upset and angry at the time when I sent you THAT letter. But you must not try to tell him the truth and I know that you haven't. Perhaps you think me over-protective of the man. It isn't that but I do know him very well, his qualities, his limitations, and also how much he can accept. And he LOVES you and DEEPLY. You are able to make him feel special and needed. I don't quite know how to explain it except that he feels at ease when bringing you your breakfast in bed, spoiling you and treating you like a child. He doesn't have that relationship with me and the fault is mine. I admit it. He and I are great friends but it's a mutual admiration society type of thing. The only one he loves in the same way that he loves you is David. To him, Marvin is a "*bon garçon*" and he's very fond of both Steve and me.

I must go to work. I love you.

Continued: 3:00 p.m.

No, I'm not feminine but I am womanly and there is a difference. I'm at my worst when I play "Mother Earth" but that tendency is leaving me fast.

You see, when I listed (was it yesterday?) what you had done for me, I wasn't kidding. When Deborah saw me Saturday night, I had spoken to her on the phone twice, inconsequentially, since our infamous phone call and she informed me that the change in me was so radical, that both Jewel and Francine and two other gals had called her up to find out what was going on? They wanted to know if there was a lover or if I was going to leave Marvin or what?

She added that she realized that there had to be someone. I simply said, "Yes." What can I say at this point? How can I explain that I've fallen, or think that I've fallen, in love with a boy/girl whom I've NEVER MET? She would lie on the floor and laugh her head off, and to tell you the truth, if I heard such nonsense, so would I! This is ME, Bébé, impregnable, uncaring, always calm and cool headed. ...I was the one who was able to break it off with Alexis and later with Deborah, and when the tears subsided (not mine, it's other people's tears I can't stand!), not miss the love-making. Neither was I lured by begging phone calls or inviting glances and what amounted to open invitations. I simply was not interested at all! Then...a few letters from you and one phone call and I went berserk! Now tell me, WHY? Give me ONE good reason, if you can, why you disturb me as you do and also WHY do I do the same thing to you? You're not my type. I'm not yours. You're much stronger than me, physically (God help me!). You're your own man, so to speak, independent from A to Z, while I feel myself bound like Prometheus on his rock!

So what made the strongest impression on Deborah, who knows nothing of all this? "Well" as she puts it (She's observant in the Jewish rites, she lights candles and observes the High Holy days and all the rituals.)—"Whoever SHE is, let her be thrice blessed! She got you out of your house and into getting a job. You look so different, not better, different and you scare me to death!"

This leads me to the questions at the end of your letter. I have already explained about the job and what it entails. I am fascinated by it and it was a stroke of good luck! My life has become a merry-go-round of a "lick and a promise" regarding the household cleaning, shopping for food, waiting for your letters, writing you letters, reading your letters, going to the office, adding to letters already started, dashing to the post office, playing the guitar, cooking, listening to David about his day with great delight, commiserating with Marvin on his problems, sending off warning notes to Steve about taking precautions (whatever they are in this day and age) and not getting girls pregnant and trying to hammer into his head THIS IS IT. By that I mean that he's at the stage in life when decisions have consequences and responsibilities. I want him to understand that he has to do things which are MEANINGFUL FOR HIM. By that I mean that his choice does not rest on our approval, his father's or mine.

I love you but must stop now. I'll finish this off in the morning.

Continued:　　November 10, 1971　8:00 a.m.

And to finish this off, I want to say this: do not, I beg you, think of my life here as one of quiet despair, it's anything but! You will have gathered by now that I am pretty funny and do like to laugh a lot, often at myself and make it very difficult for those around me not to do the same! I only tell you this because, sometimes, when something is written down, it sounds more ghastly than it really is and I don't want you to get that impression.

Yes, I am a darling, delightful and impossible, but so are you!

　　　　　　Je t'embrasse,　　Pipsi

Spain Monday, November 8, 1971
My Dearest Pips,

I arrived here this morning and was more than delighted to find TWO letters from you! Before going any further, the lyrics are absolutely FANTASTIC, but really fantastic! I'm sorry that they were not written FOR me but I do realize that I come into the picture somewhere. The words are beautiful.

The name of the horse is "Cancionero" which means

"songbook" if I'm not mistaken?

You must have read me wrong somewhere along the line because I have never been angry with you, just puzzled and I'm not puzzled any longer and I'm so glad that you haven't stopped writing.

As you say, we begin again. Now you are a very much a part of my life, and I realize, and you admit, that I'm part of yours...I certainly admit to being most disappointed if there's no letter from you. I also feel that my day is not complete unless I have re-read one or more of your letters and have sat down at this damned machine and written you a few lines, even if it means waiting a couple of days before mailing it.

Continued later: Now back to you. I have visions of you sitting wearing tiny, furry moccasin bootees, one on each big toe! The children saw them and I explained about your slippers and that I had tried to find a pair of furry slippers like mine but couldn't find your size, so I had bought these for your big toes. They roared with laughter. At least I'm keeping someone amused and I'm beginning to wonder who is the crazier of the two of us?

God, it's cold today. This is when I miss the central heating. As I told you, my blood is thin and I definitely feel the cold.

Gino is going to look at the house in the new little village just down the road from here, it's new and no one has lived in it. It has electricity and modern plumbing and it belongs to the brother of one of the maids who works here. It would also mean that I could find a maid fairly cheaply to do my housework amongst the country workers and I'm all for that! I would prefer to have my own place.

And as for falling in love with you...well...vamos a ver...one never can tell. What will be, will be, they say. But chase you into a shower I most certainly will, so be prepared!

And that is all for now, much love. Je t'embrasse très fort. Bébé

Spain   November 10, 1971   7:30 p.m.

My Dearest, Darling Pips,

There, I knew it! My letter, mailed yesterday, crossed with one received from you today in which you say "Chuck" and I wrote in mine yesterday, "Or should I say 'Chuck'"?

How are you doing yo-yo wise? Right now I feel much more on an even keel and I hope that you are feeling the same, safe in the knowledge that there will be something, IS something between us. There has to be after all the time and thoughts we have devoted to each other, but God knows where it will lead to?

Sammy is MY dog, and let me tell you about that. Last June, Celia Crossley came to stay with me for a week before flying to Central America to join John who had been transferred there from Pakistan. She was upstairs and I was outside with a neighbor, Sonia, walking her little black bitch. (I had left my front door open, knowing that Celia was upstairs). The bitch was in heat... and when I returned, there was Sammy sitting looking hopeful, just inside the living room. To cut a long story short, when I eventually found his owners, Belgians, they said that they did not want him and that I could have him and they were leaving within minutes! Well, I wanted a dog like I wanted a headache! But as Marc would say, "What can you do?" I adopted Sammy and Sammy adopted me, sort of thing. A magnificent long-haired Dachsund, he sleeps on my bed when I'm here. He is very protective of me and he adores me...and I love the damned dog!

I'm really being spoiled by the Neukorns. I received two delightful letters from Poppy. All being well, he WILL be here for Christmas and IF HE wants we will go off to Portugal or some place for a few days. (Like I said, and so did Irene, we can go to Switzerland anytime too. The main thing is that we wanted to be with him and me particularly.) He's extremely good for me. I always feel so at peace with him. It's fantastic and he is a gold mine of information. He means even more to me now. (If that's possible?)

Today I went into Pizarra to see if there was an apartment for rent and I made it known to various people that I was interested and I hope to hear more later in the week. I had a look at the house in the village here and decided definitely against it. I'll probably end up renting some studio apartment on this side of Torremolinos and traveling daily. The Hollanders are great people and all that, but I need my privacy and I enjoy preparing my own meals, etc. ...

And here is some translated Greek, none other than dear old Sappho herself!

> The blast of love
> like a windstorm
> punishing oak trees,
> love shakes at my heart.

Love and kisses, Shirley

New York   November 11, 1971

Bébé,

No letters yesterday or today and I hope that you didn't get to feeling too rotten and miserable with your sore throat? Please do take care.

Yes, I know that Poppy sounds depressed but I'm sure that you'll see him at Christmas. Irene wrote to him mentioning something about Switzerland and I think that he's waiting to see if these are concrete plans. Where, when, etc. I told him that as long as he's feeling miserable, he might just as well do it in pleasant company, knowing the minute he steps on the plane, the mood will change.

I'm enjoying my job and learning a lot. I think that if one is a good travel agent, one can certainly be a good "concierge" so that option is open to me too! I'm also a fantastic bartender and make unbelievably great drinks! I've always nursed a secret desire to stand behind a bar in a smoky saloon, wearing a large white apron and say "What'll it be Mac?" I know what it will be for me right now, back to kitchen duty, so I'll continue tomorrow. *Je t'embrasse, chere Madamoiselle, et bon soir!*

Continued: 9:30 p.m.

I spoke to Marc who told me that you had been miserably sick. I am so sorry. I have this great remedy for flu: we will fill the bath with very hot water and I'll jump in with you! Don't laugh, it's true. It has to do with metaphysical waves or something. Then into bed with a big snifter of WARM brandy with a small slice of lemon peel and a cherry pit in it. Then I turn you over onto your tummy and then give your shoulders and neck a massage. You are a lucky child because I'm double-jointed and have great hands for a massage. By that time, being pleasantly sloshed (it was a large snifter), you put your head on my left shoulder and...quietly go to sleep. (Fooled you didn't I?) You will remember, won't you, that when I have a cold, I'll need a blanket over my head while I do my Garbo (Yep, her too) imitation of "I vant to be alone" because I like to be left alone to recover.

November 12   11: 00 a.m.

Do you know that just now, I have fallen madly in love with someone else? MARIKASHA for giving me the day off! Of course I have a cigarette in my mouth, which I'm removing fast, and you had better do something about it!

I write to no one except you, oh sorry, that's false. Very occasionally now, though it used to be a steady stream, I write to Bob and Oriel, my first cousins from Holland and England respectively. Bob is the son of Sophie, my father's younger sister, who was married to a Dutchman. She, together with her husband and older son, disappeared during the War. They were transported from Westerborg in Holland to a concentration camp and exterminated. We were never able to find out where, not that it makes much difference. Bob was in Buchenwald concentration camp. (He was in the army and I believe that he was able to get hold of a dead soldier's dog tag and so the Germans did not know he was Jewish and he survived and got out alive, though somewhat crippled by tuberculosis of the spine.) He is, I think, probably the most intelligent man I have ever met, He's not married.

This is probably a good time to let you know that I detest Germans! I will never, under any circumstances, go to Germany. Once when Marvin drove three miles into Germany from Luxembourg into Switzerland in order to avoid driving the longer route of 50 miles out of our way, I was enraged! I would not speak to him for a week! I know that it's childish and I am now a bit better than I used to be about it. I no longer walk out of a room when there are some Germans present. I have quite gotten rid of my feelings of guilt for not having died like all the others. This weighed heavily on me as a teenager, although I'm not at all observant of the rites. I AM very conscious of being Jewish. It was beaten into me daily while we were in Nice. (If I had one black eye though, you can be sure that the other kid had two!) I very often annoy Marc by using Jewish expressions (have you noticed?) in "smart" restaurants.

You ask about my routine on Sundays? Well, of course, things have changed a bit now that I have a job. In other words, my time has to be rationed (not you, *Querida*, not you!), so I will have to organize my chores, etc. I'll probably end up doing two or three days worth of cooking on Sundays and freezing it. Basically, Sundays are very quiet. Marvin disappears into his den to do work on his Ph.D. He has an old upright piano in there and doesn't have to use the grand which is in the living room.

David sleeps late and takes care of his homework, etc. Steve phones and tells me his news and my five-pound Sunday *New York Times* keeps me busy. An occasional friend might pop in or there's the odd movie. Marvin is not very sociable and in truth, his time is limited.

And here we go again with this "extra-sensory perception" thing. I mentioned Garbo, and you mentioned Garbo. I was imagining you in a black velvet smoking jacket and vice-versa. This ALL means SOMETHING Bébé, so watch out! Don't be surprised if I appear around June! IF Marvin goes to Naples, I'll try to work it out, and please see what you can do about coming here for the summer!

...I'm so damned glad that you liked the lyrics. They are not FOR you but they ARE OURS! I'm having a ghastly time with the music. I have finished it but I simply don't know if it's any good or really bad? The music I have written may be too "way out" and also repetitious, but I'm happy that you like the words.

That's all Cheri. Je t'embrasse, Pipsi

Spain November 11, 1971 1:00 p.m.
My Dearest Pips,

So now it's back to "Dear Shirley"? I laughed like a drain and was delighted with your letter. If you're so much like "Charlie Brown" should I not be addressing you as "Dear Chuck"?

There you go again...."I'll tell you another time..." I WANT to know about Greenwich Village and your career as a producer, etc.? Did I tell you that I have done similar activities when living overseas in the various oil communities? It was all amateur of course but I used to enjoy it all very much. I have produced at least three shows and actually enjoyed it better than performing. Yes, I've acted too! (Apart from acting the fool, but aren't you the real jester in the family?)

You mention "feelings." Yours are fathomless. PLEASE, DEAR GOD, let this arrive on any day but Saturday! I love you too.   Shirley

Spain   November 15, 1971

Darling, Darling, Boyish/Woman, A dull, miserable, wet Monday, brightened by two letters from you! It's funny and amazing how our letters are saying the same things, but differently, and keep crossing somewhere over the Atlantic! It's rather frightening really. Each of us writing on the same subject, not having discussed it previously, but obviously thinking the same thoughts.

I do so want to go to the States this summer and I think it a great idea if you could, perhaps, accompany Marc and me. It's a wonderful thought. I can't think of anything that I would enjoy more! I might be able to leave here around July 1st and return during the first week in September, albeit that Gino still wants me to tutor his children. However, I should really renew my subscription to the Times Educational Supplement which has both national and international job advertisements for teachers. I have always had a yen to teach in the States although I am aware that there are quite a few teachers currently unemployed in the States at this time.

So now we're all straightened out...and you love me. I'm so glad! Of course my heart beats quickly every time I see a letter from you and can't wait to open and read them. Sometimes the children are working and engrossed in a project and then I get a chance to glance through the letter quickly. Then there's a chuckle or laugh and Siri will say, "There she goes, another letter from Pipsi!"

Continued: No, I'm not Catholic, which you have already ascertained, and although I was baptized in the Church of England, I never go to church. Don't laugh, because I'm serious now, I used to say "If I could be born again, I would want to be born Jewish." Maybe I have a thing about sympathizing with minority groups? Quien sabe? I have always been pro-Jewish and will probably turn out to be more Jewish than you! (I take back that ridiculous remark.)

I love what I've heard of Simon and Garfunkel but I do not have a record, so if you really want to send me one, please would you mind sending me the one that includes "Sage, Rosemary and Thyme"? Do you know the song I mean?

Yo me voy y tocar el guitarra ahorita. Much love, and many kisses, Bébé

Continued, later in the day.

Dearheart,

I have just written you a long letter but I want to keep on writing. In this way I feel close to you, so here we go again...

On the record which you are making for me, I would really like to hear you talk as well as listening to songs. You realize, of course, that I'll swoon as soon as I hear your dulcet tones!?...

"Oh no," she says, "I don't drink but it seems to me that every time you write to me, you have a cigarette in one hand and grasp the vodka in the other, and who, at nine or ten in the morning, is kidding who?

No, of course I will never disillusion Marc. He has built up his own idea of what and who I am. I realize this. As for Irene discussing my love life or sex life with him, never, she just would not! She also knows me well enough (alright darling, it's alright!) to know that the relationship that he and I enjoy is quite an unusual one. It is indeed one of father/daughter or grandfather/grand-daughter kind. I adore him, so much so that I even proposed marriage to him! (Now that would have led us into Greek dramas!) It sounds odd when written down like this...Well, it's just that I knew that I could LIVE with him, NOT in a sexual way, but in a COM-PANIONABLE way, and in case he needed someone... I really don't know how to explain it well but you will understand what I mean.. It was my way of showing him

I really do care. He keeps hoping that I'm going to meet some nice chap and settle down! I have to admit that our relationship is unique and only YOU could truly appreciate it, and thank you. Yes, he is SO PROUD of you.

I love you very much right now, very much. You ask me why it should be so? How do I know, except that it's THERE, and if anyone had told me that it was possible, for two people to fall in love without ever having met, I would have thought that they were out of their cotton-pickin minds!

Think that it's about time that I took to drinking too, so I'm off to fix myself a brandy.

I have a "friend" in New York, well, I hardly know him that well, but when I was at the Hilton, I met this young man who was obviously "gay." We got into conversation and he was waiting for phone calls, cables and money orders to come from his other half in New York. This boy is called Charles, by the way. Actually the boy brought out my maternal instincts.

I received a letter from him today. He told me that it's about time that I went to New York where all the action is. He asked after my love life and mentioned that he knows quite a few people who would be interested in me (for obvious reasons!). However, will you be an angel and go with me one night to meet him in Manhattan? I'm asking you to be my escort, and well, by then, you will have already met me and you will know whether you like me a lot or...but DO go with me please? Please do not get the idea that I frequent these places. I had never even been into a "gay bar" until I went into one in Paris in 1966. I have also been to one in Amsterdam.

God, the mere thought of all that and my brandy has disappeared! Excuse me while I get another!

Good night Sweetie. Please do not stop telling me that you love me. "Loving you, loving me, and me loving you" and why not?

For now, as you say, Je t'embrasse Shirley

Continued: 8:00 p.m.
Darling, delightfully funny Pips

... I too, have always felt strongly about the Germans. I suppose that the atrocities made a deep impression upon me as a child. I told you that I remember seeing the newsreel film showing the opening of the Bergen-Belsen Camp, and I have read many accounts of the Holocaust. I know that the first time that I visited Germany, I loathed it and felt most uncomfortable. This feeling dissipated after I had visited there more often. I used to drive through Germany en route to England, on my overland trips from Iran. The thought of never returning there doesn't throw me for a loop. I did ask Marc if he had any strong feelings about going to Germany when we had all thought of going skiing together, because Peter and Irene can fly free on military transport. Marc says that he has no objection about being in Germany because one cannot blame the children for the sins of their parents. However, he forgets that there are thousands of Germans still walking around who worked in the camps. I'm simply glad that you're proud of being Jewish.

This drinking is getting to be a habit. I've just fixed myself another brandy.

I'll mail this on Thursday. Sweet kisses, Shirley

New York   November 15, 1971   3:30 p.m.

Querida Mia,

Yes, I am also on a more even keel, though quite wild with happiness when your marvelous letters came and, I think, wild in other ways too! I am sleeping again and eating, and all that jazz, but certainly not, no, definitely NOT softening up! I'm TOUGH! Made of steel! What, in the name of Heaven, are you doing to me?

To make you feel better AND spoil you, which I intend to do with great delight, I really only smoke my cigs halfway down, so it's not too bad. And you are very bossy. And what's this about "MY SONG. MINE?" True, you do have everything to do with it...but...oh...alright, I can't stand a nagging woman—YOUR song!

You'll be glad to know that my commission for last week amounted to $2.12! When I told Marikasha to forget it, she told me to shut up and handed me two singles and six empty coke bottles, which she forced me to return!

I really am glad that this whole thing, this magic, whatever it is between us, is wonderful, and because, had you not been loving, sweet and kind to Marc, none of this would have happened! Idiot, I LOVE you and you're a noodnick! Count, just count, the number of times that I've called you "bitch" or "bastard"—either two or three?

Which brings me to my stage career. As a kid, I was always in shows at school. I also won a scholarship to a third-rate acting school. When I graduated from high school I wanted to go to the Academy of Dramatic Arts but Mama said "No." So, I ended up at the Mandell School for Medical Technicians, where I still hold the record for breaking more test tubes than anyone else! I also joined The Province Town Players in Greenwich Village, which I really loved and acted for a year, mainly Shakespeare.

When I moved to Oceanside, I joined a few organizations and immediately started acting in different shows. At that time, the two girls, Deborah and Jewel, were writing parodies and fitting their lyrics to well-known tunes. Sol Moser got the girls together with Marvin, and they wrote a show for the benefit of the library called *Oceanside U.S.A.* It was an unbelievable success. Marvin had done shows in the army and he and I had done one or two here but not on the same scale as *Oceanside U.S.A.* It was seen by approximately six thousand people! And your adorable one played the part of a "bookworm," which figures!

Then we were approached by "the civil defense" and we put on *Very Hot Milk* which was based on *Snow White*. When, after twenty minutes, as Deborah and I huddled backstage and she peeked and saw the audience leaving *en masse*, she turned to me and whispered, "People are leaving!" I answered, "I think that this must be what they mean by a "flop" and so it was. We were all very discouraged and swore never to put on another show.

Some six months later, the South Shore Foundation for Mental Health wanted a show to raise money which would then be matched and doubled by the County, ditto by the State, etc. No one could be found to produce the damned thing. There was a population of six towns, some 250,000 people, tickets, advertising and such a lot of work was entailed in such a big project so who would be fool enough to try it? Right! Me! There were six performances, an auditorium of 1,500, expenses to the tune of some $6,000 but which netted the organization $20,000! The show took the form of a riotous revue called "555-1212" which is the number one calls for information! Everyone was fantastic and the audiences loved it, and if I was able to survive that experience, I can survive anything!

Alexis was my assistant (AHEM) and on opening night, when I went to pick her up around 5 p.m. to go to the theater, she came running out of the house, fell into my car and said, "Michael knows!" I shall always remember it as my finest hour because I stared at her aghast and said, "Does that mean he won't appear in the show?" Michael, after all, was doubling in four parts! We arrived at the theater and rushed around doing last-minute details. Deborah walked in at 7:30 p.m. nervous and white-faced. (She already knew about Alexis and me by this time.) She wanted to know if all was well? I said; "Michael knows!" to which she replied, "Oh Jesus."

There was still no sign of Michael and as it was almost curtain time and Michael was in the first act, there was only one thing to do, I would have to take over Michael's four parts! (At this point, you should know that Michael is six-foot three-inches tall and weighs about 250 lbs.!) I rushed into the men's dressing room, grabbed his costumes, and rushed into the broom closet and began changing into his first costume, which was that of Christopher Columbus, and began pulling in the waist, etc. with the help of safety pins. Suddenly, I was lifted by the scruff of my neck (I couldn't move for a week afterwards!) and held dangling in the air by one of Michael's meaty paws and he growled, what surely is one of the greatest lines of this century, "By God, you've worn my pants just once too often!" I got out of that costume and the room very fast indeed! He was superb all the way through, kept his mouth shut and didn't even make a fuss when I refused his invitation to go to bed with him by saying that I thought that it was NOT a very good idea! Now, I ask you, how can you say I'm a novice? And that was the last show we did, any of us. I admit to not missing it at all. Admittedly, it was all great fun. As you were also involved in producing shows, you know that it does really have a magic all its own.

And I must stop now. I close my eyes and it's surely about 2:00 a.m. and you're asleep so I'll kiss you softly and say "Goodnight Cheri."

November 16   4:30 a.m.

...Basically my day now consists of rising at whatever, then dusting and sweeping. (I'm on my knees and if Margaret doesn't show up tomorrow, I'm sunk!), after which I prepare breakfast for Marvin and David and see them off. Then it's making beds, doing the laundry, shopping and errands, WAITING FOR THE MAIL, beginning letters, going to the job at eleven, grabbing a bite to eat before I leave. I return around three, except on Wednesdays when it's around four, continue with letter writing, cook dinner, clean up, and, depending upon who is around, play the guitar. (I will only do this in complete privacy.) Watch the Telly, read and then go to bed. Yesterday, par example, was an easy day. Marvin had a class lecture so he didn't come home until 11 p.m. I didn't have to cook dinner because I had made cannelloni on Sunday. Do you know what it is and do you like it? David and I gorged happily on the leftovers.

I love you deeply and miss you, Bébé. I wish we could hold each other, giggle, cuddle and play lovely games. And I'm sure that you're not "dumb" and perhaps I am, and so what? As you say, who needs to impress? And with you, I don't have to pretend. I shall drown with happiness in your arms and drag you right along with me!

Je t'embrasse. All my love,   Pipsi

Continued, November 16, 1971

You will be VERY proud to learn that today Marikasha offered me the job of manager! When I asked, "manager of

128

what?" she answered, "As of now, a pile of s—t!" We must all be very patient until things start to move, which won't be for a good three months.

Je t'embrasse encore une fois, TRÈS FORT.

Chuck (My mood today is indeed very boyish!)

November 17, 1971   5:00 p.m.

Bébé,

I'm listening to the "Aranjuez" concerto. It really is very good. Has he written background music for the movies do you know? The second movement sounds like it.

I have been warned by Marikasha, probably in view of tomorrow morning's "breakfast do," that travel agents are, for the most part, a very peculiar lot and that I should be forewarned and ready to be propositioned by both sexes! I'm trying to work up some enthusiastic response but...NOT being "Chuck" right now, it all sounds rather dreary and dull! You and your "Tiger Balm" is all that I want.

I'm signing off with a big kiss and a heart full of love, you're stuck with me!

November 18   2:00 p.m.

It was enough for me to be feeling soft and here you are writing on pink paper and feeling restless....Will it help at all, even with my past history, if I tell you that I really am fairly constant in my affections? That I went to the breakfast and no one propositioned me at all?

You may hurt me much more than Delyn ever did hurt you, or I hurt the others. I might do the same. Who says that love is easy? And who knows what love is? And in all of this I hear Poppy's voice echoing from my childhood, not saying, "What can you do? What can you do?" but transmitting his credo to Andre: "You don't tell a woman that you love her

unless you are ready to presume full responsibility for her!"
I agree with him, *çe qui n'empeche que je te dis quand même que je t'aime!*

Later: 3:50 p.m.   I think I'm tired! Your record is in the bag and I'm picking it up Monday, late afternoon and I'll mail it on Tuesday morning. I'm not very happy with it, you are sure to be disappointed.

No letters today, and tomorrow being Saturday, I had better have them hold any for me, just in case. I think that by January, if all goes well, and if you agree, I'll ask Marikasha if she minds if I use the office for receipt of mail. Don't you get questioning looks about the amount of letters from this end? Even though it's a short one, I'll mail this off in a few minutes. The weekend looms as damned busy (curses!) with nonsense of course, but, as you say, one has to be kind!

Steve, the sound engineer, asked me who the record was for and I answered "For someone whom I've never met!" "This no-name song" (as he dubbed it), "was it written for this person?" and when I answered "Yes," he answered, "Lucky Girl!" which makes HIM quite perceptive!

I love you, et je t'embrasse très fort,   Pipsi

Spain   November 20, 1971
Dearheart,
It's 9:30 p.m. and Irene and Peter have been gone for over an hour, having drinks with some neighbors down the street...ah, they've just walked in! So...now we are away to eat beef stew, a lovely tossed salad, no bread and no desert.
This morning I made reservations at The Ritz in Lisbon for the Christmas vacation and I'm looking forward to it very much. Marc should arrive on December

23rd here, and he and I are booked into the Pez Espada in Torremolinos until either the 26th or 27th, when we'll depart for Lisbon. I have paid a deposit because you know that Marc likes all these details taken care of in advance.

Do you celebrate Thanksgiving at your home? We worked very hard during the past week in preparation. The kids did a beautiful "tableau" on the large classroom bulletin board. It shows a forest, log cabins, a group of Native American Indians and Pilgrims sitting around a table watching a mixed group of their children dancing. The kids got a kick out of doing it and so did I. I read them some information about this era from a British perspective from a history book. I am as happy in my work right now, as you are in your office.

Tomorrow we are invited to a costume party. The theme is "The Thirties." Well, as far as I'm concerned, when one thinks of the "Thirties" one thinks of the Depression, air flights and new world records, the Lindbergh kidnapping, the film industry and Hollywood, and the rise to power of Adolf Hitler and the Nazi Party. So, I have finally decided to go as Amelia Earhart, the famous flyer. Barbie has the just the right type of leather coat and I have a leather fitted cap with earmuffs. (I used it when I owned a sports car.) I have goggles, a long woolen scarf, fur lined gloves, trousers and boots.

Thoughts, love, and kisses, Shirley

Spain   Monday, November 22, 1971
My Darling Girl,

I do promise to try and call at the next opportunity but this has its problems. There is no phone here at the

Cortijo. I don't want to phone from the local village. I doubt that they would know how to do it and the acoustics are awful. I would hate to miss something!

This is a hasty note. I'm dashing off to the coast with the family, immediately after lunch because we're off to see an American film. This leaves me very little time for writing. In fact, I'm writing this while the kids finish off some written work. I'm frustrated because I'm anxious to answer your latest letters. Be patient, they ARE on their way! Oh yes, the party was a flop! I'll tell you about it in my next letter, I have to dash now. Take care, much love, hugs and kisses, Shirley

New York   November 22, 1971

Bébé, Cheri, Sweetheart, Love,

I can think of many other endearments! It's just that I'm SO happy to be able to put pen to paper again. My God, it's been two whole days since I have been able to do so. Some of these weekends do get stupidly busy.

The next few days loom as hectic. Thursday is Thanksgiving and Poppy is coming. I like to make a real holiday dinner. Steve is coming tomorrow night or Wednesday and has to return on Friday. I have a haircut appointment on Wednesday morning, two leads to follow up on at the office and my presence is required there for four hours each day. I must pick up the record today and I WON'T listen to it or I won't send it, so I'll mail it tomorrow?

Later: 10:25 a.m.   Three letters! ...It's funny, suddenly all this data about gay bars and of course, in my last letter I told you of my experience in one! By nature, and perhaps, conditioning, I'm not blatant. Frankly, I don't even like to see straight people being demonstrative in public. Love—whether it's just holding hands and kissing gently, or "the works"—is a very private affair between two, no spectators. I'm either old-fashioned or a prude. I've had my share of gay places. The Perroquet, Lucy's place, was one and Marvin worked there for one and a half years when we were first married. The clientele was mainly men, Tennessee Williams, Truman Capote, etc. There was a Lesbian singer, Maria Kohn, who looked like a vulture and she used to sing and stare at me while touching her breasts. ...I went home with her once. She kept an open coffin, lined in white satin, on the floor of her living room. I left rather quickly!

Later: 4:30 p.m. ...after rereading what I said above perhaps I should tear this up but of course I won't, and if you want an escort to some gay bars around town, I'm your girl! (I'm spoiling you again!) One thing I DON'T do is fall in love and then try to change people. You must not do it to me either. Changes come from within, not from others. The others are only the catalyst.

I would ask you, if you will...about Peter! Typical Pipsi behavior, or so I've been told, using the fine Italian stiletto rather than the blunt hatchet. (However, I will learn more of YOU by asking about Peter and also about Irene than if I were to say, like you did, "Tell me all.")

You ask about the summer, frankly I see no desperate problems. I never do, but much depends upon you. We can write each other all kinds of intimacies yet not really know until we meet, which nerve endings will react to whatever nonsense occurs! My house is yours. You'll have your private bedroom, for that matter, a private bathroom too, depending what the boys will be doing. There will be days of fun, love-making, giggling etc. Although I will have to put some time in at the office, I'm sure that I'll be able to work that out. Nights? ...I'm afraid that it wouldn't look "kosher" if I were to spend them with you. However, I fully expect that both of us to be so exhausted it shouldn't matter too much! ...I promise you a lot of fun and probably some tears too, great joy and probably some awful arguments! And that's being fairly honest.!

Your complicated relationships always seem to be with older people, why? How old was Delyn? Irene, you say, is around 49, Pippa (nice name) much older. Your friends, La-Veta, Margaret, Elizabeth are also much older. Who else? Poppy told me of an elderly gentleman who died who lived near you and you were upset, etc. Do you not like people your own age? REMEMBER—I AM FOUR, delicious years your senior, which makes me wiser, smarter and more experienced! (A small pause here while I collapse with laughter!)

Stop drinking!

...Why must everyone be labeled Lesbian, straight, gay, homo, butch, fem, dyke etc? THAT'S what I meant when I said to Poppy that I wasn't interested in what people did in bed. Of course I admit to slight, oh so slight an interest in what YOU do!

Je t'embrasse très fort, and, for the love of god, take care of yourself!

All my love,   Pipsi

P.S. I have just reread all three letters. *Bien entendu* and what else? You haven't yet received my letter carrying on in my usual wild fashion about gay bars! Of course I wouldn't mind owning one! Now there's a thought! I could be Bar Man and you could be the cook. I'd make sure that the waitresses were pretty!

Spain   Monday, November 22, 1971   8:00 p.m.
Darling, Delightful Pips,

I did not go down to the film festival after all and the family returned earlier than expected. They said that it was lousy and we hope for something better to-morrow when there is a Japanese film showing!

Now for your letter of the 12th, mailed on the 13th. Well, I won't push it, being taken to a club I mean, it really doesn't interest me. I can count on one hand (note ONE!) how many times I have been in such a place, twice in Paris, a very good one in Amsterdam and once in London. I just wondered what New York had to offer? So, I'll settle for the letters and being spoiled.

Continued: All that work, all that entertainment of clients, plus adding tone to the place and all you get is a lousy $2.12? My God, you spend far more than that on letters to me each week! Sounds as if you need someone to look after your interests, business-wise, and you can see from what I have told you that it's no good counting on me for that. I'm hopeless!

Smoking at 4:30 a.m.! I suppose you smoke in bed too? Not in mine you don't, nor the bathroom either. In fact, if you're a wise kid, you'll give it up altogether. There will not be any excuse then will there? Watch those ears! I knew it, red again!

>*Lots, and lots and lots of love and kisses,*
>*Shirley*

New York   November 23, 1971   5:00 a.m.
Bébé,

I noticed, while walking along yesterday, that people were looking at me and moving out of my way fast! I realized that it was because I was wearing my new desert boots and when you wear a size ten to begin with.... I love to walk with my hands in my pockets. Sometimes I sort of bounce along, usually after receiving one or more of your letters. I NEVER smoke in the street and truly, I never get drunk, that was done very deliberately, as a sort of purge, like castor oil. As a matter of fact, I know of no one who holds their liquor better. Drinking in the early morning is only under special stress and why are you hitting the bottle?

Never mind, back to your letter—I'm glad that you agree about me not joining Marc on this trip. He will spoil you so I can share THAT vicariously and enjoy the thought. He is a lonely man and you will understand the very large amount of pleasure when the following happened:

These damned college applications are deadly and each one requires an essay, such as "What has most influenced your life?" or "What political event affected you personally" etc. A lot of crap! David is a superb writer and one of the schools for which he is applying asked "Which three men, or men's thoughts, have made a deep impression upon you?" And heading his list was Poppy! And it's true, he is good with the boys. He may not have been the greatest father but as a grandfather he is not too bad! So... I'm very happy that two of the ones I'm most fond of will be together.

I must go off to work.

3:40 p.m. There's not too much time to spare right now but I'll make up for it tomorrow. Your record and a letter went off this morning to Pizarra.

You are right about the teaching situation here. But you know, I haven't the vaguest idea about your job. Are you qualified for high school, elementary, or what? Are you speaking of private schools perhaps? I think public schools in England are like private schools here.

...I know the record you mean, and I will get it off by the end of the week. Simon does all the writing and his lyrics, and the music, are great. I believe that on that particular record you also have "Dangling Conversation" which I dearly love. I think that if you don't know it, you will like it very much.

I've told you, I take things as they come. Right now, there's one thought only for me...you, on your back, quite helpless, exhausted, happy, yes, very happy and completely one hundred per cent satisfied! The extent of my hopes and expectations! And I think of something that someone, a general I think, way back, who said, *"De l'audaçe, encore de l'audaçe, toujours de l'audaçe."* With you, I'll need it! As always, all my love,   Pipsi

Spain November 23, 1971
My Very Dearest Pips,

The Hollanders must be devils for punishment as they went down to the coast again to attend the Film Festival, this time it's a Japanese film. They said that it was weird. I saddled up my horse and took off to Pizarra, all alone. The weather is very good and the clouds all disappeared when I went out (and that had nothing to do with me of course!) and it was fresh with lovely blue skies, dark mountains and sights of little Spanish villages nestling against the hillsides and I thought of you! It seems to be my main occupation these days. I rode to the post office and mailed a letter to Marc.

Now let me explain about my accommodation, as you seem perplexed. I have rented my house in Fuengirola for a year. It's just too far to commute, really. When I first took the job with Gino, I was promised a little cottage which is located on his grounds here and which belongs to him. However, there's no electricity and it's a little primitive but would be great fun to fix up. Well, his son by his first wife, Jimmy, descended upon us to-

gether with his girlfriend. So, Gino apologized to me and allowed them to stay in the cottage. I had wanted to live there as I'm the only non-family member. I want some privacy and I like entertaining... (I cannot grumble too much because my living costs me nothing right now.) I have my own bed-sitting room and my own bathroom in a separate wing which is located off behind the kitchen area. Also I made it quite clearly understood before I began the job that I was NOT a governess but a tutor and that there is a big difference believe me! I also stated that any time after school hours which I wanted to spend with the children was to be MY choice.

...It obviously didn't take long to get promoted from backroom girl/boy to manager/manageress, did it? I'm delighted that Marikasha realizes what talent and what good organizing abilities you possess and what a gal you are! She has the luck of the gods to have had you dropped into her lap, "OPEN LEGS" and all, and she doesn't have to pay you a thing! Actually with the way you seem to be amusing everyone the way you do, it's a wonder that anything gets accomplished at all!

"I love you too, you nitwit," say I, as I run my hands through your hair, your GREY hair! All this "t'embrassing"— I'm squeezed to death! Nightie-night
Love, Shirley

New York   November 24, 1971 7:10 a.m.
Querida mia,

This letter will be a long one, I promise, but full of interruptions, but I'll keep writing thoughout the day. This is a luxurious feeling and I love it!

Stephano came waltzing in at nine last night. Stephano, or Stevie, when we're on good terms, which is 95% of the time, and "Stephen" when I start getting angry and "Mister" when I've really had it! Within two minutes the house was filled with tape recorders, cameras, zoom lenses, records and all the paraphernalia of his world. He is supremely happy at school, he has a two-hour radio show weekly which he engineers as well as playing disc-jockey. He is much loved by his friends, boys and girls. He has an impatient nature, really cares about David and is sometimes intolerant of his father. At the age of three, he knew what was expected and he would take off his little woolen hat in elevators and knew to stand up when grown-ups entered the room. His favorite word for me when I'm angry is "unreasonable." He is as blind as a bat without his glasses, is a pretty good pianist and a ghastly driver. Within ten minutes of being home, he was off to the movies and I have orders to wake him at ten! And that's a glance at Stephano!

Don't be a nag about my smoking and drinking. I don't pester you about your habits! *Chacun à son gout!* Besides, think of it, whenever we kiss, I can neither drink nor smoke, so bear that in mind, Dr. Hall, the cure depends on you! I STILL get the feeling that you are frightened at the thought of meeting me. Even after all these letters? I am harmless and you are an idiot! A divine, sublime one, but an idiot just the same!

Later: 11:00 a.m. Potatoes are boiling away, the cranberry and orange relish made (at 5:00 a.m.). I have finished my errands except for going to the bakery, there were too many people so I'll go tomorrow morning.

Yes, OK, so Irene will come in the spring and she'll call and say, "Pips, this is Irene," and I'll answer "Ah, Madame Hardenbergh, how do you do?" By all means, send me instructions. Do I lunch with her alone or with Marc and Peter? Do I seduce her or does she seduce me? Child, why don't you stop this nonsense? I'll never be able to explain me to you, actually I really never go around explaining myself to anyone. Perhaps another of dear Oscar's epigrams will do: "We are all in the gutter, but some of us are looking at the stars!" I've told you, I will be charming, lovely, amusing and make her laugh, I think that's enough, don't you?

I haven't read anything about war or rather, concentration camps or their exposition for the past five years. Until then I imagine I read everything that was printed. There is a fascination to all that horror, though I don't think that most people will own up to that. I think that buried deep within me, there's a very violent streak which comes out every now and again.

About leaving Marvin, yes, you are quite right, easier if there's someone else...but that is not the problem. The decision that I make is not "who is more important, Marvin or X?" the question is "Who is more important, Marvin or ME?" And yes, I AM which is in itself, a revelation. This is what Deborah sees and which also scares her. The horror for me is hurting people like he'll be hurt, but...it is true, one wants to hurt no one and one does end up by hurting one and all.

My prediction for us...we'll end up together. When? *Quien sabe*? Maybe we will be two old biddies and I'll say "Bébé, stop looking at those girls, you're drooling again!" Then you'll say "Where did you hide the bottle this time, and take that damned cigarette out of your mouth!" I just did, remove the cigarette I mean and yes, I like it, so, do it again! And that's all for today. Je t'embrasse. Pipsi

New York   November 25, 1971
Cheri,

The bird, yes love, the self-basting one, is in the oven. Outside there's a gorgeous rain and windstorm howling away. And time for two or three lines to you.

I often regret some of the things I put down on paper. You may misunderstand (and since you have the added burden of my miserable scrawl to decipher), you'll think that many of my statements are being directed particularly to you. So I wanted to say this about the Wilde quote, "We're all in the gutter" etc. I don't mean GAY people, or you with your way of life or me with mine. I mean EVERYONE! I've often been accused of looking down on humanity. This is not true. I feel very much part of it, and it is EXACTLY because I feel a part of it and I realize that every last one of us is crawling around, rather blindly I think, that I quoted Wilde. Do you understand?

New York   November 26, 1971   3:00 p.m.
Cherie (I'm hugging you very hard.),

You have no idea how beautiful I look! Truly! I'm wearing a forest green turtleneck sweater, my eyes are laughing and the hair is just what you would like and the ears are crimson red!

You must have looked great as "Amelia" and right up your alley! Why was the party a flop? Three times I've gone to a costume party and I always do the same thing—Groucho Marx! Perhaps I have a photo somewhere but it is rather frightening. I look just like him and all I need are an eyebrow pencil, glasses and a cigar! Of course I do the crouching walk to perfection!

Later: But I can only write a few lines. Steve has to get back to Boston tonight as he is in a show and has a rehearsal call for 10:00 p.m. there's a plane shuttle that gets him there in forty minutes.

Later: 8:40 p.m. I've just returned from the airport. I like very much to drive alone at night, even with the hectic traffic and the radio on playing all the hits. Some are really good.

I shall buy more paper in the morning and mail this off and write you and answer everything in your letters that came today. Je t'embrasse très fort. I wish you were in my arms...Pipsi

Spain   November 26, 1971   12:30 a.m.
My Darling Girl/Boy, Pips, Sweetheart,
Make a note of that will you, I mean the time, 12:30 a.m. and I just got up! I went to bed at 9:00 p.m. absolutely bloated with food and a distended stomach, ugh, I don't want to see any more food for another two days! I woke up half an hour ago and realized that I was thinking about you and I just couldn't get back to sleep.

...I think that Marikasha is one of the luckiest girls right now. I do not mind using the office address to send my mail to you if you think that it will work? Surely they will wonder at the amount of mail you will receive from Spain? How will you explain that?

Incidentally, did David question you when you found him sitting on the step with two letters in his hand from me? Are they musical too? I mean the boys?

I have aching shoulders all the time and I think that it's either rheumatism or an occupational hazard, writing so many letters! Right now I have a strong desire to nibble your ears... With much love, and many....well, take your cigarette out first!
Shirley

142

Spain   Saturday November 27, 1971   10:30 p.m.

Querida, OK. ...you may be thinking that you've drunk a vodka too many and I agree with you, but rest assured that the color of this paper is "eau de nil" or a lighter shade of green! I bought it this morning when I went into Malaga to get my "Residencia" permit and to collect insurance papers for my car which we'll be taking to Portugal.

...Do you have one of those cassette tape recorders? I also bought an empty cassette so that I can make a tape to send you, of what, I'm not exactly sure because it plays for thirty minutes on each side and I have difficulty speaking for three minutes! I can always sing you a couple of songs I suppose, we'll see, I'm thinking about it..

Je t'aime   Shirley

New York   November 29, 1971   5:00 a.m.

I'll never be able to send you this today. Too many things to do, but I'll keep coming back to you. I think those words, "keep coming back to you," very descriptive! It's a sort of pre-destination if you will. Don't worry about my meager pittance at the office. Marikasha simply can't afford to pay me anything right now and I must work on commissions only.

With all the jesting about plunking myself on your door-step someday, I think, being serious for a moment, that I will have to live by myself for a while. Not to live what you call a gay, bachelor life, but I will need to re-center life around me, and I don't mean this in a selfish way. It's simply that I will need time to divest myself from the nonsense and get down to basics. You, if you want it, will have sole and unique visiting rights, no curfews, twenty-four hours a day, seven days a week, etc. As it is, changes must be occurring at a fairly decent speed. I KNOW they are because people are always looking at me in a surprised way lately. Of course I don't feel it myself, except perhaps, yes, when looking back and saying "Jesus, was that me?"

...I am fully convinced that there isn't EVER a young person who feels that their parents have done a good job. Going back to my parents for a moment, whose sins were of omission, I can assure you, that having brought up my two boys with this awareness of what I had missed, I have surely made other and maybe worse mistakes, as they will with their own. It is inevitable. The only thing to hope for, by the time that they are fairly mature, is that they recognize this as a universal thing and not a personal fiasco. To tell you the truth, whatever I say about being a parent, or whatever Poppy says about my being a superb mother, doesn't make a lot of sense. If I am lucky, or rather, if they are, they will be OK and they will be able to make a decent life for themselves with some measure of happiness. Raising children is not, in any event, an easy job.

Steve told me, when I took him to the airport, that he had been quite touched by my letters dealing with sex and philosophy and about him making his own faux pas and mistakes and that at least they would be his. He also asked me WHY I had not SAID these things to him? So I asked, "If I had said the words, would you have listened?" He agreed that he would probably have told me to stop giving him advice.

Later: 4:00 p.m. I will tell you what is marvelous about a day like this! It's being able to go off to the office after writing you the above lines and without knowing whether or not the mail will bring you to me.

...I think that in my last letter I asked about pleasure for you? So, if you don't mind, are you jesting or are you being truthful! ...Really Sweetheart, I'm not concerned about it, everything will be alright, and I don't care if you're the worst lover in the world, the magic is already working so none of it will be hard. We will always joke, you and I, about "Chuck" and "Cheri" or "Cherie," boy or girl, but you know, if ever all this, all the feelings, all the needs, yours and mine, turn out to be a truly unique thing between Pipsi and Shirley, then...well, just two human beings, not male, not female, not dominant, not acquiescent, but two who can say "We" and "Us" it will be a great accomplishment.

...I think that you're a snob! You are always telling me about counts and countesses and Dukes and you're also a terrible name-dropper! Not that it matters, I mean I have, as I've told you, my own feelings about being Anastasia or the like! Do you have any idea, (of course not) of just how much I love you? In bed, out of bed, angry or smiling, singing or sulking!

As for your relationships, past, present and perhaps future, it is, of course, for me, completely understandable and follows an inevitable pattern, with which there is nothing wrong. And I gather by now that Irene has told you that she loves you and so that security is there at least?

For the rest, my love, I can only say that you are lucky, of course you both are, never mind about owing her a lot and explaining about her generosity and all that garbage, you both have something going, and I guess that it's more than most people have. Which might well be the classical moment for me to be the "*gentilhombre*" and disappear into the fading sunset! This is something which I would have done, even a short time ago, but not now, and not until you say, "That's it, go!" I also think that you don't want me to and I think that it would hurt you very badly if I did.

Je t'embrasse très fort!   Pipsi

Spain   November 29, 1971   7:00 p.m.
Darling, Darling Girl,

It's here, it's here, and I played it this morning during a break before returning to the second part of morning school, then I called the kids in and played it for them.[8] I have just played it for Barbie and everyone thinks it's great, but GREAT! And as for me, darling, I'm speechless! I adore you and you were delightfully nervous. I LOVE all the songs but of course I have special preference for OUR song of "No Title." I can see how Jacques Brel has influenced you with the tune and the lyrics in the "Spinning" song. As for your guitar playing, darling, I have flipped, but flipped and I ADORE it all and YOU. Is there ANY possibility of getting me another made? You see, the record arrived and it is rather warped, well, I should say that it's bent! Fortunately I was able to play it and it plays all right.

Why you haven't gone into this in a big way I will never know...and I thought that I would sing for YOU—forget it! I have a bigger inferiority complex than ever. You and I could go into business...a gay bar with the owners singing, we would pack them in! Mind you, I would be scared of losing you, or rather, of losing my girl! You are great, just great!

Inspired by your record I have started a tape on my cassette machine this evening, but please remember that I do not have the advantage of the studio facilities for recording professionally, but it will give you a faint idea.

---

8   Shirley had just received the vinyl recording on which Pipsi played her guitar, sang French folk songs and songs she had composed herself, including the "untitled" one with the lyrics she had written on October 31 (see page 95) and mailed.

At the rate I'm playing this record, it will be worn out before the end of the week! What do the boys think of your songs? The engineer called you "Sylvia." You have noticed, I gather, that I never call you "Pipsi" but always "Pips"?

So here are my lyrics. I made up the tune too, it's all very simple and I hope that you like it.

> I'll sing this song
> For you and only you,
> I've never sung before,
> See just how quickly you've inspired me,
> I long for the sandy shore.
> When we are strolling hand in hand
> Along that sandy shore,
> You'll play your games of make-believe
> And I will ask for more.
> So now put on your jester's cap
> And strike your funny pose,
> But let me be the one this time
> To give the single rose!

Seriously now, the recording you made is fantastic, I love it, but love it and I think that the music is great.
Au revoir cherie, baises, amor de mi corazón,
Shirley

New York   November 30, 1971   5:00 a.m.
Monsieur,

Vos manieres sout epouvantables on ne se couche pas a 9:30 pour se lever trois heures plus tard! Surtout pas pour ecrire des letters d'amour a des femme au cheveux gris! Ah la jeunesse d'aujourd'hui, pas des manieres. Les fautes d'ortographes, quel horreur!

...Nothing you tell me are "trivialities," whether it's a house you consider buying, or telling me about your job, which you seem to take great pleasure in, or any nonsense at all which passes through your head. And I hope you realize that I'm every bit as scared as you are.

I see that we are both financial wizards! You have spent more than you earn and I always spend it all at once on caviar and champagne on Sundays and beans the rest of the week! You see how we fit together, just like pieces of a puzzle!

I don't think that Marikasha will give me any problems about the mail.

...Yes, David did question me. I don't know if you're aware that everyone in this house knows about you? I may have mentioned it and it's none of my doing. Poppy came back from the trip when he first met you, he came over and told us about meeting you. He was très emotioné about the whole thing and the kids were around. The only one who knows, at least to some extent, that we have a fairly consistent back and forth flow of letters is David and he doesn't mention it. I have told him a little about you and he has heard some from Marc and he thinks that you must be "fun." The Lesbian thing doesn't bother him, at least I don't think so. David is extremely talented and does write songs. Steve is great at the piano. David plays the guitar and sings beautifully. He has won a couple of awards from Nassau County. He's very active in the school chorus and last Friday, he and his friend went to the City, to various record companies to show their demo. Steve, the engineer at Ultra Sonic cut the record with them, and gave them so much of his time and advice that both David and his friend were completely overwhelmed. He has heard OUR song. I have a single of it, just the song of course, and he adores the lyrics. After hearing it for the second time, he said that the music grows on one. Ah well, I'll wait to hear your reaction.

Could you please just feel like the cat with the saucer of cream again? My letters are meant to make you happy and certainly to disturb you a little, but NOT to make you dissatisfied or unhappy. And of course I like very much the thought of you riding your horse, with clouds overhead, and you thinking of me!

All my love, Pipsi

December

Pipsi's record inspired me, so I bought some audio cassette tapes. Using their tape recorder, the Hollander children and I recorded our first tape and mailed it to Pipsi. Excited by this form of technology, Pipsi and I both purchased tape recorders to enhance our communication. We delighted in hearing each other's voices, speaking, reading poetry, hearing laughter and singing. Pipsi was adept at writing simple "ditties" and in this way she introduced herself to the Hollander children.

Marc arrived a few days before Christmas and at the invitation of the Hollanders I took him to the Cortijo for lunch. He was most impressed with everything he saw. Gino and Barbie were gracious hosts and Marc could well understand how happy I was working together with my three students in this environment.

After spending Christmas together with Peter and Irene Hardenbergh on the Costa del Sol, we all set off on our road trip to Portugal. We stayed in Lisbon for the New Year celebration.

New York   December 1, 1971   8:35 a.m.
Bonjour Cheri,

A few years ago I went up to the William Morris Agency to talk about an idea for a musical, which came to nothing, but a few songs had been written which I demonstrated, with Marvin at the piano. The gal who was doing the interview offered me the Lotte Lenya role in the road company of *Caba-*

ret! Considering that Lenya is about 80 by now, I can't say that I was very flattered. Of course you'll have already heard THE record and are probably wondering how I dare open my mouth ANYWHERE but in the shower, our shower! I really sound better live, my voice is lower and nicer.

I admit to being in a foul mood this morning, every-hair-standing-on-end sort of thing. I have this wild desire to put all the crockery on the kitchen table and with one sweep of the hand—WHAM! However, in this plastic age of ours, what's the use? And whatever you do, don't say anything obvious or banal at this point, I'm certainly banal enough for the two of us! The Hell with it, in an hour or so, I think I'll go out and buy you something stupid and send it off. That should take care of ill humors, don't ask me what, I haven't the vaguest idea!

I sometimes wonder if we're going to burn ourselves out before we even meet? Jesus, I AM in a mood. Know what? I'll do us both a favor and I'll stop for now!

11:25 a.m. Margaret is here. Better that *she* should have the housemaid's knees. I admit that I've been kissing my right one rather often. And yes, I went out and bought you something stupid! Whether I send it is a different problem, but since, like Scarlet O'Hara, I have a tendency to say, "I'll worry about it tomorrow," I'll send this off., it's not much, and certainly not too cheerful, I'll write you a better one tomorrow. Je t'embrasse and I send you all my love, but then, you know that already! Pipsi

New York   December 2, 1971   8:30 a.m.
Darling Girlish-Boy,

Et me voila, back in a good mood again. The bad ones never really last too long, besides, I feel too self-indulgent when wallowing in them.

Time is indeed of the essence. I simply don't seem to have enough of it, at least not to do what I like best, which these days is writing you letters and reading or re-reading yours!

Marikasha has organized a meeting of all the storekeepers in the little shopping area where the office is located. She has the blood of Sacco and Vanzetti running through her veins and wants to present a united front in tackling the mayor of the town. Less than a month in my job and I have to cross swords with City Hall! It's set for tomorrow morning, in the office, and I'm to be there in my new role as Manager to hand out the usual coffee and doughnuts.

10:00 a.m. Six more errands to do and they'll just have to wait! You know, if I had met you, and you were a married woman with seven kids trailing after you, you would still fascinate me. Forget about the sex for a minute, and yes, I am being a maniac about getting you there, but...there are certain things you say, or say in a certain tone...Par example, being bossy, were you like that as a child? I know I was and why are you? Do you know? I'm not bossy any more, which is probably only because those around me always do as I wish, well, most of the time anyway.

Then you say things like "I fell in love with Delyn" and proceed to say she was jealous, with good reason, because of your love for Irene! I can certainly understand loving two women at one time or lusting after them, NOT being IN love with two! *Pas possible*. But, here again, there may be, or is, a differential in our definition of the word "love," which, by the way, I'm quite convinced neither you nor I know much about. Perhaps one suffers from blunted nerve ends? I really don't know. You wouldn't think so from our letters, but then, this is a new experience, for me anyway. Deborah once told me that I was unable to "feel" like most people! I will never starve because I'm never that hungry, never weep, because I'm never touched that deep down, never feel complete fulfillment because I'm not that open and never die because of the fact that I never allow MYSELF to live! I think that this is a pretty ghastly indictment and partly true, I'm sure. But... and this in truth, unless I'm way off and altogether wrong, the main difference between you and me, is that, as envious as I can be of other people's brains and slim thighs, or that certain *"Je ne sais quoi,"* I would rather be ME, as I am, with all the hang-ups, faults and frailties, than anyone I know, man or woman, and that is, of course, vanity of the worst sort! I plead guilty and I think that THAT way, YOU should be more like me!

A million kisses all over! Pipsi.

Spain   Thursday, December 2, 1971   4:00 p.m.
Darling Pips,

I'm listening to the Garfunkel record and specifically right now to "Dangling Conversation" and I love it, and you, and the record, and you, and love, love, LOVE you, you, YOU! And I'm devastated, absolutely devastated, just as you knew I would be. I'm holding the letter to my little nose, yes, the adorable nose, and I can smell that gorgeous perfume of yours and it smells divine, the Jean Nate. ...When I say that I was torn apart, you know damned well it's because I'm in love with two women...funnily enough both of Belgian origin, now how about that?

I'm glad that you don't have a "type." You never can tell, Neukorn, I mean, to think that YOU have not only fallen in LOVE with this boy/girl/kid, British to boot and Gentile and furthermore, you have seduced her on paper! God, who would believe it possible?

Marc arrives here on the 21st and I will meet him at the airport and we will check into the Hotel Las Pyramides in Fuengirola and we'll have a quiet dinner together I hope. Marc has tried to sweep me off my feet before, but I don't let him too much and he says that I'm impossible. Well, I hate to see him spending "silly" money. I save him lots on the tips which he leaves. I scoop them back up off the table, leaving only what is appropriate when he leaves what amounts, to a week's salary for some of these people. Then I hand it back to him and he gasps and I whistle, as if nothing had happened!

Love you, Shirley.

Spain   Thursday, December 2, 1971   7:00 p.m.
Darling,

...Tomorrow I'm going down to the coast to stay with Irene and Peter again.

...Yes, I loved being fussed over and I like having my hair brushed and washed, and my back scrubbed, and being scolded, nicely of course, and spoiled—a child? Yes. I suppose that I get on very well with kids because I'm so close to them in many ways, but then, I'm also bossy, dictatorial, boyish, tender, aggressive, a real mixture. I like to be protective. Oh well, you will just have to be patient and find out for yourself.

How did you guess? I have always wanted to go to Fire Island and "walk hand in hand along a sandy shore." That is a "must" on the agenda please!

I'm glad that you liked the brochure of Gino's paintings. Please, the next time that you're in the City, perhaps you could wend your way over to the Hollander

Gallery at 950 Madison Avenue and have a look at some of his paintings? Let me know if there is anything there that you would like particularly? I'm interested in your taste.

Excuse me while I take a swig at the brandy bottle. No, I'm not drinking too much, I just have cramps.

I've just put on Dvorak's New World Symphony. I haven't played it in ages. It's the first piece of classical music that I became "aware" of and when I did, at about the age of 13, it made me cry.

Where do you manage to hide my letters? As Irene said, "What if they were found?" (She's somewhat worried for herself too, you understand.) I have only one person to worry about finding out and that's Poppy, but you...

Thank you so very much for all the records, letters, cream and for being just you...and my finger traces the line running down the center of your forehead, the nose, the lips, and I'll move my finger and my lips will take over. "Sensuous Beastie" you will murmur and I'll say "This is no time to talk."

Love, Shirley

New York   December 3, 1971   9:50 a.m.

My Beautiful, Darling Bébé,

You are so great and the phone call was marvelous. I don't know what to say, except that there are a dozen raw eggs lying on the kitchen floor in a glorious mess! The connection was not too bad but not too good either, you do giggle. I'm so glad that you were not speechless. I missed a lot of the song and you do sound like a choir boy. I don't really know how I come across? To me it sounds like banshee screams but, whatever I say, I get paralyzed too. All of the sophistication on which I've prided myself (fool that I am!) all these years, the charm, the know-how, *avec toi*, there's no need, none, to show myself at my best. I think YOU will know exactly what I mean. It's awfully frightening for all defenses to be down and I know that for you it's the same. You see, it's the same devil which watches over both of us, if it weren't, none of this would be happening, is happening, will happen! The projection into the future, on my part, is horribly hard, because, and I hope you understand this, I've never felt that my life in itself was of any great importance. Yes, important in relationship to those I feel need me in a dependent way, NOT like you do, or WILL, depend on me, but as a presence and of course I speak of David and Stevie! And now there is this overpowering feeling of me as an entity in relation to you, two as one, no barriers but all the way, no matter if in bed, happy, angry, walking, talking, just everything, every way, any way, all the way! And of course, when we first meet, I'm wise enough to know, that some of this will show, much won't! Probably some of the things, which at the back of your mind you may be concerned about, will be as smooth as silk. The same for me, and exactly what we're NOT giving a second thought to will give us our worst moments!

And of course I know that you're not nasty, and even if you were, it would not change things! It's you, as you are, that I'm in love with, not some vision of what I think you are!

Your very own, Pipsi

New York   December 3, 1971   3:15 p.m.
Sweetheart,

I am flying! I dashed off a letter to you after the call and then received two from you.

You're obviously hopeless as a critic and obviously prejudiced in my favor. I think I wrote "Spinning" before hearing Brel but I'm not sure. Of course I'll get you another copy of the record.

I did go into song writing in a big way for about three years, really working at it every day, inspired or not, and then went off to New York to peddle them, a job which I really loathed! I received a call from Jeff Katz, who had picked up "As Love Passes Me By" and it's unheard of for a record man to do this and he was wild about it. Contracts were signed, etc. but somehow, nothing happened. Listening to it now, forgetting the tempo and all that, I find the music better than the lyrics, they are not good. I can look at a song and be very objective.

And you see, they're very simple but they say it all. Song writing is a very complicated, unrewarding business, except as an expression of the heart. Which is really funny because, as I was hunched over, sunk in misery, and working away at our song, do you know what you were doing? I do! I have photos, dated too, you were shopping with Irene! Not that it makes any difference, it's just to show you that something simple like this song, which was written a certain way as a "cri de coeur" will affect many people in different ways. A "great" song will affect all people in the same way. And if you don't understand all this jargon, not to worry, it's still unclear to me too!

One hundred per cent agreement on the gay bar, we'll make a fortune.

...I have an American accent? You must be joking? Of course I loved your voice over the phone. Poppy is right, your voice is like that of a choirboy, very clear and pure, and the lyrics are very good, surely not the first ones you've written, and poems as well? It's fantastic how you absolutely, even in that, must be the boy! But you will see that there are times when you WILL be very happy to have me looking down at you, and buying you a rose, and none of this has anything to do with changing you! I don't want to, I adore you just the way you are.

O course I've noticed about the "Pips" bit. I, on the other hand, never think of myself as anything other than "Pipsi." The few people who use it at all use either one but mostly I'm known as "Sylvia." Yes, I look very much more like a boy than I really am and I'm very soft but also very tough.

Later: 6:00 p.m. It's really very exciting at the office. The appointments are starting to come through. I must say that with my dealings, for instance, with the French Line or Cunard, I'm totally shocked at the slipshod way these companies are being run. The personnel seem so incompetent and in the case of the French Railways Office, the girl couldn't even speak English!

Thank you for today, thank you for your letters and for being very much you!

Je t'embrasse et comme je me répéte toujours, je t'embrasse encore une fois.

Pipsi

Spain   December 4, 1971   9:30 p.m.
Darling, Delightful, Caged Tiger,
*   ...This paper, which looks as if it came from a British toilet roll, is what I managed to scrounge from Irene because I've left my writing pads up at the Cortijo. I was so anxious to get to a phone. I loved hearing you and I know that I chatted on so and that you probably danced on air all day long, I did! I nearly died when I heard you say "Oh but you must have the wrong number" and I thought that perhaps you had a house full of*

visitors and that you could not accept the call. Do you know that we talked for eleven minutes? A whole, glorious eleven minutes!

I have also thought the same thing, namely, that by the time you get here or I get there, we will have burned ourselves out...all this passion on paper!

Must away, in haste, je t'embrasse très fort.
Much love,   Shirley.

New York   December 4, 1971   4:15 a.m.
Querida,

By now I'm writing with a time limit breathing down my neck as far as sending you these. In my usual manner I have left too much for too late.

Your tape is so great, it's terrific! As for now, I've only heard it once and can't wait to get to it again. I think your voice is beautiful, your repertoire tremendous and your guitar playing on a par with mine. Be patient please for my taped reply. I will get to it during Christmas week but I certainly don't know what I'll put onto it. I'd LIKE to be erotic but with your penchant for asking one and all to listen to this voice of mine (I prefer yours), I'd better not!

You are great with children, I never doubted it for a minute, that came across as clear as a bell, lucky kids!

I think you should know, notwithstanding all I've written you, that I'm NOT all hands, that I neither pounce nor grab with a lecherous leer, it's not really my style. Much more like yours, very gentle, very soft, and yes, bossy too. If I think that at times you talk too much, why, I'll whisper "hush" and close your lips with mine, as I'm doing now...now...now...

Je t'embrasse,   Pipsi

New York   December 4, 1971   5:30 p.m.

Sweetheart,

I'm dashing off this letter which is still in answer to your pink one and will try to send it off in the morning.

...The French song is quite an old one. As a matter of fact, during the war, we were traveling from Bordeaux in the same car, or perhaps there were two cars, and we were together with Julia, Jos and their son Johnny.[9] We were heading for Luchon, in the Pyrenees. We stayed there for a while and it's also where we were when France signed the Armistice with Germany. While we were driving through the mountains, Julia was singing that song. I wonder if she remembers doing it? Probably not, but I've sung it many times since and of course it's one of "Marlene's" favorites! I'll put it on a separate sheet, give you the chords and you can play around with it

Here is another $50, the only kind I ever print! Is it enough? Whatever you do, pay the phone bill. We can't afford to get a bad reputation on the Costa or we'll never be able to operate our bar. Think of a good name for the café, and Cheri, don't be obvious, nothing like "Lesbos" or "Gay Blade." I'm very bad with things like that so THINK!

Je t'embrasse, et je t'aime beaucoup,   Pipsi

New York   December 5, 1971   4:45 a.m.

Bébé,

...Your plans for taking me to Pizarra sound lovely. Of course I notice you are telling me what to do, sunbathe, walk and wait for you. (I'm teasing.) I love it all, we'll just have to wait and see... . Eventually I must make myself indispensable to Marikasha and I'm doing rather well at

---

9   Members of Pipsi's extended family from Antwerp.

it. Basically, in about a year, we'll get what are called "familiarization trips." These are for trips all over the world, usually of a week's duration and except for attending a few cocktail parties and exploring the facilities of the hotels in the area, you're on your own. Mostly I'll be dealing with Europe and Marikasha will be dealing with the Orient. Being serious for a moment, she is rather overawed by me. She is not an intellectual, though very intelligent and she certainly knows the ins and outs of the business. She thinks that I'm going to be a "crackerjack" agent. She laughs when she hears me saying to various people in authority at places like Cunard Lines, or air personnel, or Tour Directors, you know, the people with whom I speak on the phone and the information is not available, I'll say something like (and I'm not aware of this) "Listen love, get cracking, I should have had those pamphlets on my desk a week ago!" or "You can either offer something of interest to my clients or we're both wasting our time!" You do realize, I hope, as Marikasha reminded me, that a month ago I would have been incapable of this and I LOVE IT!

What I want to do is begin using the office as a mail drop for your letters and take it from there. She is certainly aware that I'm not all that I appear to be. She is only concerned with "Will she be a good agent?" She certainly thinks so and is impressed, so...I'll spend the next few months making myself indispensable. I like it all tremendously and I also think that I'm going to be very good at it. I'm very precise when it comes to making train connections, plane routings, etc. I also get on with people.

...Do you like butterfly kisses on your belly? Are you shy about being made love to? ...We are getting so intimate...and it ain't going to help at all when we meet. You are so convinced that I'll be disappointed, I'm convinced you will NOT be and I KNOW I will not! What you will have is two dopey looking "schnooks" looking for each other in a crowd at the airport! No fears, I'll know you even if all the snapshots are different, just like you'll know me.

All my love and all of me! Je t'embrasse, Pipsi

Spain   December 8, 1971
My Darling Pips,

This is not going to be a long letter but I want you to have SOMETHING in the mail when you return from your weekend. I will probably spend the weekend working as there is much to be done before Christmas and by working, I mean teaching.

We are different...I cry and you do not. No wonder you have a dormant ulcer! I am moved easily (all 135 pounds of me). I mean I'm very emotional...but I'm not ticklish.

...Sorry about playing the record to so many people. Perhaps you had better let Marc know that I asked to hear you as I had heard about your songwriting and your guitar playing? Your voice is much softer than Elly Stone's or Piaf's. Incidentally, I can be very sexy, voicewise. Actually I have never written a song before and have never made up a tune and it all came to me as soon as I heard your record. I have never written lines of poetry either, come to think of it. I think that you're gifted so don't give up, keep trying. You just need one great hit and then you're away!

Much, much love, and many, many soft kisses.
Shirley

Spain   Thursday, December 8, 1971
Dearheart,

I'm feeling very sorry for myself and very girlish and soft and I would give anything right now to be looked after and cared for. I ache in all my bones and I think that the antibiotics make one feel low and depressed. Actually, I'm at the Hardenbergh's. They had to take off for Rota because Irene was worried about a swelling in a vein in Peter's leg, however all is well.

...You ask me what I'll cook for you? I make an excellent curry, I mean East Indian curry, not some stew with some curry powder thrown in...but you won't starve! I adore caviar, Beluga that is, with chilled vodka and I love cheeses, except the American-type "Kraft" variety. But obviously you are better at it than I, so you can spoil me, and I'll fix the door handles...

...I think that Irene and Peter will go on their trip to the States at the end of April. Certainly Irene will want to have lunch with you and preferably alone, however, she'll probably settle for having Marc and Peter present unless you two can think of a way around that one. She insists on vodka and caviar!

Right now I want you. I want you to make a fuss over me. Yes, I look like a petulant child and I want my back, shoulder and chest rubbed with Vicks again. Now a hot lemon and honey drink and your cool, soothing hands on my fevered brow. The passion can come later when I'm up to it!

How did the meeting go? How is Deborah? I wonder what she'll think of me when she meets me? I'm sure that she will know as soon as she sees me, then she'll look at you incredulously and say "Not her, Pipsi, surely?"

I fall asleep thinking of you and wake up thinking

of you and your songs spin in my head. All for now, yes I love you dearly, but God knows why...who cares anyway? Shirley

New York   December 7, 1971
Darling,

This too, in haste I'm afraid. I'm in danger of going down under accumulated paperwork which I must get out of the way but at any rate, a few lines in answer to your letter of the 2nd.

I'm delighted that Irene doesn't mind me being on tape. You had told me that she didn't mind about me as long as it was on paper. I seem to have graduated up a notch. I'm also glad that she liked the song which you wrote for me, our tastes agree, I like it too! Are you sure you don't bore her with this interest in me? Or are you trying to make her jealous? I don't think that that's very kind of you if you are. And of course I'm glad that one of you, or both, as the case may be, though you TALKED of calling me on the phone, decided against it. Besides, it would have been stupid, and as Papa told you, I don't suffer fools gladly.

...I'm glad you'd like to walk through the woods, so would I and be charmed to have you take my hand in yours, and yes, you are delightfully impossible!

I will try and write tomorrow.

Much love, Pipsi

New York   December 7, 1971   2:45 p.m.
Bébé,

Some things I never forget, the taste of fresh strawberries as a child, the way I felt when writing "our" song, receiving your tape this morning just before leaving for work.

December 8   8:15 a.m.

The long interruption at the beginning of this letter was Deborah. The conversation, which I now regret, was interesting. Expected, up to a point...well, she was curious, without being nosey. The whole idea of my being involved didn't ring right! To make a long story short, I told her nothing except that I believed I had fallen in love with a boy/girl. She was so stunned and so upset that I kept filling up her glass and mine. She then proceeded to let me really have it! She said that I was insane, you were insane, and that I couldn't love anyone who was "boy." She asked me if I realized just how masculine I was? She continued by saying that I could live in only two ways, completely within myself or with a "girl" type girl. She also knew that whatever happened I would eventually leave Marvin and that I was mentally incapacitated and that if I wanted to be a fool, that was one thing, but that I had no right to mess you up. She said that I was a vestige of something that has never existed (I'm still mulling that one over) and that really all I'm looking for is someone to shoot pool with? I'm afraid that my only interjections were, "Ah, yes, you're wrong! Quite." Etc.

Well, there you have it, one reaction which I think you're entitled to know, to someone like me being in love with someone like you!

Your true character comes out in the things you say, and me opening my big fat mouth and telling you that I'm ticklish. Put away the feather duster! Why? I think that you should tell me what YOU like...you know, be nice, give ME a chance to lose my shyness. I'm NOT shy about you but still a little about me.

Let's be serious!

Neukorn traits shared by Marc and Pipsi:

a. Trying to sweep Shirley off her cocktail-
    sausage toes!
    Both saying "You're impossible!" Loving
    you. His acting like the "Grand Seigneur"
    whereas I'd love to practice "Droit de
    Seigneur" with you!

b. I "tip" like he does, which leaves me gasping
    too! I mean, fancy scooping it up!

c. We both want to spoil you, Bébé, so let us.
    So take care, my darling, as always, all my love,
    Your own Pipsi.

New York   December 9, 1971 5:40 a.m.
My Dearest Shirley,

An odd line here and there for today, anyway, and I'll hold onto this until Monday morning and then send it off.

I'm leaving David in charge of assorted animals and the house while I'm away for the weekend with Deborah and the usual crowd. He is beside himself with joy and I'm sure he has planned a round robin of orgies, lucky kid! His friends were trooping in and out last night, assuring me, with various leers, that they would keep an eye on him. This protective feeling on their part is only because they tower over him and because he's so skinny. He may have the face of a poet but I'm convinced that he has the heart of a rake!

I'm meeting Poppy for lunch and will buy a book or two and stop at the Cunard offices. This week has been deadly regarding time for myself. And when I say "myself" I mean you and me. At which point I'd like a favor from you, if you will? Would you mind playing *The New World Symphony* while I'm in the shower? I loathe it, also Brahms and Smetana and other assorted composers! And...I'm terribly ashamed, I do not know a single Hannukah song. I'm so really ignorant of any of the religious trappings that no doubt you'll put me to shame with your knowledge. Should you, on the other hand, be lacking in Gentile lore, historical and otherwise, I'll gladly fill in the empty spaces.

I'm always either writing to you, learning about you, or sending these lines off to you. And while I think of it, tell me a wee bit about Scott, Siri and Lise, just a line or two. What are they like?

Et ç'est tout pour aujourd'hui. Je t'embrasse très fort,
Pipsi

New York   Holiday letter[10]
No more dates, in this way you can make believe better.
Seulement pour les vacances!
Darling Bébé,

I must get hold of a book of St. Vincent Millay's lyrics and send it to you, it's wonderful, wonderful poetry. It's her lyrics that I love. I had them bound in blue linen but someone stole that book. I think I know who it was too! It was given to me when I was 19 by Patricia and I'll tell you about her someday. She was very special, very pretty and wrote beautiful poems. She also wrote one song which remains a standard to this day—"I'll Remember April." One of her legs was badly crippled by polio. She died at the age of thirty or so. She killed herself...I adored her. There was never anything between us except one very exuberant kiss

---

10   This is among the batch of letters that Pipsi decided to write and mail in mid-December in order that Shirley would receive them prior to traveling with Poppy at Christmas. Shirley would then be able to open the letters from her "vacation packet" daily while on the Christmas holiday.

on her part because she was very happy at one particular moment, but we were great friends. She's the only one really, that I spent time with, two weeks in New Hampshire, in a rickety old house she owned, where the two of us, in the evening, would lie around, each with a book, quite at peace with no need to say a word for hours on end. She was quite mad, or so it has been said, the final verdict being schizophrenia, but I never saw it quite like that. Nearly twenty years later, I still think of her often and miss her terribly. I never speak of her, I don't like to and I resent it bitterly when Marvin brings up her name. (He knew her before I did.) So you see, I must really feel close to you to even mention her.

All this, for sure, to impress you that your little belly is not all that I think about! It's your mind, pedantic as it may be, that I also desire! Just being greedy!

Je t'embrasse très fort.   Pipsi.

New York   Holiday Letter, sent ahead in vacation packet
Cheri,

I just looked at the calendar and realize that you might well spend the weekend of the 18th on the Costa and not go back to Pizarra before meeting Poppy. This means that I have another two days and then I had better send you all these letters or they won't reach you in time.

This whole business of your "vacation letters" took no planning. You see, you wrote "I can't bear the thought of not getting any letters" and before reading to the end of the sentence I knew that THIS was exactly what I would do.

Je t'embrasse très fort. Pipsi

Spain   Tuesday, December 14, 1971
Querida Mia,

I've damned near worn the record out! Two lovely letters from you this morning and everyone's green with envy because I seem to get all the mail.

...What a household this is! Never a dull moment, that's for sure! Right now, the black smooth-haired Dachshund bitch is on heat and they want Sammy to mate with her. So right now, I'm closeted with them both and waiting for things to happen, but Sammy is homosexual. You see, he has this thing for Irene's dog, Chico. Quite honestly, I don't think he knows what is expected of him or how he has to go about it! All the other dogs are champing at the bit and raring to go, but not my dog. Tomorrow perhaps?

Of course I know what "pimping" is. It's not just an American expression, they have it in all languages, remember Irma La Douce? How could I get through a pornographic novel without knowing something about it?

Would you please write down the words to the French song which you sang so beautifully? I'm pleased that you were feeling nervous. You and I are good at putting all the others through their paces, on the stage I mean, and then have the most awful bouts of stage fright when it comes to ourselves.

It's far too cold to go out on my horse today, the wind is whistling round coupled with the fact that I have the "curse" and the usual cramps. Now it's my turn to wax soft and sentimental and girlish...isn't it lovely to be able to reverse all these positions?

Thank God you never smoke in the street. I never did either. This should be written down for posterity, I mean, you should write a book about it, no one would *believe it. Are we the only fools who want to walk hand in hand along the sandy shore?*

This is all for now, Baby, I have some schoolwork to do. Of course I haven't commented on all you wrote nor answered your questions but be patient...

I'm sure that we will argue, but boy, won't it be fun making up!?

Shirley

New York   Monday, December 13, 1971
Querida,

This may well be the beginning of the first letter to greet you when you get back from Portugal. If it is, welcome back to Pizarra! I hope you had a lovely time!?

All that was missing from the office today was you! I mean your brilliant, mathematical brain! As I recall, you ain't good at it either! I'm hopeless and Marikasha even worse!

Arnie Beyerhof is in the "trucking" business which, in New York, has the reputation of being controlled by gangsters. Every year a "convention" of truckers goes off on what is known as a "gambling jaunt." Arnie has been doing it for years. And when he and his wife came up to my room at the weekend, when we were away, he told me to work out a deal, six days and five nights for a minimum of one hundred couples, in Paradise Isle in the Bahamas, super-deluxe. I was to present him with a fact sheet, including top accommodation, open menus, ANYTHING that anyone could want from caviar to lark's tongues under glass, cocktail parties, plane fares, business lunches, in other words—THE WORKS! My services, as an escort to handle any problems, would also be required. Apparently the men do nothing but gamble, and I mean in the thousands of dollars, so the ladies need to be entertained! *Oui cheri, mais pas à ma façon!* In other words, arrange fashion shows, horse-shows (go ahead, laugh!) shopping and other tours, etc. Of course I told him yes, I would work something out and submit a full program for his approval, and more importantly, for "Mr. Big." (Probably "Two-Gun Moe" or "Gianelli the Killer.")

Needless to say, when I told Marikasha all this, she nearly fainted! So...we began by calling the airlines, then the Bahamas, bordellos, liquor wholesalers and we get prices based on the 100-couple minimum. We get all these figures together and we add them up and figure out and eventually come up with this figure per couple and it's great! I mean, not at all expensive, the epitome of luxury, a bit "nouveau riche" to say the least, but...for this group, obviously perfect!

Now mind you, Marikasha worked at the figures on her own and so did I, as a counter check and then, to really make sure, we used the adding machine. A match to the penny! What a bargain! She is whooping with joy, screaming with hysteria and I'm just sitting there and I KNOW that there's something wrong! And the conversation goes something like this:

Pipsi:	"It's too cheap. It doesn't make sense!"
Marikasha:	"But that's beautiful! We'll tack on another 15% for our commission, the bums will never know the difference!" (Silence on my part because, with my vivid and wild imagination, I'm lying machine-gunned, dead in some dark alley!)
Pipsi:	"Look, we took the fares, right? OK. fine! The price of the rooms, right? The cost of the meals, right? The booze, the broads, you name it, we've covered everything, right? We've multiplied by 200 (100 couples) right?"

Marikasha:	"Right. We did everything right!"
Pipsi:	"NO WE DIDN'T! We only *figured it out for one night...we have to multiply it by 5!*"
Marikasha:	"Holy shit!"

We collapsed with shrieks of laughter, tears rolling down our hollow cheeks!. Of course we worked out the new figures and it's still a great bargain so we'll wait and see. And I'll continue this tomorrow. In the meantime, *je t'aime*, what else?

December 14, 7:30 a.m.

Good morning. How does it feel to be "My" composer and I "Your" lyricist? The little tune you wrote, I've put words to it and I will, of course, do it on tape. As usual, I've not given the song a title, I'll leave that to you. You realize of course, that at least, in your music, you are as old-fashioned as I am! I've added another stanza, no middle, just a repetition of the first two.

> How well I remember the smile on her face,
> How well I remember her grace,
> Her manner of speech and the song that she sang,
> I remember how our love began.
> I remember quite well the look in her eyes,
> How well I remember her lies,
> And the dress that she wore when I said, "Will you wait?"
> And the echo that whispered, "Too late, too late!"
> It was so long ago, I cannot recall
> And I cannot remember at all
> The smile on her face, or the tune of her song.
> I cannot remember where love has gone.
>
> Je t'embrasse, Pipsi

Spain   Wednesday, December 15, 1971   6:10 p.m.
Sweetie,

Thank you for the words of the song and the chords.
You have no idea of the limited extent of my guitar
playing! I have no idea how I would get an A, E, or G let
alone an E7! I have no idea of chords or their names, so
when I say that I want you to teach me, I mean just that.
You will have a lot to do in a couple of months—right
now my voice is cracked, a result of the flu I think.

I think that Deborah's reaction was to be expected. It
sounds as if she's still in love with you. Irene is also convinced, I'm sure, that you and I are so much alike that
the chemical reaction will do the rest! That is one of the
reasons also, that I keep saying to you that I think you
will be disappointed, I'm probably too boyish for you.
And yes, I am shy when being made love to so I prefer
to start off the other way round, no, you nit, none of
these gymnastic poses, I mean that I will want to make
love to you first! Let's settle for curling up under the
blankets shall we?

Look here, Sweetie, Sylvia, Sweetie, Paymer, Travel-
Agent Manageress or whatever, you are NOT getting
enough sleep! Now it is my turn to be worried about
YOU! Every time you write to me it's something like
5:20 a.m. or 3:15 a.m. Please, my love, take care, and
while I'm nagging, I really think that you're drinking
too much. All the people that I know who are drinking
as early as you are in the mornings are alcoholics!

Does Deborah live near you? Does she know that you
haven't met this boy/girl yet? Here, I have to chuckle
because, quite honestly, who would believe either of us?
People have been put away in "loony bins" for less! What
would the psychiatrists say about two people showing

this depth of feeling for each other who haven't even met? Incidentally, have you ever been to a psychologist or other shrink? If Deborah thinks that you're nuts now, what would she think if she knew about this situation?

What exactly is "Droit de Seigneur?" (Which you say you would love to practice with me?)

Again, thank you for "Snoopy." Thank you for all my holiday mail, clever girl, and the Charlie Brown books.

I adore you, you funny thing you. You are liked and loved very much!

Shirley.

New York   Wednesday, December 15, 1971

Darling Boy (Ha),

...Sweetheart, I just can't figure anything out now for the vacation, I just don't know what is what! One day it's England, the next it's Italy, a week ago Spain! In the meantime your Christmas card lies on the piano. He knows it's there. He has NOT read it. He really does live in a little world all his own and when, like now, he is deeply involved with his studies, or has a special paper to write, that's it! By the same token, I have tried to say, "Go to Naples, I'll go off on my own and then we can meet somewhere." I simply get no reaction. Also, under no circumstances will I meet you for the first time in Marvin's company. It would be unfair to both of us, meaning you and me. I just won't do it! As I've said before, I'll try to work something out. The problem is never "here" when the man is, after all, at work all day long, but when we're in Europe! He sticks to me like glue! I have, by the way, told Poppy that I'll be joining him on future trips! He was delighted! I must go off to work, I'll return later. I love you, I want you...well, what else can I say?

2:00 p.m. At the office:

I'm alone here and it's quiet...so, having taken this and your letters with me, here we go.

Do you faint dead away very often? Well, my touch is soft but I don't know about the Vicks? What happened to that great remedy of mine with a hot bath, brandy, cherry pit, etc? Of course we're going to have some fights but it's not when I get mad that you have to worry, that never lasts long, a lot of bluster and snarling. It's when I get icy cold that you have to watch out! I'm deadly! Then it takes a shovel and a pick to get me out of THAT! However, it's very rare. Anyway, you seem to get nasty too, once in a while. Are there any warning signals or should I find out for myself? Thank God, I don't cry, this way, when YOU do, I can cuddle you in my arms, kiss your hair, (or your baldy head) and whisper silly things until you smile again...I really am very tender, I just don't show it very often, I never have, but with you it's different. I guess I need you that way, someone like you, well, not LIKE you, but YOU...to know that I'm tender and silly and soft. I have, of course, been these things with others but never for very long and never comfortably. I've always felt the need to scurry back to the sophisticated shell I call home.

Since I didn't tell Marc about the record so far, I'll see what's what. Since he leaves on Saturday, he's a bit frantic already. It makes no difference though, whether he hears it or is told about it, he's not particularly interested. Anyway, he knows that I'm reticent about my songwriting, mainly because of Marvin. It's the enormous amount of mail between us I rather he doesn't find out about. As I've told you, he is a bit jealous where you are concerned etc. I'm really not interested in the songwriting business anymore. The "One Big Hit" can really only be achieved by someone who keeps working at it day in day out. I'm past all that and just want to do it for my own pleasure and yours too if you like it.

Believe me, I have my dreams, I have my illusions, but I'm so aware of the realities of life that really you never have to worry. I told you, you're not ready for me. Perhaps for bed, for excitement, for delight and for fun—yes. For falling in love? I don't know. Perhaps some day you will and then again, maybe not but we ARE friends. You do turn me upside down and things will never be the same again for me, not if it were to stop even NOW! My whole life has changed and if nothing else happens between us, I CANNOT go back. The options for me remain the same. Work, the kids for a while, and my father. I must leave Marvin, you or no you, that is not the point, it's ME! I HAVE to go. ...anyway, why do I try endlessly to explain myself? Maybe because I think I frighten you with my flights of fancy and scare you, perhaps, with my intensity? Just remember, my large footsies are planted down on earth, it's only my head which goes floating off.

Curry you say? Between the acrobatics in bed, my gall bladder and your arthritis, we're in great shape! I really LOATHE curry. We'll stick to caviar, salads (any kind) and cheese. I'm with you, I'll cook you a marvelous crisp goose (you can scrub the pot!), bake you big, fat, pork chops, the kind that leaves one with greasy mouth and fingers and then we'll go off to bed and er...ahem. And don't threaten me with your "no shower—no bed!" I'll be stark naked waiting while you're still carrying on with endless chatter in your British Way with "I say, Pip, Pip! Rather! Do I make myself clear?"

Of course the rose is a symbol. Who gives it? When neither of us cares, that's when we'll be ready for each other! I adore you and kiss you very hard!   Pipsi.

P.S. WOW! Ignore everything! I'M COMING TO THE COSTA, IN FEBRUARY, ALONE!

Spain   Thursday, December 16, 1971   11 p.m.
My Darling,

I had a great day today. As you know from my last letter, we were invited to Elizabeth Handy's for a spaghetti lunch. There were other teenagers invited and they all had a wonderful time. There's something wonderful about the ring of children's laughter. It was well worth the effort and the long drive. After leaving Elizabeth's, I took the kids into Malaga to do Christmas shopping.

When we left, we gave a ride to a couple of Canadian girls who have lived here for about three months. They are with their mother. Their father seems to have deserted them. God, you should see how they're living, it's a hovel! It's clean but the walls are streaming with water and it's so damp. The beds consist of mattresses on straw matting on the floor. There is a hole in the ground which serves as a toilet. The kids bring in all the water by hand. The mother is around my age and looks as if she's still suffering from the husband's desertion. It's beyond my comprehension as to why she has to subject these delightful kids to this, which I'm sure is not necessary. I haven't seen any situation like this even amongst the poorest people living in the "Campo."

When we got home, Lise and I made up a huge Christmas package. We had more fun fixing up this package for them than all the others put together. We found lots of clothes, all in excellent condition, shoes, sweaters, comics, loads of books, many of which look new. We also included some dog food for their dog's Christmas dinner and a bottle of wine for Mum. Lise and I will deliver it tomorrow or the next day. Fortunately, this is the time of year when we can do it without hurting anyone's pride. We are also going to invite them up here to ride horses as they showed great interest and they all seemed to get on well together.

Thank God, it has stopped raining but it is blowing gale-force winds.

I'm away to bathe. I love you!   Shirley.

Spain   Friday, December 17, 1971   4:00 p.m.
Darling Heart of Hearts,

"Joy To The World!" I received letters from both Neu-korns this morning. I'm dancing, leaping happily, skipping around and reveling in your undying love and devotion! I love you, love you, every inch of you, inside and out. It's all very frightening really, and I don't care and I want to be with you and near you....

When Gino first met me and began his crusade to persuade me to teach his three children, he told me that if I only instilled in them a love of music and taught them to sing, he would be grateful. None of them could sing when I first met them. We actually started with nursery rhymes and folk songs. Today we were busy recording as we have done a lovely thing for Christmas, readings and carols, etc. and we had a lot of fun doing it. They were all delighted to know that you enjoyed the tape.

Scott is ten, small for his age, usually monosyllabic and somewhat shy. He has changed quite a lot since I've been here. He suffers from asthma, has a good sense of humor. He rides extremely well, as all the children do. He can't sing quite in tune yet but he's improving. He is excellent at fixing things like replacing light bulbs, fixing door handles, replacing fuses, etc. He is extremely fussy where food is concerned. One wonders how he stays alive for his appetite is very small.

Siri has freckles and long blonde hair. She's somewhat of a tomboy and she's EXTREMELY creative and uses clay and paints well. She draws well and creates great poetry and prose. She is the family veterinarian and it's she who injects the dogs, cats and horses when it's necessary. She is an EXCELLENT horsewoman. She has a flock of pigeons of which she's very fond and she's NEVER punctual for anything! She is adorable, very capable, very funny and gets away with murder!

Lise is the young lady of the family, hard working, neat and tidy and she has a strong sense of responsibility. She is the most conservative in this rather Bohemian family. She likes to do the right thing. She shows a keen interest in music and today I'm going to teach her some guitar chords. She has a heart of gold and is thoughtful concerning others. She and Scott squabble incessantly, but nicely so. All three are very loyal, adorable kids and I love them as if they were my own. I sometimes wish that they wouldn't grow up.

Must away to Pizarra and look for the mail. Je t'embrasse très fort. Yo te quiero mucho, vida de mi corazón. Je t'adore. Que lastima que tu no es aqui conmigo-helas! I love you, Shirley

New York   Friday, December 17, 1971   1:00 p.m.
Cheri, Querida, Bébé,

So...I have SO much to tell you. Where do I start?

You will have received my Xmas card telling you of my trip to see you! Did you faint? Turn purple? ANSWER! Also, on the tape I tell you about it. Did you pick yourself up off the floor? There is a chance that I will be with you, or at least on the Costa Del Sol in February or March! And I will have to go and investigate...BEDROOMS! How did this happen? I don't know! I walked into the office on Wednesday—the words just came out and I didn't know what I was saying: "Marikasha, if I had to go to Spain for a week, would the office cover for me and say that you sent me there?" And she just looked at me and said, "Yes, of course. What a stupid question!" SHE is the gem, not I! And that's all I said yesterday. Then, when I came home I taped and told you about it and of course I had to tell Marvin that Marikasha wanted me to go and investigate hotels, etc. The reaction was, of course, bad but he has quieted down, and I'll finish this tomorrow. I love you, I really do.

December 18   7:30 a.m.

Anyway I told Marvin this fantastic story of how Marikasha wanted me to fly to the Costa, investigate hotels, speak to managers and talk to them about "group rates" etc. It was very upsetting for him because even though he knew I'd eventually have to do quite a bit of traveling, he knew that it wouldn't be for another year or so! He immediately said that he'd come with me! Then he said that he'd be damned if he'll let me go to Spain because you and I would end up in bed, "shacking up." Dearheart, how about it, would you like to shack up with me? Then he wanted to know why Marikasha didn't go and I told him that she wanted me to handle Europe. Anyway, he did quiet down and NOW is making plans for us to spend our vacation on the Costa and also Morocco! As you can imagine, I'm in quite a state! And also, I tried to find my "you know what" because of your erotic (rhymes with clitoric) letters and IT'S GONE! Don't laugh, Hall, it's not funny...I think it shrank, atrophied, fell out, that's what happens from lack of loving hands! Of course you've lost me as far as vibrators are concerned! You BORROW them? Well, I hope no one is suffering from any contagious, revolting diseases?!

Je t'embrasse très fort,   Pipsi

Spain   Saturday, December 18, 1971
Cherie,

Have just read your funny letter, the one you wrote about "The Truckers To Paradise" and it was hilariously funny and I laughed so loudly that the kids wanted to share the joke so I read that part of your letter to them and they too roared with laughter.

I'm writing this in the classroom. We're having school today and tomorrow because we'll finish on Tuesday which is the day on which Poppy flies in from Switzerland. We'll be having lunch in about an hour and after that, Lise and I will go to Mijas to deliver the Christmas packages for those Canadian girls.

No, I don't have a sweet tooth, except for Dutch, Austrian or French big cream cakes and gateaux or les tartes de fruits! I like marzipan and I asked Marc to bring me some from Belgium.

I'm off to lunch, I'm starving. Starving for food I mean. I'm not starved for love, not since knowing you! May I squeeze you now? I love you!

Shirley

Spain   Sunday, December 19, 1971
Querida de mi vida,

What a gorgeous day! The sun is shining from a cloudless sky. We just took a break from schoolwork and cycled down to Zalea, the tiny village near here. We certainly needed the exercise. After lunch we're going riding. I saw Irene yesterday and she's joining us today, all being well. I saw her yesterday when Lise and I went to Mijas to deliver our Christmas packages to Elizabeth Handy and the Canadian girls. They were all very pleased to see us. Their mother said that meeting us had been like a shot in the arm for them and they had not talked about wanting to return to Canada since.

Continued: December 20
Thought that yesterday's weather was too good to be true. This morning there is a very heavy mist. Yesterday, Irene and I went for a very long ride. It really was wonderful and the horses full of pep. The same one which kicked Irene, "Cervantes" by name, BIT Gino yesterday on the arm and drew blood! The kids then did some jumping. Irene and I watched while eating our lunch, picnic style outside.

... I can't believe that Poppy actually arrives tomorrow! I love him and I love you. You said something about my breathlessness and that I probably use all the wrong muscles. You are probably right, so teach me, yes?
All love and happiness, Shirley

New York   December 18, 1971   11:45 a.m.
Querida.

Before I start answering the two lovely letters I received, I'll just fill you in on what happened next with Marikasha. Yesterday, of course, I had to fill her in on all the details, in other words, I need her to back up my story about sending me on this trip, etc. as far as other people are concerned. I told her that there was someone in Spain...I did NOT say you were a girl. Anyway, you know this is all difficult to write about.

I don't know why, it just is. So, perhaps, let's just leave it at this, that the most important thing is that it's OK for you. I myself, don't know if I'm being brilliant or abysmally stupid! I DO NOT want to cause ANYONE heartache or discomfort. Time enough for all that later, if it comes to all that...and I'm speaking of you and yours, not to do with anything here. So, Bébé, think about it carefully and let me know and I will not be hurt or upset if you say "Don't"! Other than that—if you decide "Yes"—please do not start making frantic arrangements which is why I said not to disturb your schedule with the Hollanders. I must make hotel arrangements from this end and will, in fact, be speaking to managers and such.

4:30 p.m.

Back, but...the "Liebestod" from *Tristan and Isolde* is playing on the radio and if I write with that going on in the background, I WILL deafen you with outpourings of love, so...after a while, one either turns Wagner off or he'll surely do it to you!

...Yes, it's true. My father has no friends. My mother didn't either, though she used to play cards with Julia and other members of the clan. Marc has no use for people, really, though he does have "protégées," so you see, you have been quite marvelous for him, having introduced him to all these nice people you know! He and my mother were perhaps sufficient for each other.

Poppy is, of course, tremendously special in my life and I come to him late in life, in my understanding of him at any rate. He was not a father for young children. I don't want to sound cute and coy but I think he's a "man for all seasons." My admiration for him is boundless, for his knowledge, for his intellect, for the way that he looks and carries himself, for his great, great charity and his kindness towards people. I think that this is not an easy thing to achieve when one has one's own insecurities to deal with. I think that it is easy for a man who seems completely at ease with the world and his fellow men to be kind. For a man who does NOT feel that way, it is a much harder thing. He is, of course, an utter delight to be with. I hope you enjoy him as much as I do.

...I really have a problem! I can't find it! It's very discouraging! I have not tried very hard. Still, perhaps I should go to Dr. Maurice Goldenhar and say, *"écoute, Maurice, si ça ne te derange pas, regarde et dis moi, c'est encore là?"* Too embarrassing! I console myself with the thought that the FEELING is there so...After all, one doesn't usually lose a finger, a toe, or an ear, not unless one has leprosy. I'll keep you informed and NO, I certainly don't need any help in finding it, thanks awfully.

...I'm glad that your friend wrote what she did about New York. I think that I told you what a tough town it is and I don't think that you took me too seriously. I have been in many places and have never hesitated to walk down any street, at whatever time of day or night, but even I would think twice about doing it in New York! And it's not a question of bad or poorer sections, it's everywhere. It's not just a question of theft, but of violence. We have nothing like that in Oceanside, no violence. Burglaries, yes. The drug scene in the high schools is bad, an awful lot of kids are using them and it's a cross- section of all economic and religious backgrounds. To be "in" seems to be the password nowadays and drugs are part of that scene. Parents do not help the situation. You would be surprised how many of THEM have tried it for fun. I have a really strong feeling that teenagers do not like to see parents wearing THEIR style or mode of dress and American men and women do this to a great extent. I love to see the mini-skirt, hot pants, midi—all of it—on young people but which I feel becomes ludicrous on middle-aged parents!

You've said the magic word! Vacation! Both boys had jobs last summer. (I insisted!) You see, I want the best for them but it's also time for them to learn a little of the realities of life. Marc wanted to buy Steve his own car when he was eighteen and I simply would not allow it. That boy really likes the high life, theatre, restaurants, etc., and he does get a monthly allowance from Marc, as does David but they have to make do with that and whatever they earn. They like one another and get on well, which is great! I think that David's first choice is the University of Rochester. It's a fine school and I hope he makes it.

C'est tout pour aujourd'hui. Je t'aime et t'embrasse très fort. Pipsi

New York   December 19, 1971
My Dear Shirley,

Just a few lines even though I think I may have left this too late and it may well not reach you. If it does, please do the following:

Give my father a big kiss from me. Keep one for yourself. Drive carefully!

I know, I know, you're a champion on the road but I did want to wish you all a good trip and a safe one. And I hope, for everyone's sake, that the "Parador" you picked has no little bugs running madly through the bed sheets!

Do you remember telling me that "Inshallah" must be the same as "Allevei"? I have coined a new one: "INSHALLEVEI." We might as well have all the protection there is! Anyway, further proof that Arab and Jew can live together in harmony!

Have a good, good trip. I shall next be heard from when you are in Gay Lisboa, where all the Fado singers sound like mournful "Olga's from the Volga" singing about Ivan on the divan!

Much love,   Pipsi

Spain   *December 21, 1971   4:45 a.m.*
Darling Pips,

Look at the time will you, just look at the time! This is ridiculous, I can't sleep. I tossed and turned and thought, "So, it's midnight in New York and Pips is probably in bed, at least she should be."

I'm partially packed, ready to leave after lunch today. I'll collect my car, go to the hairdresser's, check in at the Hotel Pyramides and arrange some sort of decoration in Marc's room, bathe, change and dash off to the airport. I will then take him to the Hardenbergh's, where we are expected for dinner.

Barbie has insisted that I borrow her mink! She has two! Of course, I look like a Teddy Bear! I'm just not the mink type...however, I can't really wear my duffle over the kaftan or saris, so there we are! She was most perturbed to think that I might not have the "right" clothes for this trip to Lisbon, bless her, so I asked her to come and view the clothes I proposed taking. She was very surprised to see that I have, indeed, some elegant eveningwear.

December 22   4:30 a.m.

This early rising to write to you is getting to be a habit...I don't know where to begin because I'm SO excited!

First of all, Poppy is here! He was first off the plane and I flew across the hall to meet him. He looks very well and he was all smiles. I had managed to do everything as planned, although I was in a daze, I'll admit, because your tape had arrived in the morning. Now it truly is my turn to say, "There are no words. It made me want to cry in parts and in other parts I roared with laughter. I *played for the kids, the parts of the tape which were intended for them and they were rolling around the school room with laughter. But let's get back to Marc.*

He had received my three letters sent to Antwerp and one from Irene, to which he sent a reply by cable, inviting them to dinner this past evening. As Irene had literally slaved all day to get the house back to some semblance of order, they were delighted to accept. We had a wonderful evening and Poppy laughed and laughed and it was GOOD to see him so happy. He spoke a good deal about you and he told me how much you are enjoying this correspondence and I told him how you "made me laugh like a drain."

Then, when we returned to the hotel, he was delighted with his room. I had managed to find a few roses. I had placed some greenery around and my Christmas card holder, complete with my cards which all made it look festive. Of course, I had checked the mail and there was a letter from you for him. He put it in his pocket and would read it before going to bed. He called you "A sweet, dear girl!" We kissed goodnight and I held him tightly. The only thing missing is YOU!
All love, Shirley

New York   December 21, 1971 10:15 a.m. the office
Querida,

I'm imagining you getting ready to meet Marc or perhaps, even at the airport and wondering if the box with the letters reached you in time and they are packed away in your suitcase?

So....shall I come? Are we ready to meet? Don't be impetuous, think about it! I have...and I don't know. Forgetting everything else, except you and me, this is something great going on, just the way it is. Am I rushing it? ...there really is this feeling that I know more of life (though God knows you're more experienced), or know more, perhaps, about the effects that one's actions have on other peoples' lives. And this, mind you, not in thoughtless acts, but carefully planned and thought out.

12:00 noon

...If there's any question as to where all these letters will be, should I come over in a couple of months, they will be resting in a small fitted case, which can only be opened by a special combination that only I know. The case rests on the top shelf in the back room office and is hidden by cartons of invoices, ledgers and hundreds of brochures! And if that doesn't re-assure all concerned, too bad.

...Yes, I intend to get very familiar on this "familiarization" trip, which of course, it is NOT! That's what I'm SAYING it is and Marikasha is going right along with me on it! I MUST stay at a hotel, except for perhaps one night that I could stay in Pizarra if the Hollanders won't mind? Maybe you could stay with me at the hotel? Anyway, we can discuss this later. I really must go to different hotels in different towns as THAT's my cover. Next week I'll write to a few of them telling them that I'm coming to inspect and discuss terms, etc.

No, I have never been to a psychiatrist. Have you? Well, I don't want to change, I like me the way I am. It's the conditions of my life that I don't like. And I'll get out of it on my own. I think that for some, psychiatrists are great, but mostly to help their patients realize their full worth or to help them improve their self-esteem and to improve their self-image and getting to like themselves, but I like myself well enough...

December 22   7:40 a.m.

"Droits de Seigneur"? The privilege and uncontestable right of the Lord of the Manor, during the Middle Ages, to tumble any girl living, or working on his estate, and have his way with her, virgin or not!

Be well and feel happy and don't daydream too much, especially when driving! And stop thinking so much about sex! It can't be healthy! I know. I do the same thing!

Your own Pipsi

Spain   December 23, 1971   1:15 a.m.
Querida Mia,

Of course, staying up until past midnight is marvelous because I get to read your daily letter earlier! I don't know where to begin! Well perhaps I'll start with telling you about the day...

Poppy's room is at the end of the corridor, so he phoned me this morning at 8:45 a.m. I had a quick bath, dressed and joined him for breakfast. The breakfast was lousy so we have decided to go elsewhere, so no breakfasts in bed for this knave until we reach Lisbon! Then off we went to Torremolinos where Poppy had his business to attend to and then on to Malaga where we did some Christmas shopping. After that we drove back to Fuengirola for lunch at the "Sin Igual." I was quite tired after lunch and decided I needed a nap. Marc went walking. He woke me at 6:00 p.m. and away we went to do more Christmas shopping, then off to see LaVeta and Margaret. ...

Poppy told me today that you have changed from drinking the Smirnoff to the real Russian stuff with the unpronounceable name! Not before 6:00 pm. Darling, please! (In one breath I say that I'm not difficult to live with and in the next, I'm very dictatorial...I know, I know!)

Light of my life, I'm ecstatic and OVERJOYED with the news that you are coming!

Many hugs and kisses, Shirley

New York   December 23, 1971   7:00 a.m.

My Darling Angel,

Two lovely letters from you yesterday... What you tell me about this Canadian woman is just awful. Doesn't she have a family to go back to? Anyway, I'm impatient with "mothers" in general, I think they're an awful breed! In the past month I've received two phone calls from the mothers of two of David's friends. One I've never met, complaining and carrying on about both boys, when in fact, both of them are quite delightful! I was stunned, especially when one started to sob because the boy had said he'd be home by six and it was six twenty when she called. She was just out of the hospital and she wanted him to take care of her, disgusting! And the other one was carrying on because she wants her son to be a lawyer and he doesn't want to be, etc. The bad part is that these kids spend a lot of time here and had, at first, a tendency to say horrible things about their parents. By now, they know that I won't tolerate it, (even though it's often true) but they need to talk and joke with an adult, which is fine with me...up to a point, when I gently tell them to get lost. I find that this generation is wide open about their emotions—there doesn't seem to be an inner secret part of them and I don't know that I think that to be a very good thing? As much as I like their approach to physical things, the lack of inhibitions, the hugging, the kissing, I really think that a little more reticence on their part would be helpful as far as their inner feelings are concerned. David is not at all like that and perhaps he's too quiet about his feelings, though I'm sure he's not like that with his friends, which is the main thing.

You asked about the "gangsters" and their trip? We have two sets of figures to compare and we'll see which is the better buy. Then I'll present the fact sheet of costs, etc. to Arnie, who, in turn, will present them to the Mafia bigwigs. These things do have to be booked well in advance and perhaps there's a slim chance that we'll get it.

Marvin doesn't mind my working. He does NOT like the fact that I'll be traveling, or that I must attend cocktail parties or the fact that I'm not earning money! I drive to the office, which is about three miles away.

10:30 a.m. There's a Christmas Party at the office which I must attend. Our wee fridge is loaded with champagne and good French stuff at that! As Marikasha says, "As long as we're broke, let's do it in style!" My sentiments exactly.

4:00 p.m. I am sloshed on champagne! Marikasha brought in some stone-hard, ghastly homemade Italian sausage and also some twenty-five-year-old Provolone! Strangely enough, three clients walked in...they soon reeled out! I don't know whether it was the smell that did it, Marikasha's drunken giggling, Adele's hiccups, or the endless stream of booze that I genially handed out to one and all! I think I'll take a boiling bath, I'll make believe you're with me...No, I'd better not, the make-believe I mean! I had told you that I had lost "IT"—well, I've found it again!

I'm really kissing you very hard, te quiero querida, beaucoup et encore beaucoup! Love, Pipsi

Spain December 24, 1971 12:45 a.m.

My Darling, surprise, surprise,

Now, where to start? I took Marc to the Cortijo today. He was more than favorably impressed! Of course, EVERYONE is thrilled to learn that you are coming so soon! I had sort of "paved the way" as far as telling Marc about our correspondence and that we had become fairly good friends and were delighting each other and that you particularly were amusing me with funny letters. So then I played him your record—he was quite overcome! He has said on more than one occasion that he's delighted that we have become such good friends. And it's all settled! I'm going to the U.S. in the summer and I'll share my time between you and we'll have a lot, but a lot of fun! I'm thrilled BEYOND words to know that you're coming here soon.

I have just returned from the Pueblo Lopez Restaurant where I held a dinner party in Marc's honor and fourteen were able to make it of the twenty invited.

You know, of course, that by now I have succumbed and love you very much? I never was a brilliant swimmer and this tide is too strong, I'd just better go with the flow. Angel, this is all for now.

Much, but MUCH love and MANY thoughts.
Shirley

New York   December 24, 1971   2:00 p.m.
Angel,

THIS was going to be the day I'd sit and write to you! I'm at the point now where, if anyone comes within ten feet of me, I'm simply going to lash out...nothing has gone right except three letters from you, including one with the pictures of the children. They are beautiful! Wonderful little faces...just wonderful.

I had to go into the office for a minor crisis, the cooking is not getting done, I keep falling over teen bodies that are perched in every room, Deborah just called to say that she needs me to take her to the airport. I must get over to see Carmen (Carmen is my housekeeper when I ain't around.) and take her a bottle of Fundador brandy. This is just so you know (as if you didn't already!) that I'm NOT all sweetness and smiles!

I am overwhelmed by the children, they look fantastic and I can well understand how you feel about them. And here we go again...another interruption!...I love you and I'll come back to you, and that's all for today.

New York   Undated Christmas card, sent ahead in vacation
packet
Querida,

The background music is the "Goldberg" variations of Bach, do you know it? I hope you did NOT open this before today and that you are reading these lines before opening the little packet? Of course, a most Happy and a Merry Christmas to you. I admit to thinking of the birth of Christ as the best advertising campaign ever waged, and of Paul as belonging on Madison Avenue, very nifty in his grey flannel suit. But at least he chose a nice Jewish boy! My romantic nature will always think of today as "Our First Noel" even though you are there and I am here and that this letter, of course, was being written weeks ago!

OK—now open the little box...of course I hope you like it? This is the "stupid" gift I mentioned. I did not know I would buy it and basically, by now, you know I'm not encouraging you to go out wearing cravats and such! I was in a miserable mood that day and it struck me that when you ARE in that certain mood and wear a tie, you might as well do it in style! I trust you are wise enough to realize that this is no "abdication" on my part, and no Ma'am, you can't keep me in the kitchen! It can also be used for keeping together the frayed ends of a broken brassiere strap!

Many, many kisses,

And all my love, Pipsi

"I love your song, the one you've never sung before,
The one that speaks of you and a walk on a sandy shore,
With hand touching hand and a smile upon your face,
And the glint of moonlight on your shirt like a pattern of lace.
I'll take you in my arms and kiss your funny nose
And I'll be very shy when you give me the single rose,
Then we'll laugh like fools and forever banish sorrow,
But.....don't be so smug, Dear Heart,
For I will....once again....buy the rose tomorrow!"

Back to you Bebe! And this is written with all the love in my heart,

Love, Pipsi"

Spain   Christmas Day, 1971   1:30 a.m.
Querida Mia,

I don't know where to begin? I just don't know! Shall I begin with my Christmas card and my Christmas present from you? You are SO VERY sweet. I don't usually wear ties but as from now...I wouldn't DREAM of send-

ing it back, it's a beautiful tie pin and I love it and thank you a million times. Truly, because of you and Marc, this has been one of the most enjoyable Christmas holidays I have ever had.

Of course I want to "shack up" with you, you know that. How observant Marvin is! He must be congratulated. You mean he dragged himself away from his virginals and lutes and Pergolesi to make a fuss about THAT?

Poppy and I went shopping this morning (yesterday really) and I found the most divine black velvet "smoking" suit and a lovely shirt to go with it and a gorgeous small black velvet handbag. It suits me, I look good in it and I wore it this evening at Irene's. Everyone said that I looked stunning, anyway, you'll see for yourself soon!

Irene knows that you are coming. She is perturbed and disturbed and she knows that I want to go to bed with you and that I want to spend time with you...that is one of my problems. Oh Hell, I've seduced you a dozen times or more already, and I've certainly BEEN seduced, the damage is done.

Yes, I want you, and yes, I love you!
Shirley!

New York December 27, 1971 3:30 a.m.

Querida, Sweetheart,

How are you? I'm sitting really like a Russian Grande Dame, very stiff and very straight. I managed to send you a few lines yesterday morning and spent the rest of the day in and out of bed. I really slept a lot and of course, it was the worst thing that I could have done! When my back acts up like this, it's much better for me to keep moving about and be active, quietly of course, but really to just keep going.

Of course everything got done on Friday and dinner was delicious. I drove Deborah and family to the airport and coming back I listened to Christmas songs and sang right along. The roads were deserted and it was lovely. Saturday afternoon was spent at some cousins of Marvin's and there were many small children around and a lovely little baby so I had a very good time. And here I am writing to you again. Joy! Joy! Joy!

I don't like Schubert either! If you're wondering why I have this limited taste in music, it's because I think that a lot of the nineteenth-century music became too saccharine sweet for me. I like Bach and pre-Bach. From the time I arrived in the States until I married, I would listen to classical music every night for a couple of hours or so on the radio. I never heard or knew any "pops." To this day, I can hear a piece of music, a symphony or sonata or concerto and whistle right along with it. (But not as well as you!) I don't like modern classical music, not for me the Schonberg or Shostakovich. What I like about the Rodrigo is the lack of flourishes, it's very simple and to the point. All this of course, from a person with no real knowledge of theory or anything about music notation.

I'm like a turtle on its back with MY back in its present condition. Usually it doesn't last more than a few days. David's *"cri de coeur"* when he saw me leaning sideways was "How do you do it?" And yes, he had a glorious time while I was away on the weekend and yes, the house was a glorious mess when I came back!

It sounds as if you're giving Poppy a wonderful time. And I know about the two girls who own the Pueblo Lopez Restaurant, Josie and Helen, because Julia told me. She said, *"Et ça se voyais quelles etaient Lesbiennes!"* I felt like saying

"*Et moi? Ça se voi aussi?*" Julia, I assure you, has her suspicions about me. She's too much a woman of the world not to. They're a very sophisticated bunch those Antwerp women, very chic, soignée, and very involved in charitable works and they do a good job.

All my love Dearheart, but all of it and many soft kisses all over your sumptuous body. And a loving, deep one for that marvelous mouth of yours!

Pipsi

December 28   2:45 a.m.

So early! That's only because I woke up and decided I'd better take a hot bath and move around a bit. I have a feeling this is one of the times it's going to take a week to get better. Not to worry, by the time you read this, I'll be climbing trees and vaulting fences again!

Having reached this point in our relationship, do you REALLY read pornography or were you teasing? I was once given the job of sneaking into this country a book called *La Ravageuse*. I read it on a plane on my return home, which is no place to read a book like that! Besides, with those damned French books, you have to cut the pages open and as I read further into the book, I really became quite frenetic and bits of paper were flying around the cabin like pieces of confetti! That was a very good book. I don't know what happened to it.

December 29   11:25 a.m.

Before I say anything else, I want to tell you something. There are going to be many times with you and me, that one or the other is going to do or say something which is going to either annoy, or make the other one uncomfortable, for whatever reason, it's not important. I cannot ever be deeply angry over something like that—I mean your playing the tape or the record—annoyed at that moment, yes. Listen, Bébé, and try to understand. I received my father's first letter this morning. He says that he was "moved" by hearing the record and why didn't I tell him? So off goes this letter to him explaining, but his letter to me I've torn up because if Marvin sees it, there will be need for explanations. Plus I'm annoyed because I've had no news from you and besides, my back is no better and I look like a crab crawling along! Of course, the idea crossed my mind after I sent you the tape that I should have written and said, "What I say about Poppy is between you and me." I didn't so after all, how are YOU to know? For all I know, you did a good thing, what's the difference? I have my own vision as to my relationship with Marc! Keep him happy, keep him laughing, have great discussions on politics, philosophy, economics, etc...just not too much...well, love, I guess.

As always, your very own Pipsi!

Portugal, Lisbon   December 28, 1971   Hotel Ritz
My Darling softened boy/girl,

Right now it's extremely difficult to write letters. Last night I wanted to but I was just too, too tired! It had been a rather long, hard drive on horrid roads. It rained a good deal and the windshield wipers failed to work! We had had a bad skid, which frightened me rather and for ME to admit that it was a bad skid, it must have been! It was through no fault of mine and fortunately, I was driving very slowly.

What a marvelous girl you are to think of all those daily letters for me, but now, yes, I have to admit...yes, I opened more than my quota last night! You see, I had this terrible thought, "Imagine if I got run over and had not read all those letters of love?"

I wore the tie pin! Yes, the gold pin sent to me by a dear friend/lover/boy/girl/Manageress/lyricist/plumber/songwriter/partner on Christmas Day. Marc admired it for its simplicity but I did not tell him that you had bought it for me. I played the record for him though and he was quite moved. I said, "There you are Poppy, you did not think that you would sit in the Cortijo and hear the voice of your daughter!" He is a sweet, gentle, dear and loving person. I'm honored to be his "nieta." (what does that make you to me relationship-wise?)

Je t'aime et tu sais je suis très heureuse que tu m'aime! Shirley

Lisbon, Portugal   December 29, 1971   11:45 p.m.
Pips,

I'm truly sorry, I'm mortified in fact and I want very much to say that I was/am sorry. I certainly presumed too much and I had no right to let Poppy hear the tape as you had not given any instructions permitting me to do so. You are right, I am a child or should we just say immature! I felt very miserable after the phone call, extremely miserable in fact to also learn that so far you have not received any of my communications! As for letting Marc hear the tape, let me just say this, I thought that it would be nice to let him hear from your own lips, those beautiful words relating to him. He was, of course, quite moved but he did not cry. He nearly did but I told him that he was not to because it would upset me if he did and that I would not have played it if I had thought that it would upset him and make him cry. I just wanted to do the right thing and you are probably very angry and like a child, your scolding me made me close to tears. I was very choked up and in fact I couldn't say much to you. What else can I say? I'm stupid and immature and full of remorse, and full of love for you, that's why it hurts so! Shirley

New York   December 30, 1971   3:00 a.m.

Love, Dear

I'm flat on my back in David's bed. He's sleeping at his friend Richard's house as they have been busy since yesterday preparing for their New Year's Eve Party. So if the writing is worse than usual, it's the position I'm in.

Your letter was marvelous. It's lying at the bottom of a drawer. If I BEND, I'd get it but my condition is the same and I'll try to stay flat as much as possible today. I'm glad you like the tie clip. ...I don't understand why you cried with the tape? Did you like my Dietrich imitation and was the sound clear?

Trying to look ahead, it would be best to book for around February 20th or perhaps March 10th? What is best for you? And I must book the hotel from here. It's a new little "minipackage." I will want to see various parts of the Costa, preferably the less popular places, IF they have hotels. Be an angel, find out if an introductory letter from Marikasha will be sufficient documentation for me to be able to look at accommodations?

Business is booming! We can't believe it and keep hugging ourselves with delight! Yesterday, the landlord of the building, an unpleasant creature, said he wanted to go on a two-week trip in mid-January. I mesmerized him with the fascinations of Marrakesh, the quaintness of Fez, the brothels of Agadir, etc! After he had left, Marikasha said, "My God, is there any place you haven't been?" I answered, "Oh, I've never been to any of those places" and we quietly collapsed with joy! At any rate, if business keeps up like this, Marika-sha will put me on salary in March. I don't know how much, it really depends upon how many days I'll be working.

I've warned Marikasha that the volume of mail might be, shall we say, heavy! No problem. She is, of course, pondering about me and I think she probably guesses as to what is what. She told me two days ago about a friend of hers who is a Lesbian, and this and that. I was noncommittal, although she wouldn't give a damn about what I do. Somehow I would rather not have it out in the open with her, though it's bound to come out sooner or later. We have such a great relationship going, I don't want anything to spoil it from the point of view that she might get "cute."

I want you to promise me one thing, PLEASE: no fuss, no parties or dinners in my honor and all that stuff. I can't wait to meet the Hollanders and the Hardenberghs, but please, no big deals about any of this, just some nice, quiet days together. And truly, I must do some research while down there.

Je t'embrasse très fort.   Pipsi

Top: Shirley with the Arab who helped to get her VW out of the sand when she and Delyn drove from Abadan to Dohar, Qatar, 1968

Center left: Shirley holding Laveta's granddaughter. Fuengirola, Spain, 1971.

Center right: Pipsi in her backyard. Oceanside, New York. August 1971.

Bottom: Pipsi with Ralph in her back garden. October 1971.

Shirley's parents, Rene and Ernie Hall, Spain, 1971.

Marc Neukorn, Pipsi's father, Spain, 1971.

Peter and Irene Hardenbergh, Shirley, and Marc Neukorn in Lisbon, Portugal, December 1971.

Shirley and Pipsi together in
Marbella, Spain, February 1972.

January

On December 31st New Year's Eve I managed to phone Pipsi, unbeknown to Mark and Irene. I wanted an intimate conversation with her. When the phone rang Pipsi was in the middle of taping for me. She was also experiencing lower lumbar pain. Apparently she had a muscle spasm and had not yet seen her doctor. Subsequently she began a few weeks of physiotherapy which helped the condition.

Upon my return to the Cortijo after my vacation, I learned that Gino had organized a skiing trip for us all to go to the Sierra Grande, near Grenada, in mid-January. This meant a change in our school routine. We would ski, weather permitting, and do lessons at night. During poor weather we would do schoolwork. We traveled by road driving our respective cars.

Portugal, Lisbon January 1, 1972
New Year's Day!   12:00 noon.
Sweetheart,

I know that you will be up, after all, it's already 6:00 a.m. where you are! How marvelous to think that you will be here in less than two months!

Now let me tell you about last night's little adventure, and this is TRUE, every bit of it! First of all I must admit that I looked dashing, really. I had been to the beauty parlor and had the works! Yes, your Bébé was shampooed, pedicured, manicured and massaged, like a pedigree bitch at a dog show! Then of course, I was dressed in my new black velvet suit, which I love....

We went to this "Fado" restaurant called "Severa" for the New Year's celebrations and there were some VERY interesting characters there! To begin with, there were two gay girls with two gay boys as escorts, who eyed us and obviously discussed us when we entered, and one of them was dressed in a brown velvet suit. It seems to be the fashion. She flirted with Irene and came over and kissed Irene on the stroke of midnight! At the next table, there was a most elegant brunette, about 45 years of age, who reminded me very much of Deborah Kerr. She had three dapper young men with her. They were bearded and frankly they looked as if they would have been more at home studying the Talmud! Her jewels, my dear, were all quite large, obvious and quite beautiful! As the lights lowered she stared at me and I stared right back and thought, "Well there go my New Year's Resolutions!"

To cut a long story short, I was returning from the tiny crowded space they called a dance floor, where I had been dancing with a young child of about eight years (No, I DON'T have a "Lolita" complex!) when "Madame" stands up from the table where she had been sitting and walks right into my arms! I kid you not! I nearly collapsed but somehow regained my composure and said, "At last!" She then held me closer and proceeded to brush my cheek with her lips. I gently pulled away and asked her if she was on holiday here? She spoke Spanish and French and told me that she was Belgian! (Another one! See how I seem to get mixed up with these Belgians?!) She said that she lived on the Costa del Sol and I replied, quite casually, that I did too. Then she said, "You must phone me!" and informed me she was returning to Spain on January 2nd. I asked her where she was staying. "The Ritz, room 740. You have that? Room 740!" I have to admit I really enjoyed dancing with her. She wore a long black gown and was most "soigné." Irene was furious and she couldn't believe that the woman had asked me to phone her at the Ritz! She said if I wanted to have an experience with three young "gigolos, together with Madame...just go ahead and phone!" Well, I did try to phone but found myself asking the operator for Oceanside instead!

This morning, when I was telling Poppy that I could not reach her after she had invited me to phone, he said, "Can you imagine?" I asked him if he, while he was downstairs, would try to find out the lady's name. He came hurrying back with her name and he said, "Now be careful, dear child, with that Madame Reneé Goddard!" I told him it was the first time that I had been propositioned by a woman in such a public place!

For all that...you were closer than ever and this time our phone connection was excellent most of the time. I love you, at least the voice, the wit, the humor, the grey hair, the letter writer, the song writer...looks like I'm doomed!

Happy, Happy New Year!
Much love, Your Bébé

New York   January 2, 1972
Angel,

BE one and rub my back please. I'm bone tired and every one of them aches.

When I get to feeling like this, which is about once a year, I go to Maurice and he gives me a Vitamin B12 shot. Invariably I bounce right back and drive everyone wild with great zooms of explosive energy. Yet, as he says, no one has proved that it does any good really, which goes to show that it's a case of "mind over matter."

I have your perfumed oil-and-powder letter IN IT'S EN-VELOPE at least two feet away and it's operating full blast! That's strong stuff! Très oriental! I can't figure out who is the worse lecher or roué, you or I, which is certainly promising for the future!

Are you having a great, fantastic time? I hope so. And Hall, put those tips back on the table! You have no couth, none at all!

> Twenty kisses from old chapped lips and all my love, Pipsi

Lisbon, Portugual   January 4, 1971   11:00 p.m.
Querida,

Now you have another reason for loving to go to the office—receiving mail!

Another night of cinema going for Irene and Peter who decided see a Roman Polanski film. Poppy wasn't interested so I stayed to keep him company. He has just gone to bed. He has laughed a good deal on this vacation and has said, more than once, that he is very sorry that tomorrow is our last full day here. He is already talking about a return visit in the Spring! He has talked a good deal about you this time, mainly because he sees that you and I have become friends. Everyone, but everyone is dying to meet you!

Perhaps you should prepare yourself? You know that you are going to be met by someone who is fat, bossy, wrinkled, sometimes "boy," sometimes "girl" (though I'll admit to feeling very "boyish" lately). There is so much

to show you...and I wonder if I'm going to be a big disappointment to you? At least Poppy seems to think that
we'll get on together like a house on fire!! (Consumed by
flames of passion no doubt!)

I look over my shoulder and out of the window. The
full moon of a couple of nights ago, is no longer full.
The city lights are twinkling and I think of you across
that ocean. These days I never stop thinking of you. I
eat, sleep and dream of Pips. I see your grinning face
and hear that voice, oh that beautiful voice! And your
laugh has to be the nicest laugh I have ever heard.

Hugs, caresses, kisses and embraces,
Shirley

Portugal, Lisbon   January 5, 1971   11:45 p.m.
Dear Heart,

The day after tomorrow I'll be in Fuengirola and
Benalmadena. The day after that, up at the Cortijo and
there I'll find letters from YOU!

What a marvelous thought. Are you really coming?
Are you really?

You know, dear, sweet Marc said today that when I
finish with the Hollanders I'm not to rush into just any
job. He says that I'm to take my time and I can always
go and stay with him in New York for as long as I like....
He is SO sweet and he gives me a great feeling of love
and security. I love him very dearly, from the bottom
of my heart. He talks so highly of you. This evening we
heard about your trip to Russia with him.

We are BOTH insane, but ain't it fun? I'm sorry, my
Sweet, but I'll have to end, I'm extremely tired.

I love you very much, Shirley

New York   January 5, 1972   2:25 a.m.

Dear "Piggy,"

I say, you are a hog! Imagine reading all those letters one after the other in one day!

Yesterday, I received from you, one letter, one tape and one card, the one with the knife in the back, which of course, was perfect for someone in MY condition! Actually my back condition seems better. I saw Maurice yesterday. It is not a damaged disc, nor, thank god, is it arthritis. It seems that the muscles in my lower back have lost their elasticity, partly through my own fault. So, starting next week, I'll have to start doing back muscle building exercises to get it back into some form of decent condition. I say that it's "partly my fault" because I favor my right side. I don't stand straight but always lean on my right foot and I slouch a bit. This is caused by the "empty" feeling caused by the removal of my kidney. I sleep on my right side.

I think that you have to do a little bit of growing up. Yes, yes, I know you don't want to and maybe you won't, but I think that it's something you should try! I love the "child" in you and don't want to change you, but it's time, I think, that you stop being a goose about certain things! Blondes for example! Yes, but you know there are blondes here too, sweet and willing and with better voices, so I'm not about to be overwhelmed by a new one. It's interesting that you equate falling out of love with YOU and IN love with a blonde! That's the reason I say you are young! You're speaking of anything BUT love! One doesn't fall out of love just like that, it's a long, dreary process, I know it well.

So you see, I MUST come because, maybe, after a week, it will penetrate that dense little head of yours, that it is YOU, pendulous, bald, chunky, cute and rather stupid sometimes, also very wise on occasions, but it's YOU, Shirley, that I'm aware of and interested in! And...if it doesn't work out between us, it certainly won't be because of a blonde fluttering her eyelashes at me. ...

Je t'embrasse très fort. I love you, Pipsi

New York   January 6, 1972   2:20 p.m.
Dear Bébé,

I should say "Pen Pal," the appellation given you by Marikasha. I found your very funny letter waiting for me at the office. But, Dearheart, why send Poppy to do YOUR work, when, by lifting the phone, you could have gotten the information from the front desk? I really think that you're in a rut. Try another nationality for Heaven's sake! Russian ? (You can have my body but not my soul!) Hungarian? (The recipe for an omelette—first you steal two eggs!) Danish? (But Shirley, how do you know that I'm REALLY a girl?) Anyway, is the charming Madame Goddard Flemish or Walloon? I certainly don't see why Irene got upset? "Brown Velvet" kissed HER at midnight...anyway, it all sounds like great fun and New Year's Eve Resolutions are made to be broken, otherwise they're no fun at all!

Certainly, many are envious of my trip to the Costa and there are a few offers of joining me. I smile and state gently, but firmly "Sorry, but..."

Much love, Pipsi

New York   January 8, 1972   4:30 a.m.
Angel,

Received the lovely letter and the photo of the four of you yesterday, many, many thanks! I agree about Portugal, I found it a dull place, but "What can you do?"

Now don't laugh, but Marvin is much more concerned about Poppy MARRYING you, than you and me in bed! He's convinced that Marc is very susceptible to your charms and he will make you Madame Neukorn the Second! I don't THINK that Marvin has any idea about me but he does realize that women are attracted to me. For instance, he's convinced that Lucy is, and always has been, after me. Then very often, when we meet new people, he'll say "Why do you always end up in a corner with the most interesting woman in the room?"

I still haven't told Marvin THE date. He knows it's the end of February so I'll tell him next week. He's been quite good about it and of course he can't wait to meet everyone. He doesn't know about the summer yet and I'm holding off on that for a little while, just as a question of timing. Believe me, I really think that I handle him quite well and I'm sure that, except for the odd moment here and there, you'll have fun with him. He is an interesting man in many ways and of course, at the piano, with a couple of drinks, delights every-one. He is very shy with women. I think he will like you and of course I appreciate your writing the occasional card to both of us. As far as noticing any difference in me, I'm far too good an actress for that.

Seven exciting days and six romantic nights! It's the best I can do and as I've mentioned, I've had to book the hotel as it is a package. If this Sirocco Hotel is not nice, I CAN upgrade it to a better one, whichever is recommended by the airline. I told Iberia that I wanted a first-class hotel, so they said "Sirocco." I must come back with a report. Actually, we're aw-fully ignorant about the Costa and I do expect to have a lot of clients interested in going there this summer.

Oh yes, the two little "Peanuts" books came to the of-fice and thanks again and don't spoil me so much! I think this is all very complex, your talks with Irene and all that.

I sometimes picture myself as the sacrificial lamb. I think I understand, and then I realize that I don't at all, I mean your relationship...And yet, I have some talks with Deborah which perhaps clarify some aspects of love but that is from her point of view which perhaps is similar to that of Irene in her relationship with you. But of course, YOU are the puzzle in all this!

Poppy's praise of me...how I wish he would stop! Half of it is true I'm sure but how dull for people to have to listen to all that. It is true, strange as it may seem, "I am a girl of principle" and if that ain't a laugh, what is? I am also an incurable romantic and whether I ever find it or not, I'll go to my grave believing that two people can love each other on an equal footing in every way and forever...so you see, Querida, you have here a young/old boy/girl, naïve/cynical, romantic/realist on your hands...and really, don't ever be shy when I talk too much, just hit me over the head and shut me up!

All for now Bébé and that word suits you, no, not because you're immature. I'm not exactly grown up, it just fits I think.

Je t'embrasse très fort, Pipsi

New York   January 9, 3:30 a.m.
Querida,

Of course you should say "Oh Lord"! I mean about Papa talking to Marvin! I can see it now, "Yes Marvin, I heard Pipsi's tape and record..." and "Shirley and the children send Pipsi tapes."

Heart of my life, I adore you but you talk too much! I KNOW that you don't understand my way of life but Marvin is NOT Marc, who is very naïve, and as you should know by now, believes in only what he wants to and shuts his eyes to everything else! If you could possibly understand that, left to my own devices, I can work everything out, so that by the time spring comes around, even Marvin will be impatient and looking forward to meeting you! After all, I've worked it out to be able to see you next month, PLEASE, let's not ruin it!

Yes, I also like the way David looks and he is a lovely person. He is very much his own person. I have never known him to do something or follow the crowd because it is the people thing to do. He's having a wonderful year—the discovery of girls, driving, being involved in the school show. (He has the second lead in their production of *Fiddler on the Roof.*)

At the office we had a very busy 10 days between Christmas and New Year's, which is unusual. A Mr. and Mrs. Milton Goldberg walked in yesterday wanting to go to Europe. As it's their first time, she said to make it something special as it might be the only chance she'll ever see it. She's about my age, looks like a sick woman. The husband took me on one side and said that it should be an easy trip, not tiring and all that. So I want to make it something very special. They don't have much money, etc. and Marikasha blew up and said not to waste too much time on it and that I should have gotten a deposit from them. Then I blew up and told her that I would handle my clients exactly as I saw fit! She smiled and said, "Good. Now perhaps you realize what I meant when I told you that it would take about three months and then you'd tell me to go to Hell!" This is of course what she wants, she doesn't like a "boss-employee" relationship. We do work well together. We should know about the "trucker's trip" in about ten days. I doubt we'll get it but keep your fingers crossed because it's a $60,000 deal, which ain't hay!

You asked about my clothes? I'll let that go for another letter but I'm hopeless because I LOATHE shopping! I do NOT wear pantsuits, only pants and mostly turtlenecks. I think

I'll have to wear skirts (yech) when I speak to Managers and Representatives or else, seeing us together, the staff at every hotel on the Costa will think I'm preparing a mass invasion of "Our Crowd"! (Did you read the book? It's about the Jewish aristocracy in the United States.)

Behave yourself *jeune homme, je t'aime beaucoup, vraiment beaucoup.*

Hugs and kisses, Pipsi

Spain January 10, 1972
My Darling, Sweetheart,

Let's begin with your letter which was mailed December 21st. Sweetie, you had better know now that I have no idea either of the names of various "types of bits" or names of horse tackle! Having learned later in life to ride, I did not learn in the "OLDE ENGLISH RIDING SCHOOL!" I have never had a formal riding lesson in my life. I've picked up and gleaned from watching other riders. I feel confident enough to handle most horses and enjoy riding and will even race around a track if I have to but I do not jump or know anything about the rudiments of dressage. I ride because I really enjoy it and being out of doors and looking at the countryside.

Look Sweetie, will you please let me know on which flight you're booked and have you booked the hotel yet? If not, do you want me to arrange it? As I'm off to the Sierras I can't do anything about seeing any hotel managers right now but I will do so when I get back. It's all arranged here that I can stay with you because I will make up the teaching time before and after, and I plan on working every Saturday from now until you arrive.

...*No, I have never been to a psychiatrist, but when I was in hospital in Iran a psychiatrist came in to see me but I'm afraid I was not very helpful. To begin with, he only spoke Farsi or French. I don't speak Farsi and my French is not that good. I told him that I knew what my problem was and that he could not help in any way and to please leave me alone. He did!*

Irene will be pretty busy when you are here, thank goodness. She is expecting visitors from Washington and they will want to go off on excursions to various towns and possibly to Morocco so you may not even meet. She believes that you're here on a familiarization trip too. She said, "She worked that one alright didn't she!"

Sweetie, I'm going to bed now as it's past midnight and I have a million things to do still. I'll take your letters with me and answer them as soon as I can!

Shirley

Spain Sierra Nevada   January 10, 1972
My Darling Girl/boy/Cheri/Cherie

So we have finally arrived here at the ski resort! Gosh, you would love it here, especially on a day such as this with blue skies, the grandiose mountains covered in glistening snow...

Right now I'm playing your tape for Lise. Once again, she has a bout of bronchitis. As Lise is not well, I have suggested that the family go off as a unit tomorrow and I will stay with Lise most of the time and go and practice on the nearby gentler slopes and limber up.

Imagine my surprise a few moments ago when I walked into the hall and saw Marianne, the owner of the "Pourquoi Pas" gay bar! We were delighted to see each other. She is here without her girlfriend, who is back in Torremolinos looking after the business.

...I ordered a book from Blackwell's, the Oxford bookseller. It's The History of a Death Camp. It's about Mauthausen. The British woman author took twelve years to write it and I understand that it's a factual account. I've only read the Foreword so far.

Continued: January 11,

Lise is somewhat better today but still with bronchitis. I've suggested that the family go up the mountain to the "real" slopes. I have to admit to having done a total of three week's skiing in my life! I am already aching in every limb, especially my back and stomach muscles.

We have agreed that the kids will stop skiing each day at 4:00 p.m. and report for lessons at 5:00 p.m. What with trips to England (though educational), holidays, sickness, etc. we have some catching up to do and need to make a real effort.

This is a "quickie" Darling as I'm off into the sunshine again and for more exercise and also to mail this.

In haste and, as yet, all in one piece. How about you?

Je t'aime beaucoup Querida Mia.   Shirley

New York, January 10   [tape excerpt]

Hello Dearest,

I have a lullaby, written a very long time ago and probably my first protest song. I'll play it because I rather like the tune. The words could be better ...because ...I have a horror, a real horror about patriotism, the kind that kills people. You know—"He dies for his country" and all that sort of thing? I shudder, because I think of what is left behind. Basically, really, every country has its heroes. I imagine it's the only form of consolation to say about young men who have died for their country? I think that it's ghastly and that it is a horror.

> Child of sorrow hush your crying
> Child of sorrow dry your tears
> Daddy lies for freedom dying
> Daddy's gone but Mommy's here.
>
> Child of sorrow hush your weeping
> Child of love so warm and true,
> Daddy lies for freedom sleeping
> Mama's here and holding you.
>
> Child of sorrow hush your wailing,
> Child of sorrow born in fear,
> Daddy's gone, there's no use waiting.
> Daddy's gone but Mama's here.

...You will probably be thinking to yourself that I seem to be a person of strong likes and dislikes? Well, there are not too many—but a few things send me right up the wall. The war in Vietnam is one of them, of course. I have very strong feelings about very few things, and they deal mostly with what people do to one another. Inadvertently, I think, it's the little man, the average "Joe" who is thrown this way and that by the powers that be. Those powers, whether they are functioning under a flag that proclaims democracy, or a flag that proclaims communism, it makes no difference, because it is the little man who suffers. It is the little man who gets it and he gets it right in the teeth. So yes, about these things I have very, very strong feelings. And what I wrote you once, you know, it is also true, for instance that Mr. Muskie is now certainly going to run on the Democratic ticket. Of course, labels don't mean anything to me, Democrat or Republican,

I couldn't care less, I vote for the man, certainly not for the party, if you know anything at all about American politics?

I'm completely against the war in Vietnam, against our intervention in Vietnam, which does NOT make me in any way a supporter of North Vietnam. One has nothing to do with the other. I can say there are many things wrong, very wrong, in this country, which certainly does not make me a supporter of either the USSR or Communist China.

But, anyway, what did I start to say? Oh yes, I mentioned Mr. Muskie and I am definitely going to volunteer to work for him. I think he's a very, very good man. Unfortunately my past history is always the same, inasmuch as the person for whom I work always loses! So, you know, I get the feeling that when I approach the party headquarters and they see me coming, they would rather barricade the doors! ...

Well, that's it love.

New York   January 11, 1972   2:30 p.m.
Dear Electronic Genius (Ha!),

I spent the morning at Maurice's. My back is doing fine but it will take another week to be perfect. Anyway, since I must attend this cocktail and dinner in New York tonight, Marikasha told me to go home and get back to the office around 5:00.

Yes, I know you are bossy, and I guess you're a little plump. I'm surely more wrinkled than you, *et moi aussi*, I feel very "boyish" lately. Am I as masculine as Deborah sees me? No, I'm not, but I am in a mental way and yes, certainly, in that way, more so than you. I still haven't told her. I am, of course, far more serious than anyone suspects, so you know, when you say "EVERYONE'S dying to meet you" I know that you all expect to laugh and you will, it's true. I am funny or rather, I see the funny side of things. I'm not very demonstrative and certainly not in public and VERY rigid about certain things where I'm concerned, I mean my own mode of behavior. I have my own set of morals for ME, not for others, not even the ones that have been or will be involved with me.

Thank you for my single rose, and in case you've thought about it, don't! I mean don't meet me at the airport with one! *Tu vois, moi aussi, je suis bossy*! Actually, meet me any way you like and do what you damned well please.

Many soft kisses. Pipsi

New York, January 12, 7:15 a.m.

That cocktail was quite a brawl! I fed one friend bourbon and introduced her to a charming guy from Staten Island! The last I saw of them, they were gazing deeply into each other's eyes! Then MY adventure started! A lovely voice behind me said, "Do you often play Cupid, *Tête Grise*?" I turned around and found my nose in direct contact (it WAS very crowded) with a small-bosomed chest enveloped in a cream cashmere sweater! Now I ain't small, with heels, figure 5 feet 5, so I look up, and up and really I think I have never seen a more beautiful woman! She was at least 6 feet 1 inch, a Mulatto from Kingston, Jamaica. Of course she turned out to be a model and a dancer and the girlfriend of the president of the company who was throwing the party. Rather a nut I think but very nice and my God, WHAT skin! I kept calling her "Hester," which is not her name, I can't remember it, and she kept calling me *"Tête Grise."* She was fluent in French and INTERESTED! However, I told her that I was very involved with a girl on the Costa and she answered, "Yes, but she is there and I am here!" So I said, being stumped, "What can you do, what can you do?" Then, getting bored, I spied a nice young lady with broad shoulders, slim hips who had been gazing at Hester (and drooling) and I called her over. She didn't walk, she ran! I asked her name, "Charlie," she said, so I said, "Chuck, this is Hester, or at least I call her Hester, take very good care of her." And I left THEM gazing into each other's eyes! And so much for *"Les Aventures de Pipsi, Agente Voyageur"*!

And now back to your lovely letters!

As far as I can tell, the summer vacation would be probably the first three weeks in June. I must be back on the 24th or 25th in time for David's graduation! We'd probably stay on the Costa for about a week and then spend about ten days in Morocco, which Marvin wants to see rather badly. I do know that he's now terribly intrigued by you and the Hollanders and Irene and Peter and is anxious to meet everyone!

...As to why I'm under your skin or why I love you, I really don't know. I don't think I ever will! Perhaps we'll find out a little of what this is all about when we meet? We'll talk, God, how we'll talk! We'll also kiss, cuddle, hug, and love! It's going to be marvelous you'll see.

Now—your New Year's Resolution said that you would stop pestering me about the cigs. And vodka! I only smoke my cigarettes halfway down really and I don't drink that much! I don't need the vodka.

I adore you BÉBÉ and I really can't wait to be with you!
Je t'embrasse très fort. Pipsi

New York   January 13, 1972 4:30 a.m.
My Darling Opinionated Bébé,

Papa and I spoke for half an hour yesterday. He adores you and I heard about Estoril and the Casino and a fainting man and you catching him.

Poppy also yelled, "Silence in the ranks" when I protested his high-handed ways with me! This because he wants to take me "shopping"—MERDE! I think that he's afraid of my appearing on the Costa looking like a slob and speaks of pantsuits. Oi, Oi! He also intends to stuff my pockets with $ bills and was very, very, stuffy about "when Marc Neukorn's daughter" etc. So we yelled at one another and there will be more of that when he comes on Saturday! I did remind him that I certainly knew how to entertain people, and that it didn't HAVE to be orchids and champagne! I mean sometimes a single rose and a glass of red wine is just as good. At any rate, you might get your caviar, unless we decide to buy two bicycles and pedal furiously and disappear into the sinking sun! I think HE's beginning to worry about me living up to my reputation!

I love you. Pipsi

Spain   Sierra Nevadas   January 16, 1972   6:00 p.m.
Darling Pips, Pipsi, (THAT's a concession!)

How rapidly the weather changes here! It was snowing and rather misty most of the day. Now it's clear, with blue skies with brilliant sunshine but an icy wind. I must admit to not doing much skiing today.

...Oh yes, I now know about the "Borscht Belt" because I asked Barbie this morning and she mentioned the "Concord." That reminds me, did you see the report of the robbing of safety boxes in the Hotel Pierre? Didn't you have your wedding reception there? When did you realize that you were no longer in love with Marvin? And where did you go for your honeymoon? And when were you FIRST aware that you cared for women? (You did say, "Ask away.")

...I'm enclosing a ghastly photo of "Dear Marlene." Much, much love and many kisses, passionate, wet, soft and dry. Shirley

New York   January 14, 1972   5:00 a.m.
Cheri,

I've re-sealed a letter written yesterday. I wanted to add a few lines and send it to Pizarra! Nobody tells me anything! I thought that you would be in the Sierras for ten days. Marc told me yesterday that it's for two weeks...I'm confused, which is not unusual for me!

Are you having fun? And do you think that after this, you can STAY PUT for a while?! Here there's a mixture of snow, sleet, rain, and howling winds and I love it.

Six weeks from tomorrow! I'm very, very, nervous. Don't be deceived by my bantering ways. I keep looking in the mirror every now and then and pull my hair in despair. I'll be the bald one, not you! To think that the usual thing that attracts at first glance is how one looks and we're working in the opposite way! Yes, I know, this worries you too. Never mind, that's the least of it.

Take care Angel, I love you and you're very precious to me.

Je t'embrasse très fort!   Pipsi

New York   January 16, 1972   5:30 a.m.
Querida,

Did you know that this is a quote from Marc addressing me: "Next to you, Shirley is elegant!"? Are you? As you can imagine from this remark, Poppy was none too pleased with the way I looked, but don't take it seriously, should he mention it in his letters that I'm tense. It's not true. But...he dragged me off to shop which turned out to be a complete fiasco and I've told you how I loathe shopping!

I seem to be living in some sort of great vacuum, which makes Poppy's remarks about "being tense" nonsensical. The days are very busy and pass in a flash, they also seem to pass like a slow motion film. There is, it's true, this *feeling* of nervousness about seeing you but I can't say that *I* am nervous. Never mind, I'll go on and on if I start like this.

Continued: January 17   10:00 a.m.

10:30 a.m.—Tell me, have I been very wise or very stupid in making arrangements to visit you in February? Or will we only know after? Anyway, I'm having the day off because, as I had expected sooner or later, Mr. K had a massive hemorrhage in the wee hours. I managed to get Marvin to drop him off at the vet's office. I expect a call within the hour telling me, of course, that he should be put to sleep. I wanted to do it about two months ago but the reaction from everyone was ghastly. The net result of course is a total mess. Mr. K, whom the kids found and brought home some eight or nine years ago, has been particularly *my* dog. He was wonderful with everyone, especially the neighbors' children but always making sure that he knew where I was before wandering off on his own. He's about fourteen now, but in his younger years he had the illusion that he was "Superdog" and he would slide Steve's bedroom window open (on the second floor, this house being a split-level), tear open the screen and launch himself into the air, landing nimbly on the driveway. When Norton, the cat, was laid up with a broken hipbone, the dog never left his side and used to lick the top of Norton's head at odd moments. When the other cat, Ralph, was a kitten, he would jump on Mr. K's back and off they'd go like the wind! Anyway, he's an awfully nice dog and I loathe seeing him in this way.

Perhaps tomorrow, when I get to the office, there will be a letter from you? One gets used to receiving letters frequently and so when one hasn't received any in four or five days one begins to wonder—I know, you've had the same experience in the Sierras. I hope that you minded as much as I did?

All for today, all my love and many bear hugs and tender ones too of course!

Je t'embrasse très fort, Pipsi

Spain   Sierras Nevada   Monday, January 17   4:15 p.m.
Darling/Querida/Mi amor,

No skiing at all today. No post delivery or collection either. The snow and howling winds have continued non-stop since yesterday. My car has completely disappeared under the snow, so has Gino's! The children and I have been studying this morning and I'm waiting for them now so that we can continue with more school-work.

I believe that we will return to Pizarra at the end of this week. I think that a good deal will depend upon the weather, if the sun is shining then we will stay until the last minute but if it's snowing and the visibility is poor then we'll probably head for home. Of course I'm anxious to get to my letters which I KNOW you will have written me.

I plan on teaching every day from now until February 26th. That gives me at least ten extra days of teaching. Gino and Barbie said that it was not necessary but I want to do it and then I can enjoy that week with you, but completely! We have one commitment and that is the day after you arrive—Siri's birthday, which I've promised we'll attend. We will most certainly play Sar-

dines. I'll have to think of a few other interesting activities and games for the kids. I'll chauffeur you around to the hotels, oh what fun! And you're going to love the Hollander house and my little village of Pueblo Lopez!

I am impressed with your French verses. I am very lazy where languages are concerned. I SHOULD speak, read and write far more Spanish than I do and my French is very rusty.

Much, but too much love,   Bébé, Shirley, "Hall"

New York   January 18, 1972   3:00 pm
My Darling Bébé,

How is Lise? Why does she have so many chest coughs? Give her my love will you? And also, is Irene OK?

I have only sent you one card to the Sierras. I hope you miss my letters? They'll all be waiting for you in Pizarra with my news as to where, how, when etc. and probably some instructions as to what to do about the room! Be prepared for the future, I mean I will always say to you, "Bébé, I'll take care of everything" and then come to you and say "Bébé, please do take care of what I've messed up!"

Yes, I'm in one piece, the back not quite perfect but getting better every day...I'm really very healthy...

Continued January 19   4:00 a.m.!

Horses yes, skis, no thank you! The fireplace for me, the slopes for you...Take me to the "Pourquoi Pas" for a drink. You have an unbending influence and will make me pliable where I have been rigid. Does the thought please you? I don't know, maybe you'll prefer me without too many changes, perhaps, anyway, just a bit of softening on the sharp edges?

...This morning, *je prends mon courage a deux mains* and I'm going to Lord and Taylor, we have a branch here. Ugh.

And also to Saks in Garden city, about twenty minutes away. When Marc is insistent, wow, he's insistent! Let me know, really, if there is something you want or need or would like to have...and as for the kids, don't worry, I'll figure out something, no problem. You certainly love that family and I like the thought that you are happy with them.

You sound, somehow, less frightened of meeting me. You may well be speechless but I don't think you'll faint! Am I right?

Je t'embrasse très fort.   Pipsi

Spain   Sierras Nevada   Thursday, January 20, 1972
Cherie/Cheri
The day before yesterday, Scott broke his leg, poor chap! Hence no letters written to you yesterday! The weather was bad because it had snowed continuously for two days and the visibility was poor. However, the chair lift was working, so Gino decided to go skiing with Jimmy, Faith and Kenny, an American boy, Scott and Siri. It was on their second run that Scott got his ski caught by the tip in some deep, fresh snow and CRACK, over he went! Fortunately I had spent the morning, together with Lise, digging out and clearing the snow from my car. I warmed up the car, then put the back seat down and installed a small mattress, sleeping bag and a pillow inside. After the local doctor had given Scott some painkillers, Gino drove him down to Grenada. No one else was allowed to drive down the winding road as we were literally snowed in, however, Gino got permission to follow the snowplow. Once at the hospital, it was discovered that Scott has a spiral fracture of his tibia and they put him in a plaster cast from his toes to

his hip!

The weather today is foul, so Siri is working and I'm writing to you. Scott has to go to the hospital again this morning as they want to take another X-ray to see if they need to insert a pin. They remain in Grenada and we are waiting to hear.

Much love and many kisses. Shirley

Spain, Sierra Nevada, January, 21 1972   6:15 p.m.
Cherie/Cheri, Pipsi, Pips,

You know, my love, you take up most of my thoughts both during the day and during the night too and this is a poor state of affairs. I'm beginning to wonder how I existed before you came on the scene? I thought that I was happy enough?

...I still have no idea of the time of arrival of your plane but guess it will be 8:00 or 9:00 a.m. So I expect we'll drive to the hotel. Which hotel? Then you can have your "private" bath...not even your back scrubbed?

Then it will be entirely up to you but I might venture to suggest that we go to Fuengirola to visit my little village of Pueblo Lopez and walk around some. We could have lunch at the "Sin Igual" then go back to the hotel for a siesta. By then, I know that I'll be quite exhausted not having slept for ages with all the excitement of waiting for you to get here! And certainly you'll be exhausted too? Then a bath, maybe together this time? We'll dress and go out for dinner, perhaps at La Hacienda, maybe to the "Pourquoi Pas" for a nightcap then to bed.....Ahhhhhh.

By this time you will have me pleasantly sloshed? And if your ears are red, so they should be. While I, *at this moment, have a peculiar feeling in the pit of my stomach. Yes, of course I love you and you're SO damned sure about it too!*

This will probably be the last letter that I'll write from here. What can I say that you don't already know? Je t'aime, Cherie.

All love, Shirley

New York   January 22, 1972

Dear Heart,

YOU don't have to call me "Pipsi" and anyway, you may well call me a few choice names by the time you get finished reading this! Not to worry, it's nothing important.

I found two beautiful letters from you waiting for me at the office. I go in on those Saturdays when Poppy doesn't come out to visit. I admit that yesterday I did not write, somehow I felt too tired. I felt ugly, slightly miserable and annoyed, etc. I think I need a haircut! My back is really OK. I'm no longer stooped over, just tilting forward a bit.

...Yes, my wedding reception was at the Pierre and the honeymoon was three days somewhere very near New York. We came back and found out that Lucy had lost her liquor license. The Club, called The Perroquet, was closed and Marvin was out of a job!

As to your question of when did I realize that I was no longer in love with Marvin? I'm quite sure that I've mentioned that I NEVER WAS! And certainly let's not go into the idiocies of an 18-year-old girl. Think of it as a mental precocity and emotional infantilism! I think I've always cared for women. I certainly always fell for my teachers. I always liked to be around older women and certainly never knew pleasure with any man and, by now, you know there have been very few.

I think I knew that I liked women a long time before do-ing anything about it, the penalty of really being very shy! The irony, of course, is that I'm so good at it, was so good at it, whatever, whereas, with men, I'm a piece of wood. I should say "was." I don't, and haven't in fifteen years, except for Marvin.... I did say, "Ask away" and I've answered!

Many thanks for the brochure AND for Marlene. I think she's rather fantastic, après tout...."Après Tout"—that's not bad! If "Pourquoi Pas" is a good name for a bar, why not "Après Tout"? Think about it!

Yes, I know about Irene's operation, that it went OK and that Marc sent her long stemmed roses. (Bless that man, he is so great.) She wrote, well, an amusing letter which I've an-swered (out of vanity, love, I bow my head in shame) just to show how it SHOULD be done! I still have to mail it. It's just that I don't want to come to the Costa under false pretenses. I mean with all my moralizing, etc., maybe I give an impres-sion of great innocence and lack of know-how. And really, I'm awfully good at playing these games but I'm just not very interested, it's too easy...again, vanity!

You and I are going to be very, very happy and also un-happy on occasions, but mostly very, very happy! And if all of this is being idiotic fools, well the world needs those too, I don't think that there are enough of us around!

Je t'embrasse très fort,

All my love,   Pipsi.

Spain   Cortijo De las Yeguas   January 22, 1972
Light of my Life,

Last night I listened to your tape and I loved it, but loved it! You do not sound nervous anymore and you talk to me as if you had known me all, but all of your life!

Yes, yes, I talk too much. I apologize and will try to be more careful. I'll really try. What more can I say? Yes, I'll play down the closeness of "you and me" when communicating with Marc. He says that you were not well, in fact he told me that you looked awful and that you were extremely tense and nervous and that he noticed it in your driving. He also said that his children will not listen to his advice. (He has the same problem with me!) "What can you do?"

Obviously, Marvin does not KNOW Marc at ALL if he is worried that Marc might make me the second Mrs. Neukorn! Of COURSE we were holding hands. I LOVE Marc very much in my own way and I am loving and affectionate with him. Actually, he's the only man that I have felt that way towards and it's all pure tenderness...

I love you VERY much. Bébé

Continued:

After lunch I rode my horse. I rode alone and thought of you a great deal and hoped that when you are here that the jonquils will still be in bloom.

You are SO funny! How would I know if Madame Goddard was a Walloon or if she was Flemish? She spoke French, we conversed in English and Spanish and she lives in Antwerp.

...When I returned from the Sierras, there was a letter from the Iraq Petroleum Company. They have offered me the job as Deputy Head Mistress (no laughs, Vice Principal in your language!) at the Community School in Abu Dhabi in the Persian Gulf. It's a great opportunity career-wise, so I spoke to Gino because the post would mean beginning there in September. He says

that he definitely wants me to stay here if I'm happy...
and he knows that I'm happy. Anyway, Abu Dhabi is so
much further away from New York and...and...and...
  I love you, you sweet, adorable, very mature,
  Pips. Bébé.

New York   January 24, 1972   2:30 a.m.
Querida,

   For once it's not my fault, the hour I mean. I was awak-
ened about an hour ago by a sound of fast click, click, click.
Wondering who the Hell was tap dancing through the house,
I got up and found David pecking away at the typewriter. So
I had coffee and he a glass of milk. We shared a raisin bun
and some jaw-breaking yawns then I packed him off to bed
with the promise that I would wake him at 6:00 so that he
can finish his work. As I mentioned, this is the last few days
of exams and such and beastly reports to be handed in, etc.

   Yesterday was quiet. I did nothing except my *New York
Times* crossword puzzle and of course reading the damned
thing. It weighs about 50 lbs. on Sundays! I made a huge
pot of clam chowder, do you like it? I don't. I thought erotic
thoughts about you!

   I am REALLY NOT very bright, and this is not false modesty. I only SOUND like that in letters, not even when I speak. So
it's you, much more than me, who is building up an image.

   "My Spinach experience in Sweden?"

   I was visiting Kickan, a former governess, who decided
I should have the experience of one of the great saunas. We
had gone on an excursion and were planning on lunching at
a fabulous hotel which also had a fabulous sauna. Actually
she was looking for an hour of peace and quiet away from
me. So I was sent off alone and upon entering the sauna area

I was greeted by a huge, massive woman and shown into a cubicle. With deep grunts, she gave me to understand that I was to undress and she disappeared. So off come my clothes and I look for a sheet or towel in which to wrap myself. Nada! Then "Grunts"—all 300 pounds of her—reappears, looks at me open mouthed and goes off in what can only be described as a fit! Peals of laughter emerge from her mouth. She's waving vile, fat fingers towards my breasts and screaming idiotic words in Swedish in my face! And then she disappears again! I'm left just standing there, stunned really. To begin with, I'm never very comfortable when I'm naked and I thought that I had committed a horrible faux pas. Anyway, in my usual indecisive way, I was thinking of putting my clothes back on when I hear a commotion and my friend reappears with two cronies who look just like her. Now there are three of them staring at me and laughing hysterically while I stand naked, looking very dumb, and saying over and over "Hey, what's the joke? What's so funny?" Then I finally realized that they were actually laughing at my meager bosom! (Not to worry, it has grown a LITTLE since then.) Well, I thought that they were being VERY rude and I simply said, "Screw you!" (What happened to my exquisite manners?) I was turning around to get dressed when I'm picked up by "Grunts" and tucked under her ham-like arm. Then, this "show off" carried me about twenty yards into a room with a large tub filled with steaming water and spinach (actually it was algae) and left me there! I seemed to breathe in fumes of iodine, etc. After about ten to fifteen minutes, just as I really beginning to relax, she reappears, kneels next to the tub, picks up a handful of the green stuff and starts to rub my arms, my shoulders, my back etc all the while, chuckling away! By this time, I'm eyeing her very carefully and wondering just how FAR she's going to go! By now she's doing my legs, and my belly and my hips and I'm chuckling and giggling because I'm TICKLISH! When she got to my abdomen, I figured that's it! So I arose, rather like a Botticelli Venus, except that I was covered with slimy green algae and I head for the shower area. I cannot locate any faucet handles or taps of any kind to turn on the water. I look around and she's at a control panel, so, OK, what do I care, let HER turn it on. She did, yes sir! A blast of FREEZING icy water is sent in a jet at me, then the temperature rises to almost the boiling point and with blasting force! Then she wrapped me in a huge towel and CARRIED me back to my cubicle where she had the nerve to give me a not-too-gentle whack on the rear before leaving me to get dressed! I then joined everyone for lunch. I'll admit that I was all pink and rosy and also so exhausted that I fell asleep while eating my Swedish meatballs!

I DO remember that I leave a month from tomorrow! Will YOU remember that I love you, every bit of you and that an awful lot of it has nothing to do with sex? And there can never be "too much" love.

As always and ever, Pipsi

New York   January 25, 1972   2:45 p.m.
Dear, Dear Bébé,

Received your letter telling me about Scott and am now wondering if YOU are in one piece? Stay put, will you please! I'm very sorry about the boy and will send him a card.

It's bright and sunny, blue skies and it's 50 degrees this morning but there's a fifty-mile-an-hour wind blowing and I'm sure we'll have snow before the week is out.

In case you still haven't reached Irene, don't worry, she's OK! As I've told you, she wrote me from the hospital, clever wench, in case you're furious and in a rage.... Good! It's exactly what you deserve for talking so much about me!

I'm TEASING, but "What can you do, what can you do?" You can do what I asked you to, though maybe you had not received it, and that's to tell "Madame" not to write. I'm busy etc. etc. Yes, I know I didn't HAVE to answer, but you know my reaction to having "red capes" dangled at me...

All my thoughts, all my love, all my hugs and kisses,
Pipsi

New York
Dear Heart,

What fantastic letters you're writing lately! DON'T STOP!

The least difficult thing in the world is to BE happy when one is NOT in love. The trick is to BE in love and BE happy!

You know, your telegram was waiting on my desk. Marikasha was all shaky and pale, she was afraid that something was wrong. By now she feels like Cupid. She's off to Jamaica for a few days' rest around March 23 and leaving me in full charge! She may well be out of a job, me too, by the time she returns!

Bébé, all for now. I hope you feel smug and comfy and smirky at the thought of how much I love you? Stay that way! Je t'embrasse très fort

New York   January 27, 1972   3:30 p.m.
Bébé,

I sent you the telegram yesterday—it's the Hotel Riviera in Torremolinos and of course you'll have to go and take care of things, but not yet. I received my voucher but it says nothing except that I'm booked in a deluxe hotel and it IS the Riviera because I checked that by phone.

The truckers' convention fell through, some kind of power struggle within the higher echelons and though I'm a wee bit disappointed, it's for Marikasha that I feel badly. She's very tired and it would have boosted her morale. Instead, we spent the morning telling each other some dirty jokes, which she enjoyed. She taught me some rude Italian gestures and I'm trying to break her of the strange habit of saying "Halvah" instead of "*Allevei.*" Do you know what Halvah is?

Have I told you that I don't like thin women? Actually, can you imagine, I've become a fanatic! For me to be attracted, a girl has to be 37 years of age, about five feet four inches tall, going a bit bald on top, has to have a weird accent, a mixture of English and lovely rolling Rs. And yes, ahem, er, eh, well, yes, yes, a large, pendulous bosom! I know, but I can't help it! Oh yes, she has to be a bit boyish too!

The one thing (and my imagination is very active) I cannot picture, are your blue eyes. Really! I love you Bébé, will this month ever go by?

All hugs and kisses, and LOVE,   Pipsi

New York   January 28, 1972   4:10 a.m.
Bébé,

Now admit it, you haven't received a letter written this early for quite a while. I'm only going to put a few lines down for now. I woke up around two hours ago aware of that eerie silence which often means snow! And so it is, falling nice and easily, so I stayed in bed for another half hour, then took a hot bath, had a cup of coffee, put on my boots and duffle and took a walk around the block, accompanied by my two idiot feline friends, Ralph and Norton. Naturally I thought of you, so what else is new?

I spoke to Poppy last night and I'm meeting him for lunch

on Thursday. I think that he may be nervous about the two of us meeting...for various reasons but NOT the one you and I are nervous about. I think that it goes a little deeper than just the fact of having spoken so much about me, he wants me to impress one and all.

Well, he's VERY involved with you of course. You say that we Neukorns have the ability to make you very sad and very glad. And you, in turn, have completely changed our lives, his no less than mine. He is a far, far happier man since knowing you, you've done a lot for him, you really have.   Je t'embrasse très fort.   Pipsi

Spain   Cortijo de las Yeguas   Friday, January 28, 1972
Darling, Darling Pips,

I'm feeling most virtuous right now. I went riding, all alone and enjoyed it because YOU were very much with me. Riding alone, for me, must be similar to your walking alone along the beach. I began riding alone when I was living in the "boondocks" at a place called "Banda-Mashur." Delyn was, by that time, living in Masjid-i-Suliman and Irene had moved to Tehran, and there was absolutely no one with whom to really talk in that outpost. I used to fly to Masjid-i-Suliman each Friday afternoon, on a company plane and return on the first plane on a Monday morning.

Anyway, to get back to this afternoon...I took this long ride, followed the river, passed the bull ranch and through the lemon trees and an orange grove and thought, yes, Pips will love it here and I hope that you're game and will be fit enough to ride one of the horses and we will go for a gentle walk along one of these familiar paths...too far to go walking hand in hand and too steep. I felt virtuous because I cleaned all the tack afterwards and it took a good hour!

Much, much love, kisses, hugs, nibbles, thoughts, so many of them!

Je t'embrasse très fort, Bébé.

New York   January 30, 1972   5:45 p.m.
Sweetheart,

...By the time you receive this, we can say "This month, we meet!" It's fantastic. In all honesty, thinking about it, the way it came about, I mean my asking Marikasha, the way I did, I'm quite convinced that it was pure animal instinct at work! And I don't mean sex! Just a sort of self-preservation kind of thing, an inside warning that it was time for me to "see and feel," realizing that it could NOT stay at this pitch without KNOWING. When I say "knowing," I don't mean fantastic, earth-shattering revelations, though this too may well happen. Rather, an acceptance of fact. "Yes, it is not a dream, there is, there really is something here." As far as the chance that there isn't, by now, you know that I DON'T worry about that at all! You do, but less than you used to, but you still do! If it is so, then better we should find out now and in this way it affects just the two of us.

Anyway, Bébé, Darling, I'll just keep on saying it, I love you, am IN love with you, and please, test the mattress, I want only that you should be comfortable!

Hugs and kisses,   Pipsi

February

F — fabulous feelings of love
E — excitement and expectations for our future
B — belief in ourselves
R — remarkable awareness of each other
U — unique
A — airmail liaison
R — risk-taking and reassurance
Y — yearnings

Spain   Cortijo de las Yeguas   FEBRUARY 1, 1972

You no doubt know that it is February now?! Three cheers, January over at last. I just know that when the 26th arrives, I'm going to long for that week to last forever and ever!

...Gino is flying to New York tomorrow and he'll mail this and the tape. I've invited Barbie and the children to lunch tomorrow at the Sin Igual as they have never been. I want to take Barbie's mind off the fact that Gino's going to the States.

I did not ride today because I was busy staining the bed frame and closets in my room, but also because my horse has a very bad cut on his leg/hoof area. Apparently he caught it in the manège gate and, being terrified, he pulled and pulled. Gino had to call in the vet. It happened while I was away and Siri, who acts as the vet around here, bathed it this morning. Now I'm going

240

down to bathe it again before nightfall, so excuse me please...
Later: I have just found another poem[11] *which I simply must copy out for you! It's by an American, Amy Lowell.*

THE LETTER

Little cramped words crawling all over the paper
Like draggled fly's legs,
What can you tell of the flaring moon
Through the oak leaves?
Or of my uncurtained window and the bare floor
Spattered with moonlight?
Your silly quirks and twists have nothing in them
Of blossoming hawthorns,
And this paper is dull, crisp, smooth, Virgin of loveliness
Beneath my hand.
I am tired my Beloved, of chafing my heart against
The want of you;
Of squeezing it into little ink drops
And posting it.
And I scald alone, here, under the fire
Of the great moon.

So, my dear sweet, love, another day has passed...I have to keep myself busy. Words cannot express how much I'm looking forward to meeting you.

Yours, with love, kisses, caresses, nibbles, smiles, frowns, bites, pouts, thoughts, all my thoughts, Bébé.

---

11   As found in *The World's Love Poetry*, Michael Rheta Martin, ed., Bantam, New York, 1960.

New York   FEBRUARY 1, 1972!   4:40 am
Darling Bébé,

I've never written "February" with more tenderness! I love you, I love you, twice because I didn't write yesterday. It's a busy week, this coming one, and I think I had better polish the damned silverware for this dinner party on Saturday.

Continued: 9:55 am.

A question: when were you a barmaid and what kind of bar was it and for how long?

I don't know if I'm clear-headed or light-headed—anyway, I feel good. My back is really fine and it's sheer pleasure to be able to stand straight once again. But...step by step is the only way I can think of you and me. Now I'll do the few dishes so that when I return from work and before I go to the Pan Am wing-ding I can sit quietly and write some more.

Later: 2:15 p.m.

I certainly ain't sitting quietly...three letters from you, red face, red ears, wiggles.

I called the Manager of Atesa and I'm muttering on the phone *"Espeçe de Chameau"* and he screamed at me that he'd never been so insulted in his life! How was I to know that the idiot spoke French!

Marikasha offers to set up a cot in the backroom if you come over. "I want you to be happy," she says.

...As far as variety being the spice of life, forget it, I don't believe it for one minute! That's a continual search and usually one born out of fear. A fear of being left alone, of being betrayed, of being rejected when one is told "I don't love you anymore"—so a fear of many things. In the long run, to be virtuous simply means to be loved by someone whose love you return! Very rare, not because it can't be found, but because you need, for that, a childlike trust and a belief in love or words spoken in love and I'm afraid it's very hard to do just that... For myself, I can only say that I wasted a hellish amount of years on the wrong sex, which is why I AM inept and incompetent and THEN concentrated on the wrong women. I became the teacher without ever having been the pupil! And neither one was, or is, a Lesbian, whereas you and I are. And the only difference between you and me, is the fact that you found out, or accepted it in time and I didn't. I'm sure that I'm more at ease, more tolerant and more easygoing with men socially, than you are. However, it's with women that I feel a sense of love, understanding and tenderness and with whom I am emotionally connected. Why I haven't and don't have affairs (like certain nits I know) is that I've always been far more cerebral than clitoral. In truth, playing games is a dull thing for me. I happen to do it far better than anyone I know, so there you have it! However, I'm NOT playing games with you.... Don't worry and don't worry about ME! I mean about not being in love or loving ME! If it comes to that, it's not your problem and I can handle it. Anyway, in itself, without the sex, the relationship is fantastic too.

But I am NOT shy about making love to you, every way, any way, it's the reverse I'm shy about. But not very much with you I don't think. I don't know? And I haven't made many suggestions, though there's a few hundred running madly around in my brain! Anyway, from your letters, YOU sound like quite the lover and I'm beginning to feel inadequate, which will never do! You speak much about your mouth, tongue, etc. and I of my hands...And you can beg all you want, but that first bath/shower I'll go in alone! And I'm not at all convinced of how well you've been made love to? You sound far too domineering for that. Maybe it's time for a change!

No vodka, it's not necessary and I want to lay your mind at rest!

4:40 p.m.

And there was a half-hour interruption because Deborah popped in with money asking me to book her to Detroit. (Her son lives there.) She also told me, once again, that it seems that at the first cocktail party, I was spotted as a real "Butch"—this came through the grapevine (Francine telling Jewel who then told Deborah). Of course I told her I was attending another tonight and if, indeed, I had been "spotted" at the last one, where I had been wearing a skirt and turtleneck, I would certainly be "branded" tonight with the outfit I plan on wearing!

I'll be back in the morning!

February 2   5:00 a.m.

I'm back, I'm back! Well, I was neither quiet, sophisticated or charming but I must have been funny because I had people gasping for breath at my jokes! It wasn't much of a party and I was glad to get to bed!

If I'm not telling you anything about the final plans for the trip, it's because I'm off to settle things, once and for all when I get to New York tomorrow! Your letter with your reaction to the Riviera hotel filled me with rage and that's when I called the Atesa manager "un chameau." So I must go there and to Iberia, to Global, and for lunch with Poppy. I'm exhausted at the thought of all this and I'm trying to make time to go to Gino's Gallery but I'm not sure I'll be able to manage it.

I'm acquiring a reputation, due solely to my accent, which I'm wise enough to REALLY put on at odd times, and so I'm being offered various jobs at posh travel agencies! Actually it was such an offer that led to my amusing everyone last night, but for now, I'll stay with Marikasha! She's very good to me, my time is my own and she's being marvelous about "us."

I love you and want you in my arms to nibble, to caress, kiss and whisper silly things to.

Je t'embrasse très fort Pipsi

Spain   Cortijo de las Yeguas   February 1972
  Darling, Sweetheart, Angel, Querida—After that special week when we'll be together, we might never send tapes to each other again and we might start writing those ever-so-ordinary letters such as "how are you" and "how is your mother". And are you smiling and convinced that Bébé is deliriously excited and quite mad? As I write this I realize that in three weeks you will be here and you say to me on one side of the tape what you're going to do with me and I know what I'm going to do with you—tumble and play like two puppies and hold hands and laugh and have fun and kiss you all over—after all, I have to live up to it, being sex-oriented I mean.
  There ARE sports other than skiing!
    Love you, Bébé.

New York   February 2, 1972   2:25 p.m.
Querida,

There were no letters from you today so I'll start answering the third one. I've finally come out, oh well, by telling Marikasha the facts, I mean about you being a Lesbian, etc. She said that she guessed about me a long time ago and anyway, the offer of the cot in the backroom still stands!

I think I'M the one who should "pop the question"! That's because I'm older and taller of course. ...But you know, there are SO many things to discuss. I certainly am rather taken aback...I'm not even there yet and we're already discussing marriage? Don't you believe in engagements?

Listen, no puppies for me. I'll gladly adopt Sammy and share him with you but for here and now, I'll make do with Ralph and Norton.

All, but all of my love, Pipsi

New York   February 4, 1972   3:40 a.m.

Angel,

I drove to the office to pick up my mail, two from you and did you make that "Snoopy" cut-out yourself?

I've just looked up the word "vain" in the dictionary. It means the same as "conceited." So when you say "conceited and vain too," you're saying the same thing. And of course when you say, "How far does this vanity extend?"—not, dear Hall, to the collecting of scalps as love trophies. It prods me occasionally into putting people down when I think that they're stepping out of line.

...Why are you scared? Why do you speak of these past five months as though from here on in, it's downhill all the way? And why am I asking so many questions? Actually a nice little spanking would do you a world of good! Ah well, I said I'd beat conceit into you if necessary.

And now to my accomplishments of yesterday!

The people at Atesa were really very decent and I spent an hour with them discussing business. Then I went to the French Tourist Bureau, Olympic Airways, Brentanos....It was raining and I wore my "tally ho" outfit and then went to the Chantecler. I had two vodkas and Poppy had three whiskies! We then proceeded to devour pate, Dover Sole, salad, strawberry cake and coffee. He approved of the way

I looked! We spoke of you of course, and I have a tentative date with him and Gino for lunch next week. Then we went in search of the raincoat. IT's not exactly my type, but "What can you do?" I then grabbed a cab, took the train, and went to the office and came home and read your letters. I cooked a roast, played "our" song. I ALWAYS mess it up! I eventually fell into bed at 8:30 p.m. I was asleep in five minutes.

Now if you're wondering what feast I'm preparing, I'm making it easy for myself. I have neither the time, nor the patience for culinary delights. The hors d'oeuvres will be shrimps *rémoulade*, bean and tuna salad, and guacamole. The main course will be: filet mignon with Madeira Sauce, spinach pancakes, salad of greens and watercress. Desert will consist of strawberries with Grand Marnier and cookies. There will be an excellent Burgundy to wash it all down! You know what? I wish I were cooking it here for you and me. I would wear the apron and you could come and put your arms around my waist and I would say: "Bébé, leave me alone, go ride your horse, go practice your chords, and don't be pesty." ...Ah, but you wouldn't stop because YOU'RE the bossy one! Then, of course, I'd end up by turning off the oven, tearing off the apron and I would take your hand and drag you to bed... How I wish it were NOW, this very minute. As long as I'm THERE, consider yourself kissed, caressed and tasted, all with soft, soft lips and gentle hands. I'm completely lost with you, in you, and yes, I know, you like to throw me for a loop! You manage that very well indeed, but this is for YOUR ego, but you know this very well too, don't you!?

Je t'embrasse très fort.   Pipsi

Spain   Monday, February 7, 1972
Angel, Lover, Darling, Cheri,

OK. OK. So in a matter of minutes my mood has changed yet again and here I sit, feeling very girl and protected and loved by you. ....How funny that I should receive this letter from Marikasha's office in which you tell that you told MARIKASHA . I'm not at all surprised that SHE wasn't surprised! I realized or knew about you BEFORE you ever wrote to me...well, let me say that I had my suspicions.

By the way, Barbie knows! She's certainly not dumb and yesterday, while we were so busy re-arranging my room and talking about this and that, like the placement of the oriental rugs, I mentioned about Delyn and that I'd spent almost five years with her. Anyway, she teases me somewhat and we do laugh a lot together. She says that you'd be better off staying here. We'll see, we'll see!

So—how was your dinner party and did you get the silverware polished? I hope that I'll hear all about it in your next letter?

"WE" are discussing "MARRIAGE"? My GOD, Neukorn, what the Hell did I write. You have me real worried!

...Yes, I would say that you do and will, I'm sure, get on better with men than I do. My favorite is Poppy. You have no idea just how good that man is for me. I like Gino too, in his way. There aren't many occasions where I have the opportunity to spend time with men here, however, in the oil company world I did.

In answer to your question: During my school and college years and then during the vacations, even whilst teaching, I used to work to earn money. Frankly, I needed to. So I have experience in the following jobs: Child care, shop assistant, live-in governess, educational tutor, house cleaner, British postal worker sorting and delivering mail. I have also worked in a factory where they canned fruit and filled jars with various preserves and jams. I have also worked in holiday camps and hotels as a waitress, bartender and as a chambermaid. All in all, it was a marvelous experience and an education about life and the value of money and how hard it was to earn it! If I wanted to go on vacation or travel, then I needed to work to earn enough money to fund it. I remember going on my Lambretta scooter on a tour of Normandy, Brittany and Paris on one occasion, which I enjoyed. ...

And I'm not shy about making love to you, but maybe I'm shy about YOU making love to ME! So—where do we start? I'm teasing, really, because, as you say, everything will take care of itself.

All love, Shirley-Bébé

Spain   Wednesday, February 9
Pips, My Dearest Love,

We are booked into the Hotel Pyramides! I will check in on the 25th! Certainly it's an improvement on the Sirocco and the Riviera and Marc seemed to like it and so do I. The meals are not great but then we're not having "pension" and we'll most likely be taking all our meals out anyway.

Pips, come soon. Take care Darling. Please try to get some rest before you hit the Costa del Sol because six nights is not very long and we have an awful lot to talk about! Let me kiss you, very gently,   Your Bébé.

New York   February 10, 1972 4:40 a.m.
Dear Bébé,

No letter from you yesterday. The service is getting vile, maybe it's because it's winter, which causes everything to be delayed?

Tell me a private thing, the vibrator, was that something you thought about yourself or did you get the idea from a book? The reason I ask is because Marikasha asked me if I had ever read *The Sensuous Woman*? Well, I hadn't, so yesterday at the office, she hands me a copy and I leafed through it in about twenty minutes and of course, I got completely hysterical. So I was wondering if you had read this book?

Continued: February 11, 1972   4:00 a.m.

Two weeks to go! I must say that this week flew by and I hope that the next two will do the same. Steve comes home tomorrow for "Intersession" and he'll be here for at least ten days. This means that there will be constant trooping in and out of the house with friends and possibly new strange-looking characters.

Poppy is coming for lunch tomorrow. I find him very edgy about my trip! I understand, vaguely, why. He wants us to meet of course but I think there's also a feeling of nervousness about the whole thing concerning my entering the picture of this special relationship you have with each other and also will I live up to all this nonsense he's been spouting forth about me? Oi! Oi!..

        Je t'embrasse très fort, Pipsi

New York   February 13, 1972 5:10 a.m.
My Darling Bébé,

Steve is fine really and looked decent. He was clean-shaven and his hair met with Poppy's approval. He is really doing well, not only from a scholastic point of view but generally all around. He is going in rather heavily for acting, much to Marvin's despair, but I feel that whatever he does, he must be the one who decides. Within the extremely wide field of mass communications there are so many different avenues to follow. He is certainly trying his hand at all that the college has to offer. He has a nice way about him which can draw attention to himself without being pushy. For instance, George Segal, the actor, was lecturing at college and during the coffee session afterwards, they started to chat and then Steve sat at the piano and played the theme from Segal's latest movie. He does this sort of thing easily and casually.

David's performance is towards the end of March and he's busy every day after school with rehearsals. That and his discovery of girls keeps him walking on clouds! I've had to bring him down to earth a few times, which might bring a smile to your lips! Where the boys are concerned, I'm rather quick to see or sense things which I may think are not too good, and I don't hesitate to tell them so. So much for Mother Goose!

My dinner party was a huge success. The food was truly excellent. Blanche brought a wheel of Brie and then we had a great time singing old French songs, Viennese operettas, etc. Marvin excels at this and does it with such happiness. He is at his best either buried in some twelfth-century manuscript or playing the piano at a party.

Let's not think about the time from March to June! The limits of my life are bound within two Fridays. For now, at any rate, they are the horizons of my world. And no, no doubts are creeping in!

> All, but all my love! Je t'embrasse très fort!
> Pipsi

Spain   February 15, 1972
Dear Pips,

All ready to go again—"Stop the world I want to get off"

No, I have never read The Sensuous Woman—how about bringing it with you?

I'll explain about the vibrator when you're here. I first used one long ago, in 1965, but I was pleased to learn, at a much later date, that I wasn't the only one and that thousands of women had used them. I'm not as inventive as I thought I was.

Two weeks from today, Tuesday 29th , you will love me even more and me you, of course! Or, we'll be thinking "Gosh, how could we have made such a stupid mistake!?" God knows I want you here—I'm VERY excited.

I love you. Bébé

New York   February 16, 1972   8:20 p.m.
Bébé, Cheri,

Hello, goodnight, sleep well. I think that's all I have time for...

Poor David, he's having love problems. I just walked into his bedroom and he was on the phone obviously having a bit of an emotional scene. So I walked out. Then he came and explained: "Yes, I feel THIS way and she feels THAT way, and there's this other boy" etc. Of course, I was very wise and said, "Oh...ah...I see..." for about five minutes. His answer to all my "ohs" and "ahs" was that I was very understanding and he appreciated my good advice! Mind you, I haven't the vaguest idea of what he was talking about but I did look profound when I said "Oh."

...Are you sure you're not Jewish? Sometimes on the

tapes you have a Jewish intonation! After all, you can't tell, maybe your great-great-grandmother fooled around with a young man from my clan? Ah, you don't think so? MY great-grandmother CERTAINLY did! Forgive my silly mood.

Continued: February 17, 1972   5:10 a.m.

Have I told you...no I haven't, well I've bought myself a *Travel With Berlitz* little book. See, in case we have an awful, long argument while driving, and you throw me out of the car and leave me stranded, there's no problem, I'll be able to take care of myself!

...Please go and light a few candles to the local Saint or Virgin of Pizarra. We don't need any awful storms or strikes or such! Maybe I should go to Temple on Saturday?

Je t'embrasse très fort.   Pipsi

New York   February 17, 1972   3:30 p.m.
Monsieur,

This is in answer to three letters dated the 12th,14th and one dateless!

I don't think you realize how much happiness you give Poppy and how it's hard to put it into words, so certainly, we'll talk about it when we are together. But you have whirled him around and brought him down from his celestial plane. You make him very, very happy!

What do you mean "I'm going to adore you"? I do now! And yes, people will stare...I don't know if they'll smile, I have a feeling they'll be gnashing their teeth and turn green with envy. We'll probably get kicked out of the hotel, what fun!

I'm in full agreement, let everything go on strike when I'm WITH YOU. I'll smile at Barbie and say, "Listen, you said I could stay here and *me voila*!" And you can teach me how to clean the tack and while you teach the kids, surely I can find some way to earn my keep? And if we both bounce up and down on that new bed of yours, it's bound to soften up!

Yes, but all kidding aside, how is your family—your parents, your sister, your brother—faring in England? The reports about the coal strikes make it sound pretty dismal with everyone living by candlelight. I hope that all is well with them?

You know, I'm a great believer in destiny, exactly the sort of thing that's happened with us. Although I'm a far greater believer in genes playing a very important role in one's development, rather than childhood environment, we are ultimately shaped by people with whom we come in contact. So that, today, YOU, Shirley, are a sum total of the relationships which you have had with people. By this I don't mean parents particularly, as much as the close, emotional, character-making relationships one has encountered in one's life. So when you say, "Where have you been all my life?" chances are that, had we met ten years ago, we might have passed each other by without a second glance. There is "a time for all things" and I think, long ago, I quoted an answer to the question "But I thought you loved one another?" The reply was, "Yes, but at different times." So for us, perhaps it goes back to a forgotten day, when you showed a "white-legged, Stravinsky-looking Marc" the way to the loo at the Marbella Hilton! In space, in time, in importance, nothing at all, and yet look what it led to...from that time to now, to you and me and to next week...to Lord knows what! For now, I can only say that there is no more doubt in my mind whether my coming was wisdom or sheer idiocy. It's by far the wisest thing I have ever done, perhaps the ONLY wise thing I will ever do. Never mind the reaction, the future, whatever, for now and for us, it is—well it just IS!

Pipsi

New York   February 18, 1972   Noon.   from the office
Bébé,

Angel, I'm writing this from the office because a heavy snowstorm is supposed to hit us tonight so I'll mail this on my way home. Better to have storms today than next week! Oi, Oi! This may well be the last letter you receive because of the pending storm. I may not be able to mail another until Monday, which you may not receive before you leave for the coast.

My flight number is 958, New York-Malaga. My arrival time is between 8:00–9:00 a.m. Angel, I'll be on my way by the time you receive this.

Je t'embrasse très fort, Pipsi

Spain   Saturday, February 19, 1972   10:15 a.m.
My Darling,

One week from today and we'll be together! If all goes well, we should be checking into the hotel about now. You will be unpacking while I run your bath for you. Ah, what a thought!

Maybe this will be the last letter to you before you leave. I'll try to get one more written, perhaps over the weekend, so that you'll receive news from me almost every day.

YOU may be able to live on stale bread but not me darling!

One week from today, I'll be handing you a glass of vodka, while I sip an aperitif before lunch and I wonder if you will have seduced me by that time or if we are saving that pleasure until after lunch? Not really a good idea, not on a full stomach, darling!

Love, kisses and caresses, Bébé.

Spain February 24, 1972
Darling,

I seem to be floating. There are a million things to be done before I leave for the coast tomorrow and I'm not ready. I can't believe that YOU, yes, YOU are coming and that NOW you are READING this and I'm here WITH you!

I have just opened my well-worn book of The World's Love Poetry and I have found something so very appropriate.

>HOMECOMING
>By Sappho of Lesbos – (600 BC)
>You have come. Well done.
>I longed for you.
>You have given fire to my heart which burns now
>For you. Welcome! Be welcome—
>For all the hours of our separation.

Just two days...ah, bliss.
With love and longing, your Bébé

New York   Sunday, February 20, 1972   4:00 a.m. [12]
Querida,

If this is being read, you're either in a fauteuil or sprawled on the bed and I'm taking my bath! I think I'll faint, or did I do that already at the airport, or did you? Or are we both speechless and gauche?

Truly, I can't conceive of going through the next few days without writing. Tomorrow is a holiday and post offices will be closed.

---

[12] In the days before her departure, Pipsi continued to write letters and hand-carried them to Spain. She presented them to Shirley in the hotel bedroom on February 26, prior to taking her solo bath.

Anyway, I thought that this would be a good idea and should insure me a few minutes for my quiet bath, which I sorely need, without your mumbling "Come on, Neukorn, hurry up!" Or for that matter breaking down the hotel bathroom door! Yeah, but what to wear when I emerge from this damned tub?

I went to the office in dreadful weather. The canals had overflowed and water was halfway up the hubcaps. The wind, rain and driving snow here are unbelievable. I went to the library and took out a book entitled *How to Fight a Bull*. I locked myself in the bedroom and managed to impale myself on my makeshift *muleta* (a yard-long ruler with a bath towel draped over it!). Then I tried to write some four-liners but I simply was not inspired, simply nothing doing. My mind is a complete blank and I feel quite numb and dumb. Perhaps I'll have better luck on the plane? Blah, today will be a tough day to go through. Like you, I don't like Sundays and the weather is so awful that I won't be able to get out and go for a walk by myself. Thank God, Washington's Birthday or not, the post office is open tomorrow and I'll go in to the office.

Je t'embrasse très fort.

Your own, Pipsi

New York   Tuesday, February 22, 1972   4:20 a.m.
Dear Bébé, also Angel, Sweetheart, Love, Goose,

Tell me, did we argue about tipping the bellboy? *Dieu Merçi*, it's Tuesday! Maybe there'll be letters? I spent three blessed hours in the office yesterday, just Marikasha and I and no customers. I admit to looking forward to the five days in March, from the 23rd thru the 28th, when Marikasha goes to Jamaica and I'll be in full charge. I realize that it will be a "sink or swim" situation but since I have to do it sooner or later, I may as well take the plunge! And speaking of swimming, how am I doing with my bath and are you comfy? Are you excited and happy? I am!

Right now, as these words are being written, I'm very calm and stupefied. My ears have turned WHITE, oi, oi! I hope I have enough self-control so that I did not grab you in some lewd manner and throw you on the bed as soon as we were alone? ...I'll do THAT after lunch, and here we go again, my ears and face are burning brightly and are you smiling? Yes, I'm hurrying up, I'll be out soon...

Continued: 3:30 p.m.

Grr. Snap! Seven letters from you, sheer heaven. And I was so happy...and then I made my big mistake! I called Iberia! Iberia has been able to do what NO ONE has been able to do and that is to reduce me to a raving, screaming maniac! What it takes is my phoning Iberia to once again confirm my reservation and having them answer "We have NO reservations in that name!" Get the picture? So if I sound mean, tough and nasty, well, sweet love, three hours on the phone with them will do it every time. Talk about frustration!

February 23   12:30 p.m. from the office.
Darling Bébé,

I came into the office to find Marikasha on the phone with our Iberian rep. He was SO apologetic that I'm to check in on Friday and then go to the V.I.P. lounge where "Veronica" or "Hermana" will be waiting for me!

So...as Marikasha puts it, "If you're going into the V.I.P. Lounge, you're going to look like a V.I.P.!" Well, I still won't feel easy until I'm on that plane and taking off.

Yes, I think that you could pour some of that vodka now and don't make it more than two inches! I'll be out in five minutes. Allevei and Inshallah!

Our week together passed all too quickly. Pipsi's visit proved to be a wonderful experience; our respective expectations were higher than we had hoped. We were truly compatible and shared a great deal of fun and laughter. The Hollander children had by now established their own relationship with Pipsi through letters, tapes and gift exchanges. The day following her arrival we drove up to the Cortijo to help Siri celebrate her birthday.

The Ides of March were evident even at the beginning of the month at the Cortijo. Numerous visitors and some obvious marital problems between Gino and Barbie taxed everyone's patience. The children and I concentrated on our schoolwork.

March

In the plane   March 3, 1972   2:15 p.m.

Bébé,

THIS plane IS going to be late. I have just settled down in my seat and they're still loading. The plane is crowded but not too bad. A little old lady has the window seat. In my usual, gallant way, I helped her with her safety belt and promptly squeezed the middle finger of my right hand in the buckle! The seat between us is empty except for our respective handbags. I'm in my aisle seat and I'm looking down at my leather and brass ankh. The tears are somewhere around. I can tell because this page is a bit blurred, but at least they're not running down my hollow cheeks. There's a kind of strange lump around my breastbone. And now this plane is rolling! OK. we're up and I'm still keeping an eye on Gino's sketch which is tucked in among blankets and pillows. I think that NOW, I should say to you "I am SHY Bébé, I AM shy!" I am, about telling you what this has meant, these few precious days. I don't know how—it's so much, too much, in a way. I've learned what it means to be HAPPY, all of it. I think you KNOW, certainly not just the sex, though, heaven help me, the way you look THAT certain look, can and does drive me right up the wall. You see, your letters have made me so very happy that I, too, knew it would have to be pretty good. It certainly couldn't have turned out to be bad, certainly not. But you see, for me, it turned out to be a kind of miracle! It's a miracle because you ARE—not what I thought, in some

259

remote dream thing, what love should be like—but because YOU ARE what I was talking about when I've written to you, "It doesn't matter if I never find it, I'll go to my grave believing that it exists!" And it does, yes, for me, it does.

And now they're coming around with drinks and I'm about to order a sweet vermouth! Get that smug look off your face Hall! It's very good, red, on the rocks and with a slice of lemon in it. The lady who is sitting by the window just told me that she doesn't usually drink whiskey but she is a bit nervous, so I told her that if there was anything I could do not to hesitate, etc.

There are many things which I have liked these past few days. These include your friends and your acquaintances, the gay, the straight, all of them, some more than others of course! The children? Well, I don't even have to say it! Given time, I mean apart from acting the fool, the four-liners and all that, we would be great friends, I think. Barbie is very special, not because she was so unhappy, and yes, I'm an old softie that way, but she's quite a girl all the way. She uses profanity well and very few women do! LaVeta is the other one. Those two are my favorites. Mammacita and Luis are nice and I loved their restaurant, the Sin Igual. I liked it that we could hold hands and kiss and just sort of make funny jokes and it felt SO natural for me. I did not have a second thought about it or worry about who might be watching, only when we walked near the Cortijo, in case the little ones were watching. I'm rambling, I'm sure I'm rambling, and I do NOT look like Radclyffe! I'm going to eat, I'll be back later. I love you, God, do I ever love you!

You say I'm frail, I'm not, really I'm not! I'm not as strong as I like to believe I am. (I certainly realized that while sailing through the air!) but I am not quite as weak as you think me. The tears, and yes, it's still blurring this paper, because you have touched ME, not a part or portion of me, but ME! I do not worry about being weepy when Marvin meets me at the airport because I won't be. I DO worry about the possibility of it though, when seeing Poppy tomorrow, because with him too, though in a different way, you have touched him deeply. I just hope I don't mess it up!

I have to say this, I think you KNOW it but I have to say it, for both of us: My jokes about giving you two years to sow your last wild oats, though they're not so wild, I joke about, it's true, but I am rather serious about it. Just as you were when you told me to ask you after the divorce, or separation or whatever. (And being a fantastic flirt myself, I've just paid for the little old lady's whisky and she's all aflutter and blushing!) I'm serious when I say you're not ready, you do not know! Rather like David really. I give that boy of mine two years to toughen up a bit, to learn to know the ME within himself and to think, "I'm more important now than anyone else." Well, you know what I mean. And I give YOU, another boy of mine, the same two years to decide what will be what. Obviously two years seems to be the magic number.

But, dearheart, please do this for me: Understand that what I write to you about all my emotional and sexual feelings of love come from deep within. I don't want you to ever believe that anything is a ploy to make you fall in love with me. You wrote once, "You'll do everything to make me fall in love with you." This I have NOT done. None of what has happened during these past few days were ploys or wiles to make you fall in love with me. Nothing which I write in lyrics or music or letters will be done to MAKE you do anything of the kind. Nothing that I express or write to you about, whatever it is, conventions, or meeting "Hesters" at cocktail parties, or seeing Deborah, etc., will be written to make you jealous. This sort of thing I have NEVER done and actually, I wouldn't know how! So PLEASE don't worry about telling ME of the time spent with people you love. I know you're not doing it to get me all worked up, I know this, so just keep writing like you've always done, chattering away (You do chatter Hall, you do chatter!) and talking about whatever you want to, whatever it is.

I have seen you in different moods, at least some of them, with different looks to your face. Your body changes too. When you move to "Sugar Sugar" and you're dancing, I think it's fantastically cute and sexy. Sometimes you lumber along like some great Teddy Bear. Your back is much straighter when you're riding than when you're walking, and of course, I LOVE the way you ride! (the horse—you gnat, but also my leg!). I like the way you move your hands when you speak and sort of twitter and shake when trying to explain something to someone who refuses to understand, also the way you stamp your foot. The look of your face above mine is marvelous, looking down at me. I love the look of you when you're flat on your back and terribly excited, THAT is beyond words. It's just unbelievable! I must stop for a while...I'm tired, but I'll come back in a little while.

Continued: 6:20

No, I haven't slept, I've just been sitting, thinking about you and seeing you and remembering. All this should teach you a lesson! Don't ever again, get involved in a correspondence with a woman of a certain age! Now is the time I should be quiet with my guitar, a pencil, a piece of paper and try to work out a song. Then perhaps, all the tight feelings in my chest, and the burning feeling in my eyes, could be expressed in a language far better suited to these feelings than in this letter I'm writing.

God, I hope that Marikasha is busy, busy!

I want you, reading the paper, falling asleep over it, enjoying your roll and coffee, saying "I love you and do you love me?" or looking dashing in your velvet suit, and you are, fantastically so, or running like a nut across the grass in your "Lucy" sweatshirt...and since this cannot be for now, and since I can't be ALONE, then I want my desk piled with work and my guitar—and you know, this little "Woodstock" is gonna be just fine. Never mind my red blotched eyes, it's really self indulgence. My QUIET tears will return, those that neither show nor hurt quite like this.

Did you have to open up the faucet?

Yech, I hate being like this, it's stupid and sounds and reads "cheap"! Now YOU wanted an airplane letter, you're getting it! Anyway, it's far too exhausting! I'm beginning to sound like Poppy with those heavy sighs of his that escape every now and then. I'm not going to write much more, I really need a couple of hours to pull myself together and this ain't the way to do it! By now, I'm beginning to get angry with myself, for acting in this way! I feel like throwing up! What's a nice Jewish girl doing with an Egyptian symbol around her neck?

And in all this, do you believe, Querida, do you FINALLY believe after these few days, that yes, I love you, adore you, will keep on writing just as before? Has it penetrated that little baldy head of yours? And you know something? You and I, we both spoke on tape and wrote of the purity of this relationship, of how we knew one another perhaps better then than we would now...Well, I think we were wrong. The purity IS and the sex and sensuality WERE certainly active! And I think we DO know each other better! I didn't REALLY believe that you were conceited and you are! You are! You thought I'd be much bigger and I'm not!

I shall now proceed to pull myself together. This will be mailed first thing in the morning together with all my love, my every thought and my eternal thanks for everything!

Je t'embrasse très fort,   Pipsi

Spain   Saturday, March 4, 1972
Darling,

I'm at the hairdressers and I want so much to drop a line to you. I'm on my way to collect the car. All day yesterday I felt that something was definitely missing... YOU, of course! I hope that you had a pleasant flight? Did you smoke lots? Never mind, one has to lapse SOME-TIMES.

After I left you, I drove up to Mijas and had a light lunch with Elizabeth. Then we shopped a little, at least Elizabeth did, and I walked around in a daze! I took her out to Sin Igual for supper. It was very good and I sat in the seat in which you sat the FIRST time, and HOW I missed you and MISS you!

There is so much to say but I want the peace and quiet of my room, my picture of you and you around me, so the hairdresser's is a not a place that I find conducive to writing! I have a lovely image of you, sitting in the car, talking and looking at me in the light of the street lamp, just before we went to the Pourquoi Pas. It's what I call the Radclyffe Hall look.

I smell of you. It was a great week, it really was! Thank you for coming so soon. I love you, the feel, the smell, the taste, the contact, everything!

Your Shirley-Bébé

New York   Sunday, March 5, 1972   4:30 a.m.

Dearheart,

Poppy was here and we had a lovely long talk. He is VERY happy that we got on so well and wanted to hear everything we did, every minute of every day! I told him a lot, including not only that you stayed with me but also small incidents such as pinning you down and me sailing through the air!

We also spoke quite a bit, or rather, I did, about ME and MY situation with Marvin, etc. He does realize, I think, that things are not good. I told him that I felt quite indifferent about Marvin, blah, blah. I don't know if it made a very deep impression on him; he changed the subject and went on to other things.

Now for your advice, and think it out! Poppy's plans are to take you on three separate trips rather than one long one. He's suggesting Mexico, Bermuda and the Caribbean and he said that he would love it if I could come along on them. I could tell that he meant it and, need I say, I would love it!

... I asked Deborah to have dinner with me tomorrow night and I have decided to tell her the whole story. In all fairness to Deborah, considering the vague rumors that seem to be occurring about this "Woodstock" I think that she should know a little bit more than she does at present. We have been too closely associated for too long a time. I don't want her to be put in an awkward position, without being well prepared for it. (Did I tell you that Francine is supposed to have said to her boss that I'm a Lesbian?)

And this by the way, this part of it, has nothing to do with you, only to do with leaving Marvin. The other, yes, that has to do with you, when the time is right and it cannot hurt the boys, I will not lie about our relationship or make up stories about trips and such. Those six days and nights made me very aware of honesty, and I'll part with some of it when I feel

I must, but I will NOT give it up entirely.

And now to important matters! How are you? Is your little, round face blotchy? I LOVE the way you look, I hope that the photos come out well. I have creamed my cuticles, using the Vaseline from the little tube. I feel very lewd when I look at that little tube! Do you think I'm overly sensual? I think I'd like an answer to that.

All my love, your own Pipsi

Spain, Cortijo de las Yeguas   Monday, March 6
10:30 p.m.
My Darling,

So here I am at last, alone except for the sounds of you, just you and me here right now, at this moment. Back to my old routine and, I hope, the same sort of letters.

Tomorrow we're all going to Seville. Gino is driving us all down and we may stay overnight. That means that I will be unable to get to the post office until Thursday morning. I have missed you very, very much and I continue to miss you. Barbie thinks that you're absolutely marvelous, so do the kids. In fact everyone who has met you thinks that you're great. I love you and again, I say, I'm missing you!

I've been looking at your photos again trying to decide which ones are REALLY like you... miss you....I wish that you were here in my little bed, warming it and me instead of the electric blanket. Was the week as you expected it to be? Was I as you expected me to be? I did warn you that I was bossy, that I was very "boy," that I was fat, that I looked my age, that I was nice, that I was honest, that I was conceited too, that I loved you.

Your smell lingers on my clothes.

There was so much for which we had no time. You are just as I expected and great fun to be with, as well as being serious and I love that certain look you have which looks like "Radclyffe"...yes, the name "HALL" will suit you...or Neukorn!

I must get some rest now, set the alarm clock and prepare for tomorrow...I'll mail this from Seville.

Much, much love, Your Bébé

Spain, Cortijo de las Yeguas   Tuesday March 7, 1972
My Darling, Angel, Sweetheart,

We did not stay in Seville. Gino took one look at the new hotel where he was going to paint a mural and decided that it would be better if he put up canvasses. His work only took him an hour, so Barbie and the kids and I went off to a museum and then on to a department store.

I feel terribly empty—everything is different now, my room where you have been, my car, the schoolroom, the house in fact...I want you here in my bed, or just sitting reading and listening to music and not talking just knowing that we're there together. I want to look down into your big brown eyes and I want to nibble on YOUR lower lip—and I want you looking down into my eyes and holding me and saying "Yes, Bébé, come, yes, come, Bébé, come!" And on that pleasant note I'm going to bed because I've been up since 6:00 a.m. and it has been a long, hard day!

All love, hugs, kisses and caresses, Bébé

New York   Monday, March 6, 1972   3:10 p.m.
Bébé,

Avec toi, mes mains etaient toujours chaudes! It's true
and now they're cold again. The office is busy and Marikasha
sends you her love. She wanted to know if it was OK for you
and me. I wore your blue-green shirt and lit my cigarettes
with your lighter and hers with matches. You spoiled me too
much with all your gifts, Bébé. But, on the other hand, I'm
sipping a very light, sweet vermouth WITH soda! I haven't
had a drop of vodka since being with you. No problem, no
problem at all!

You know, after I went through that damned gate, I
turned around and you were walking towards the exit, your
back was to me—you looked very small, not so very strong at
all. I feel very protective towards you, I really do!

I'm off to do some cleaning and I'll finish this off in the
morning. All love and kisses!

Continued: March 7,   7:45 a.m.

I had dinner with Deborah and we had a long talk. I told
her about you, etc. Of course, she had plenty to say—not
about my leaving Marvin, she remembers me telling her this
a long time ago. I told her then, that when David went off
to college, I could start making my plans! She was horrified that people on the Costa should know about me, furious
that I had told Marikasha and she ended up by telling me
that I'm not "real"! She says I don't exist, I'm the product
of someone's imagination! I was very indignant for a minute
and then roared with laughter! I know you think me intense,
I certainly hope YOU think I'm real? She agreed that I'm Lesbian through and through, but she is aghast at the thought
of my living openly as one. I tried to explain to her that this
had nothing to do with you, meaning that, primo: I was leav-

ing and segundo: if it did not work out for you and me, I would live alone and probably drift into some kind of relationship with a woman. It's very hard for her to understand because she is straight. For her, the idea of going to bed with a woman is utterly distasteful, which is probably the reason she always saw me as a man, at least, in bed. She says that I'm very faithful, which may sound strange, but on that we agreed. I really am. As far as protecting herself, she said that she'll simply say the same thing she's been saying all these years when people question her about me, namely that I'm a very private person. That's all she can say, *and* that she has never discussed intimate things with me. It seems that the gossip about me is far more widespread than I had imagined. So that was that. It's been months since we've been able to spend a few hours together, just chatting, and usually positions are reversed, she talks and I listen. Perhaps it's hard for you to understand this relationship, though I should not think so! I can only say of her— "she's a good kid!"—which is one of your expressions. She is, and so much for that!

Sweetheart, I'm holding your face in my hands and I'm kissing your mouth very gently. I love you, Bébé, I love you. Pipsi

New York   March 7, 1972
Dear, Dear Bébé,

Your card and letter written at the hairdresser's came today. Thank you, thank you! I've listened to side one of the tape you had made for me to listen to while I was in the bath. And yes, your voice is sexy, much more so really than on tapes...boyish a little but NOT masculine. There too, we don't seem to have been troubled, I mean with the Cheri/cherie bit! ...There is so much of you I don't know. I catch some glimpses of different Bébés and pouf...it's gone. You say on the tape "What will become of us?" What are you afraid of? Me, in our relationship to us, or you? If I said to you now, "I want us to be together starting now and really for always?" could YOU, at this point, say "Yes?"

...And my Lord, what do you mean, you DIDN'T use the vibrator?! You ARE sex-oriented and quite insatiable, and let me know if it's working OK.

You mentioned Irene and posting my letter. Last night, while sitting across from Deborah and thinking of Irene's photographs, I was really amazed at the resemblance, physically anyway, and the "genre" is so alike, both bronchial with low voices.... And now I'M the one smiling! All I know is that if you're not my "type," would someone kindly tell me why I'm so madly in love with you? Because I'm brilliant of course and because, deep down, I KNOW—that you'll be very happy to take care of all the cooking! Oui?

Je t'embrasse très fort,   Pipsi

New York   Thursday, March 9, 1972   5:50 p.m.
Dearest Bébé,

...Well, I have just spoken with Poppy for about an hour. He read me your letter. He's certainly getting things ready for your arrival! A new mattress, one-and-a-half-dozen new pillowcases! I broke up completely and said, "No one buys one-and-a-half-dozen pillowcases!" He answered, quite pompously, "I do!" He was quite upset that they don't make sheets with scalloped edges anymore! My God, we're going to have a good time with him! And had I told you that when he invited me on one of the summer trips he said, "You will not mind sharing a room with Shirley?" I'm afraid my voice cracked when I answered, "Oh no, not at all." I told him tonight that I call you "Bébé." He wanted to know why. So I said it was because you're small, curvy and cute like a Bébé and he laughed!

I love you, and miss you and I wish you were here in my arms right now!

Je t'embrasse très fort. Pipsi

Spain   Thursday, March 9, 1972

Darling, I have just re-read your letter of yesterday, the one you wrote on the plane. I love that letter. I'm SO pleased that it all worked out and that you were happy. I'm glad too, that you're giving me two years in which to sort myself out because, if you asked me to choose right now, I couldn't! Can you understand that? And how can I feel so deeply for two different people? And the sex part is NOT what I'm thinking about. Anyway, I AM confused, so let's not talk about it right now.

I was happy before but I'm happier now, and confused! I realize that life is much easier for me than for you. I can be, and am ME! You can only be YOU with Marikasha, to a certain degree. Thank God for Marikasha in more ways than one! I am very glad that she knows.

Love, luv and love, Your Bébé

Spain, Cortijo de las Yeguas   Friday, March 10, 1972
My Darling Angel,

When I returned from Pizarra, I went into the kitchen...don't faint! I have made a British traditional Shepherd's Pie and then "bananas and custard" by special request from Lise. I had made it for them when we were in England and they enjoyed it so much that I prom-

ised to do it for them again sometime. Today seemed as good as any other because Gino and Barbie have gone to Malaga with Scottie to the visit the doctor. I wonder if he will return with his cast removed?

Continued: Saturday   11:00 a.m.

Scott's cast has been removed and he has a rather thin, wasted leg! He'll have to do some exercises.

It's pouring with rain. We're having school today because we spent a day in Seville. They all enjoyed the supper which I fixed for them and of course, it was a pleasant surprise for Barbie. Gino is amazed that I haven't smoked "pot." He thinks that one should have an "open curiosity" about these things. I disagree. I have never wanted to try it, perhaps an inherent fear? Anyway, I'm still not interested and where does one stop? Should one have an "open curiosity" about the hard stuff too? God forbid! There are many things in life which do NOT interest me and I have NO desire to find out! Fear it maybe, but a little fear is a healthy thing!

All for now, I'm rushing off to the post office.
All love, Bébé

New York   Friday, March 10, 1972 4:40 p.m.
Dearest Bébé,

I've only time for a few lines now. ...In answer to your question about the boys' summer holidays, Steve begins his around May 24th and David a month later. I'm hoping that they'll get jobs out of town. This is not so much for you and me but because we get on each other's nerves after a while. It's not their fault or mine, it's just the age.

At any rate, they will have jobs, they're too old not to! I have told both of them that I'd much rather see them do something they really like, never mind how much or little they earn than do what Stevie did last year. He worked in the camera department of a large store and hated it! I think you will enjoy meeting both boys and David is very much looking forward to meeting you this summer because he's more aware of you. He will know within a month's time if he has been accepted at any of his selected colleges. He's won a Regents Scholarship and he's pleased. He's having a marvelous senior year. After *Fiddler* he is directing a play for the Thespian Group and, as you can imagine, not too much schoolwork is being done.

Now for Marikasha! When I came back, she wanted to hear about you and me and our plans in that direction. So I told her that if, after my leaving Marvin, you said, "Yes"—then we would live together. And of course, this is what is worrying her. I told her that I would not leave her high and dry, that I would train someone to take over my job, etc., for her. Of course, from a business point of view, she depends to a great extent on me. Not that I'm so good yet, but she knows I can handle clients and she IS training me to be Manager. The funny thing is that I know a girl who would be very good at it and who has expressed an interest. All this, of course, because I think that I'll be happier living in Europe, with you, or alone. I've had it with the States and it's a pity. I really liked this country a lot. I don't anymore, nor do I like the people very much either.

I'm due at the office at 9:30 until 12:30 and then I must rush into New York for a matinee of a rock version of *Two Gentlemen of Verona*. It's supposed to be excellent. On Monday I'm meeting Poppy for lunch and I must go furniture shopping with him. Grr, grr. Snap, snap! Tuesday there's a Breakfast to attend and a Seminar in the evening and a cocktail party for business. I don't like that much activity.

I adore you, and yes, yes, you DO deserve me!

Je t'embrasse très fort. Pipsi

Spain, Cortijo de las Yeguas   Saturday, March 11, 1972
My Angel,

I received a wonderful letter from you today, a million thanks. I never tire of you telling me that you love me and what is more, I BELIEVE you. I KNOW it to be true deep down in my heart and I suppose you are the kind of person I have been searching for—but I'll say no more about that right now.

I cannot understand why Deborah should be horrified at the people on the Costa knowing about you? I suppose she must be very straight. Does she think it a good thing to live a lie all one's life? As far as we know, we only have one life to live, so why not be honest as far as possible with ourselves and others? Of course, our damned stupid society has frowned upon homosexual relationships and therefore many people have led wretched lives because of guilt feelings, etc. As soon as I found out that there were hundreds of people just like me, and hundreds of people much more peculiar than me, I did not feel so guilty. I am so VERY pleased that all the people who care about me—ME—like me as a person and are not too concerned about what I do as regards sex, so long as I get it, enjoy it, am loved and love in return and hope that I'm not hurt too much and that I don't hurt anyone.

I get sick of having telling untruths about myself. The last time that this occurred was when I went to England for an interview for a post for which I had applied. It was in Sierra Leone. Naturally, after the interview, I had to undergo a medical/physical. So I went to the doctor, who was a rather sweet, elderly gentleman. After the physical he asked me a few questions such as:

"Are you on the pill?"

"No"

"Well, do you take any precaution at all?"

"No"

"Don't you think you should? After all you will be the only single woman, apart from a secretary and there are many men there on a bachelor basis."

I just didn't have the nerve to tell him that I might end up seducing the secretary! I allowed him to give me the names of various brands of the "pill" and the address of the clinic where he thought I should go to be fitted with a loop or a coil. You see, the job was MOST important to me at the time, or I thought it was and I realized that if I came out with the truth and said, "Oh, all of that is no problem because I'm a Lesbian" it might ruin the chances of being offered the post. (On returning to Spain they called me up and offered me the post but I had given it a great deal of consideration and realized that the school situation was not a good one for me, and also, there would be no other SINGLE women.)

As I said, all in all though, I think that it's better to be honest. I could not be otherwise—Irene does not agree with me—too much conditioning I suppose and great feelings of guilt.

Oh, and I think that you're very "REAL" and I think it's about time you begin to LIVE, not merely to exist! I do think that you are intense, and tense and emotional and I love it all and the tenseness began to fall away, but the time was too short. Why shouldn't you live as happily as you know how? Does it matter whether it's with whom? Different race, different religion, whatever so long as YOU are happy? Anyone who CARES about

YOU should WANT you to be HAPPY. But it's nice to know that you're the faithful type—
        Bye-bye my love, until later. Much, but much love.   Bébé

New York   Sunday, March 12, 1972   6:40 a.m.
Dear Bébé,

I received two lovely letters from you yesterday and I'm glad mine reached you, perhaps the service is improving?.

Well, I've told you about Deborah, so by now you know about that. We went to see *Two Gentlemen of Verona* and you MUST see it this summer. It was really terrific! After the show, we had cocktails at Deborah's sister's, three glasses of champagne for me and an indifferent dinner, pleasant enough I guess, it's just that I keep getting lost with my private thoughts and have to be recalled to reality. To be truthful, Marvin notices the change, very much so. In fact he keeps telling everyone that I've become serious since my trip.

...Sometimes I think perhaps you should have known me a few years ago— tougher, sort of untouchable, unwilling and unable to feel too deeply, but you are stuck with me as I am. You have changed me so much, not only since meeting you but way before, you've made me "REAL." It's the only way I can explain it.

As ever, je t'embrasse très fort, Pipsi

Spain, Cortijo de las Yeguas   Monday, March 13, 1972
My Darling Girl,

The weather is still lousy. It poured with rain most of the night and it's cold and damp and miserable. Barbie and Gino have gone off to Torremolinos and I'm fixing "savoury-rice" for the kids' lunch. No, don't get carried away by the fact that I can cook plain food, but I will make an effort sometimes, I promise!

I received a long letter from Poppy who says that you were full of lavish praise for me. (He sounds VERY pleased that we get on so well.) He also says that business was not as good as he had anticipated and he has decided to stay home. Anyway, as I've told him, I would rather he stayed home than go gallivanting around the Caribbean looking at all the girls without me! (being the selfish sort!) Well, I'm off to the kitchen. All love and kisses. Shirley/ Bébé

New York Tuesday, March 14, 1972 1:45 p.m.
Dear Love,

I don't know what's going on! Since Saturday night there's been sleet, snow, hail and thunder and lightening! It's very unusual weather. I'm home early because of the official breakfast I had to attend, after which I went to the office.

...Bébé, you do NOT make me feel pangs of jealousy. I KNOW what the situation is. And, as I've told you, I KNOW you need the two years. I may occasionally act the fool, but I'm not, really. What you MUST come to terms with as far as I'm concerned is that I'm on my way out! Nothing to do with you, and this, too, I've explained. It seems that all I'm doing is explaining to you, to Deborah, to Marikasha even—my leaving is a question pure and simple, of me, myself, for survival or rebirth. I HAVE to go. And this is what you must understand. I'm not your responsibility. I'm not leaving because of you. I'm not leaving because I love you! Will you please get that through your little head?

Can I understand you being in love or loving Irene and myself?

Yes, I guess I can, and though I rarely give advice because I don't believe in doing it, let me just say this: Don't rush out to meet your emotions or sort them out. And secondly, and most important, when someday you make up your mind, do it ONLY because of the way YOU feel! Not because of any other idiotic reasons, such as gratitude, or being charmed or whatever. I may well be Marc Neukorn's daughter but I am NOT Marc. I'm me, very romantic, very gentle, very much in love with you, but Bébé, you can't even imagine how strong and tough I really am and there's nothing in the world that can, or ever will, get me so down that, given a wee bit of time, I don't bounce right back up again. So please, worry about you, worry about Irene, worry about the world, but don't worry about me. OK? OK!

And have you read about Muskie? I'm not yet listed as one of his supporters and the poor man is lagging behind! What can you do? Throw the full weight of my charm behind Nixon! THAT should ensure his rousing defeat!

And while I think of it, I leave for Milan on May 29th and will be back on June 20. The furthest destination is Vienna. I DON'T LIKE the idea of being in Austria however!

Angel, don't worry about being confused, it will, one way or another, be OK. And since you don't have to make any decisions right now, or for a long time yet, forget it! Let's fool around instead! You in my arms with that special look on your face and me, telling you once again, I love you!

Je t'embrasse très fort. Pipsi

Spain, Cortijo de las Yeguas   Tuesday, March 14, 1972
My Angel, Sweet One,

Today you have a "breakfast" and a "cocktail" with "Go-Go tours." Here it has rained all night and it's pour-

ing now, but pouring! Irene came up yesterday to check on the horse because we have had the vet in to give him injections. She also asked me to go to lunch tomorrow.

...It is almost certain, let us say 95% sure, that Gino and Barbie will fly to New York on Monday. I've asked Barbie to phone you. They are due back here on March 29th, so I'll be in charge of the kids the whole time. I hope that we get through a lot of work as well as having fun!

...I'm overwhelmed with all these feelings for you and for Irene too. I AM honest with you too and I will always be so.

I love you very, very, much, Your Bébé

New York   Wednesday, March 15, 1972   12:20 p.m.
Dearest Bébé,

What a nice letter! No one writes like you, really! Great, that you think it's great, I mean, about me coming on the trip with you and Poppy. I don't know any of the details, length of time, etc. but worry not, I WILL manage to get away. He really does want me to come and is now referring to it as "our trip"—meaning you, Poppy and me!

I've told you about Deborah's reaction! She is really far more upset about my telling Marikasha than about you and me. She can't reconcile herself to the fact that I'm leaving. And it's no good comparing the situation between Deborah and me with you and Irene. I haven't been sexually involved in quite a while. It's also true that she loves me and I love her. She knows I'm very devoted to her and she knows that she can, and does, come to me with various problems. I'm only telling you all this and probably repeating what I've said before, because there is NO comparison between the ladies, except for bronchitis! Are they the same type? Yes, and they both love us! So what else is new?

And don't say that Irene is a little worried because this happened to her before. By your own admission, you walked in on her and found her in the arms of some visiting general, and you went straight to Delyn. And since I gather that this sort of thing doesn't happen anymore, you're not involved with me on the rebound, which is the way you started with Delyn, I think?

I DO wish that you wouldn't worry about being confused! At best, you must have expected it. Don't let it upset you. And as for Irene being splendid, I never for a moment thought she would be anything else, not from what you've told me. ...All love and kisses,

Your own Pipsi

New York   Thursday, March 16, 1972
Dear Bébé,

Hello, and this IS the first time in days that I've been able to sit quietly at this hour and write a few lines. David is home, going to school late and the dress rehearsal is tonight AND he's very excited. It certainly is going to be good. All the youngsters are very talented and both the Director and the Musical Director know what they're doing. Add to this, a really fantastic Art Department which takes care of the sets, plus a very competent orchestra, and of course the tremendous élan and enthusiasm of the kids. It's just great! The auditorium is very large and seats around 1,300 and acoustically it couldn't be much better. It is, of course, a large school with over 3,000 students. If one can ignore the misty clouds of pot that float around, it's really rather nice!

I shall now have a wee bite and a cup of coffee and take

the boy to school and make my usual tornado-like entrance into the office.

Continued: 2:00 p.m.

And thank you for your lovely letter! Wow, when you get on a soapbox, you really let go! So let's take THAT first. Yes, Deborah is very straight, this I've told you. The thought that people should KNOW about me, yes, this is what upsets her. I certainly feel no guilt and frankly I don't give a DAMN WHO knows about me. I would NOT like the boys to know about me YET. I don't think at that age, especially with David, it would be the best thing in the world. As for Poppy, I don't know what his reaction will be. You see, to me, other than the mechanics involved, I feel no need to do anything else but LEAVE! There's really nothing to be said except for an explanation to the kids and then it's just "Look, I don't love your father. It's not his fault, it's not mine, that's just the way it is."

I'm happy, I'm happy, FAR happier than I have EVER been and yes, by nature, I'm faithful, so if that's what you need, no problem, no problem at all!

    Je t'embrasse très fort, très fort. Pipsi

Spain, Cortijo de las Yeguas   *Thursday, March 16, 1972*
My Darling-Little-Big-Man,

 At last the sun is shining. There has been SO much rain and as the clouds were lifting this morning, I saw a great deal of snow on the Ronda mountains which rise behind the Cortijo.

 ...Time, time, time, there's not enough for you and me! I need more time for us! I am SO excited to think that you are going on holiday with Marc and I.

 ...You know, it's a most pleasant thought, I mean that you haven't written sexy love letters to anyone be-

fore. As a matter of fact, except for a few to Delyn, nei-ther have I. You see, all my life, I suppose, I must have been searching for my twin soul, a Woodstock-Charlie-Brown-Radclyffe Hall type, who loved me so deeply and sincerely, with tenderness and passion, one who could be SO endearing, one who thought the same thoughts and felt the same feelings, one who needed no explana-tions, one who could be moved by me, who needed my love, care and protection, in a different way from the way I needed her care and protection.

I love you very much and I miss you now, very much. Your Bébé

New York   Friday, March 17, 1972   6:00 a.m.

Sweetheart, I found it, I found it! No, NOT THAT, the Ro-drigo! I've been up since 4:00 a.m. trying to put all the re-cords in their proper jackets, and the Rodrigo WAS in its jacket with the others instead of its usual place.

Now, I'll share some nice news about David. As I write this, only you and I know. He has been accepted by the Uni-versity of Rochester! It's a fine school and certainly one of the ones he really wants to attend. Since he's not at home yet, he knows nothing about it! He'll be very happy.

I must stop for now, it's a busy afternoon because of the play tonight.

Continued: March 18   8:25 a.m.

I didn't get home until 3:00 a.m. and I was up at 7:00 a.m. The show was fantastic and I don't mean just David! The whole production was nothing short of miraculous, from the chorus on up!

As ever, with kisses and hugs, Pipsi

New York   Saturday, March 18, 1972   5:00 p.m.

Dear Bébé, Angel, Sweetheart,

SIX letters from you from the 11th thru the 14th, also one from Siri and one from Elizabeth. Now I'm going to answer them in a methodical way, because you approve of neatness (ha).

Yes, I really am going with you and Poppy on one of the trips. ...Marvin's reactions? Nothing much, only that he finds me very strange and serious. I don't think he had the time to miss me very much and anyway, he's getting used to my going my own way. David was just fine. As for Poppy, I told him of the many things we did and how tremendous I thought you were. I also tried, in a certain way, to at least start preparing him, very gently, for the fact that I didn't think that my marriage was much. I did say that I was completely indifferent to Marvin, etc. It's not too important except that I must get him used to, very gradually, to the idea that I WILL be leaving Marvin. I'm very aware of his age and of how great he is and I want to be as careful as I can be, not to give him sudden shocks or cause him pain. You will never know how much I long and wait for September and for David to go off, so that whatever type of thing starts to occur, the boy won't have to see it. Perhaps this is the Jewish mother side of me, I don't know.

Yes, Francine called up the office to speak to me and Marikasha told her that I was in Spain. There are a lot of rumors around about me but it's not important really. I'm getting the sort of thing where women come up to me at these cocktail parties and say "Are you Sylvia? I've heard about you." This isn't that new to me, there's only more of it. I admit to getting a certain amount of pleasure in answering, "Yes, I'm Sylvia and what you've heard is all true."

6:45 p.m.

...And never mind about Gino and pot and all that. Patricia gave me a marijuana cigarette when I was 18. I smoked it and nothing happened and I haven't tried it since nor do I have any desire to. I've said this to you before but I think there is a mania, perhaps especially with American, middle-aged people, where they go berserk, aping everything the kids are doing such as pot smoking, fashion, lingo, etc. I don't like to see it and frankly, I don't think the youngsters do either.

Je t'embrasse très fort, Your own Pipsi

Spain, Cortijo de las Yeguas   Sunday, March 19, 1972
7:30 p.m.
My Darling,
...So—you go to Milan on May 29th! How are you going to survive from May 29th thru to June 20th without letters from me? Is there ANY possibility of you dropping by here, ALONE while Marvin does some research or something?

And you say, "Worry about so-and-so, and worry about this and that but don't worry about ME." Darling, OF COURSE I worry about you. ...You know, when I was driving back here today, I was wondering about "us" and thinking, "I wonder where she would like to live and what does she propose WE live on?" What bright suggestions do you have Neukorn? If you think that I'll become your housekeeper while you write songs, forget it! So come on, my love, come up with some bright suggestions. I'm not too thrilled with the idea of a bar, although I have to admit that the name IS good—the "Apres Tout." I mean, I'm not a "nighttime" girl and I'm NOT prepared to leave YOU there tending bar! And WHERE are WE going to live? I really want to know, what do you think? In haste, with all love, soft kisses and caresses of passion too. Your Bébé

New York   Monday, March 20   3:00 p.m.   the office.
Dear Bébé,

    Marikasha was just called by the staff at the junior high; her son may have appendicitis, though it's more likely a virus.

    And I had an emotional phone call from Francine this morning, pledging eternal friendship and telling me all the fantastic things she's been hearing about me? She also asked why I never call her and I did get her to admit that I never have called her. Blah, blah. (Yes, I'm home now and the kid has a virus.) Francine then proceeded to tell me that she wanted our "relationship" to continue as it always had and told me to call on her for help if I needed it while Marikasha is away, etc. THEN, the manager of her office, whom I met at Mahoney's, got on the phone and the two of them proceeded to carry on like raving idiots. I don't know what's going on but something certainly is. Sylvia said that she didn't know that I sang sexy French songs and Francine kept screaming that I wasn't to sing them unless she was around! (I practically never do and certainly not sexy ones!) Either they were sloshed or it's that time of the month!

    And that's all for now.   All love, Pipsi

New York   Tuesday, March 21, 1972   5:10 p.m.
Dear Bébé,

    Did you know that the "Three Musketeers," you, Poppy and I, will leave New York around July 12 or 14 and spend seven days in Mexico City, one night in Taxco and six in Acapulco? I think the ONLY problem you and I will have is the need NOT to waken everyone in the middle of the night—I mean chatting and talking of course! Anyway, I just spoke to Poppy and this is his proposed itinerary. He's off to the cemetery tomorrow as it would have been my mother's birthday. We seldom go together as we each seem to prefer going alone. I usually go around the time of her death and at Yom Kippur. It's probably strange for a kid who wasn't brought up that way. It's some kind of vestigial tradition I guess.

...Once and for all, as far as Marc is concerned, you will never understand how happy I am in the special relationship that you two have which is unique unto itself. I enjoy hearing my father talk of you, knowing that he loves you in the way he does. I love what you tell me of my father, I do. For myself, I have to see it...because it is a two-sided view which I get. I get yours and then I get his and I haven't got my view yet. Seeing the three of us together is essential for me to be able to know how to speak to him in a certain way and what I'll have to tell him, eventually, about my marriage, about my leaving Marvin. ...I love the relationship which you have with my father. OK? OK!

As far as my love for you is concerned, I also want you to understand something. There is one thing only, that I can REALLY say that I want more than you, and I WANT YOU DESPERATELY, but more than you (and forgive the dramatic expression) I WANT MY FREEDOM! Once I have it, I will be fine. I'm fine now, but once I have my freedom, that's it, you know. Oh certainly, I could be unhappy not having you or whatever it is, but I will be far, far happier, there is no comparison. I have known this for a very long time.

It's just that once I'm alone, actually by myself and alone, I will be "home!" And so, you know, I keep my eyes, on September. This is not a question of stopping my responsibilities towards the children. Hopefully they know that it doesn't matter whether they are eighteen, twenty, twenty-five or thirty, or whatever age, if they need me, I'm there!

Je t'embrasse très fort, Pipsi

Spain, Cortijo de las Yeguas   *Wednesday, March 22, 1972*

My Darling Girl,

The weather is still behaving oddly. It looked as if it were going to rain but it didn't. So this afternoon, I took the kids onto the back road, which is as good as deserted, and I taught them all to drive the car, Gino's of course! They did extremely well. Of course, it IS understood that they will NEVER, not ever, drive the car unless they're with an adult. As we live so far out from the village, I decided that in case of a dire emergency they could cope and get some help. They did better than any adult I've taught! I just felt better knowing that all three could drive if it were REALLY necessary.

You should have received letters from all three children recently. I have no idea, by the way, of what they write. They write letters to many people and they always look forward to their mail. Living in this rather isolated place, this form of communication becomes important to them.

Your Pixie-Bébé

New York   Thursday, March 23, 1972   11:15 a.m.

Bébé,

...No, my darling, not a chance of my "dropping in" or coming over and leaving Marvin behind somewhere. It will be difficult enough getting away just to write to you. I loathe going on this trip because, here at least, our lives are quite separate, especially when he has school. I get very fidgety whenever I'm with Marvin for any amount of time. And again, I repeat, you will enjoy him to a certain degree. As Marikasha said after she heard him play the piano (at the opening of Mahoney's), "He's fantastic!"

Now "Practical Annie" "Yiddishe Mama" etc. to your pertinent questions:

WHERE I would like to live is immaterial, and really, I leave that to you. Probably in Europe eventually, after perhaps being here for a little while first. But, basically, life is not so pleasant in the States at present, and economically, very, very expensive.

As to what we would live on? Well, it depends upon a few things. First of all, I have about $5,000 a year, which at least for two years, has to go towards Steve's and David's education. There, you see, I'm a woman of property! Secondly, there is no problem about sinking from between $10,000 and $20,000 into a business. I have enough capital to use as a collateral for that. And for god's sake, keep all of this to yourself. I'll explain all this in the summer. So if you think of a business you'd like to go into, we could always discuss it, I mean apart from the "Apres Tout"! Then, too, I don't really know how you really feel about teaching? I mean, if it's really something that you love, and want to continue, then we'll adapt ourselves around that. I'll get a job and you'll teach, wherever that might be. Or, on the other hand, if you want me to support you and you want to lie on a sofa eating chocolate creams and...no, forget it, not your genre at all! All I can say is this: There is money to invest into a business. Come up with something brilliant, but it should be something we KNOW SOMETHING about!

Think about it. I can and am willing to work hard.

All love, hugs and kisses, Pipsi

Continued: March 23   8:00 p.m. in bed!
Querida,

I am tired! Can you imagine, I was at the office for eight hours today! You know what I found out? It's another ball game when you're the boss! I loved it! And I had some unexpected aggravations but it was a fantastic feeling, very nice and I like it! So, unless you decide to continue your teaching career, think of a business and the two of us can be bosses! OI!

Your own Pipsi

Spain, Cortijo de las Yeguas   Thursday, March 23, 1972 1:00 p.m.
My Darling Pips,

What a dismal day. It's simply pouring with rain, yet again, and it's cold and damp.

...If I close my eyes and think about you and that week, OUR week, various visions float across my mind. First, I see you coming out from the bathroom, all scrubbed, you looking at me, wearing your (now mine!) blue pajamas. Then I see you looking at me, no, SCRUTINIZING me across the table at the Lepanta patisserie where we stopped for croissant and coffee after I picked you up from the airport. You sitting and listening attentively at the "Hacienda" while I rambled on; you, sailing through the air; you running with the kids; you sitting on the horse, you looking down into my eyes, you at the other end of the bathtub, you striding along saying "But I'm tall, yes, I am!"

After lunch, we're going out onto the back road so

that the kids can practice driving the car. After that, we're going to light a large fire in the living room and Lise and I are going to practice our guitar playing!

Later: 7:00 p.m.

I like the "Yiddishe Mama" side to your character, your concern for your boys I mean. It's one of the things which I admire about you. I don't see you as being "overly" protective. And you know, if you ever decide that you need to leave Marvin after September, you can always come here! You know, Barbie has said so, so it's no problem at all.

As for Irene, I wonder? I truly wonder? Sometimes, like when we're in the Pourquoi Pas or with the girls from the Pueblo Lopez Restaurant, she shows a certain possessiveness where I'm concerned, etc. She'll walk hand in hand with me or with her arm across my shoulder, which is fine. Then, on other occasions she gets very uptight and says naïve things as, "Oh, do you think so-and-so suspects anything?" As Barbie says, "She should be sleeping with you because she's certainly getting the credit for it!"

Yours, as ever, with love and all my thoughts these days!

  Shirley Bébé

Spain, Cortijo de las Yeguas   Friday, March 24, 1972 7:30 p.m.
Darling,

This afternoon, I spent about an hour and a half riding the very "difficult-to-ride" horse, called Mara Hata. This is the horse on which Gino was riding when he broke his nose, on three separate occasions! She reared slightly a couple of times but nothing really worth mentioning and I sang to her the whole time. I always sing to so-called difficult horses and there was no problem, no problem at all!

...As for Francine and her office manager, Sylvia, they both sound sloshed and of course, intrigued. Don't they know ANY other Lesbians?? What ARE all the things which they're saying about you?? You always do that...dangle a carrot I mean.

I'm thinking about it very seriously, and YES, I can honestly say that I love you...and I'm waiting to see what your suggestions are as to where we should live and what we should do to earn a living, etc. What bright ideas have you come up with?

I'm just finishing a glass of wine before supper. Why can't you be here now? Now I'm beginning to think that I can't do without you! What an admission!

> *Yours, as always, with love and kisses,*
> *Bébé*

New York   Saturday, March 25, 1972
Querida,

What fantastic service! Your letter of Wednesday and Lise's were in the mail, ain't I lucky? It may be fairly quiet for an hour or so, so I'll get started in answering you at least.

Yes, of course Deborah has, as I've told you, noticed a change in me and so has Deborah's sister, Dianne, whom I hadn't seen in a while. Deborah used the word "implacable." The point is that I feel "out of it." I'm not going through the usual motions, and I think that this is what people are noticing. Not that it's been overnight, it's just gathering speed. I'm being accelerated or I'm accelerating, me within myself. I don't like it when I'm not in control of a situation. And when I say not in control of a situation, I'm not talking about you in this instance, but within oneself. I don't feel that I am in control of my own plans! And I feel that my actions actually are too fast for what I had planned and intended to do. My "toughening process" is moving very fast! My indifference is showing much faster than it should.

The approximation I had given of two years for "David's settling time"—this is animal instinct—no different really from a Mama Bird knowing when her babies will be ready to fly. And I MUST restrain myself from saying "fly" before I feel he's ready!

I am by nature NOT a philosopher. I think I'm very impulsive in many ways—not really too wise! I think the wisest thing I ever did and I will ever do was to go to Spain for that week! And that was done by instinct too! We women are sometimes not too logical, but what I've said to you just now—this business with me being in control of my emotions and so forth—believe me, I hope that I can last the odd two years, school years or not. I just hope that I can. I just DON'T know.

> All my love, and hugs and gentle kisses,   Pipsi

Continued: 10:45 p.m.

My Darling,

Well, I'm in bed! ...I hope you understand that when I say "Can I take two years?" or "I feel as if I'm moving faster than I thought I would" this has NOTHING to do with you or your questions of "Where?" "How?" "When?" "And on what!" None of the things which you say to me are pushing me or making me feel pressed for time. Do you realize this? Do you understand that if I mess up my "exit," so to speak, it won't be because of YOU but because I was not as strong or as capable

as I thought I might be? And I am being totally and completely honest when I say this. I KNOW what the situation is
for you, I KNOW your doubts, your fears, and all that! I know
WHY they are there, why you're mixed up! And this is why I
had said to you, "Don't worry about me." I mean, don't worry
about my handling MY end of this, MY leaving, MY taking
care of David and Steve. This is MY problem, only mine. You
have others, which I can't help you with.

I'm plodding like a mule but I'm not one, nor am I blind to
actions and reactions. If we decide that we will be together, at
that point, NOTHING, but NOTHING can really interfere. Do
you think that I'm not aware that my kids might, well, let's
say, reject me? Or my father? Of course, it could be, it might
be possible, but I'll tell you this: It would not last for very
long. If it did, it would really mean that, perhaps, after all, I
had not done a very good job of being a mother, or a daughter.
I don't worry about that sort of thing very much, you know.

Je t'embrasse très fort, Pipsi

New York   March 28, 1972   4:10 a.m.
Bébé,

As you will have figured out from reading this letter,
yesterday was very busy to say the least! Thank God Adele
walked in during the afternoon.

She just stood at the door and took in the scene: three
phones were ringing, five clients were milling around, I was
writing a ticket with my right hand while pointing with my
left, showing a Mrs. De Paul where Baden-Baden was on the
map. The point is that I loved it! I've learned so much in
the past few days about handling problems and people and
knowing when to get tough (yes, sometimes I'm tough!) and
when to be coy and when to cajole. Anyway it's been a great

experience and I hope that Marikasha can go to Hawaii in April, there's an Agents' trip she's trying to attend.

You know, even when it's like that at the office, like yesterday, quite hectic, you're NEVER out of my thoughts—I seem to manage all the problems and doings, with you very much there, in a strange way which I can't explain, as if you were keeping me calm in hectic situations and smiling at bewildered clients. Which, in turn, soothes everyone else and really creates a happy feeling! So you see, from your little room in the Cortijo, and from such a distance, you contribute to the welfare of travelers all over the world, and Marikasha Travel Inc. says "thank you!"

Tomorrow night I must attend a "Seder." I don't enjoy these things very much, the saving grace is that my six little grandnieces and nephews, ages 2 thru 6 will be there, and since I always sit at the children's table (to everyone's relief) I'd better remember to wear a pair of really old pants and an old shirt. It's very messy trying to feed chicken soup "mitt" noodles to little ones! And Matzohs, if you have the right technique, makes fantastic confetti!

Je t'embrasse très fort! Pipsi

Spain, Cortijo de las Yeguas   Tuesday, March 28, 1972
Evening
My Darling Girl/Little-Big-Man,

To answer your question, I don't know where I want to live. I like sunshine and so that is quite a factor. I do not think that I would enjoy living in a city, I haven't tried it in a long time but somehow I don't think I would like city life...I hate traffic and noise, it bothers me... And the thought of running a bar horrifies me. And if you think that for one minute that I'd leave you be-

hind to tend bar, then forget it! Like you say, you would drink all the profit away! I have no brilliant ideas. How about that? And if I decided to set up housekeeping with you...(of course, I'm laughing at THAT way of putting it!) I would not live on the Costa because I do not think it fair to Irene...So I don't know. I don't have an income, so I suppose I will have to teach, unless I win the lottery. I suppose I could find about $10,000 and that is about it. Oh well, we do not have to worry or think about these things right now. One thing is for sure, I do not want you to support me.

And do you realize that we'll be together, I think, in August and we can celebrate the anniversary of the beginning of our correspondence? I sent you a letter in August and I was smitten by your reply! My God, time flies and one wonders where it went!

Much love, Bébé

New York   Wednesday, March 29, 1972   3:50 a.m.
Sweetheart,

Deborah was in the office yesterday. She came to bring me a sandwich, which was very, very sweet of her. She seems to have gone through a horribly rough week with her daughter. And I joke about myself being a "Jewish Mother"—which I possibly am, to a vague extent, but you know, SHE really IS that way! She and Adele engaged in a long discussion about how tough it is to be a girl today. Nowadays, of course, when a girl goes out with a boy, after one date the boy wants to "pop into the sack." So what does a girl do when she doesn't want to? So I said "She stays home and reads a good book!" But no one took very kindly to my remarks.

But Deborah is really very, very protective of Jodi, who,

after all, is well on the way to being nineteen! I suppose I think somewhat differently and of course, I'm the mother of two sons, but Deborah turned to me in a rage after something I had said (and which I thought was rather innocuous) and responded, "Do you know about the underground sex scenes in Boston?" I told her that I didn't know what the underground sex in Boston was and that when I've been to Boston it's all above ground! There must be some 165 colleges and universities in Boston and you know, there's this huge cloud lying above the city of marijuana smoke or pot or whatever they use and she tells me of an underground sex scene. I didn't even bother to ask her what it was. She proceeded to tell me, "Don't you realize that your son is probably involved?" Hah, my Steve? So I listened to all of this but I just gave up after a few minutes.

I suppose if I had a daughter I would realize it is a very different society in which they are growing up. It's a different time now, not that I approve of all this, but the parents have to adjust one way or another because this is the society of which they are members.

Hugs and caresses and one great, big, fat kiss
Pipsi

Spain, Cortijo de las Yeguas Thursday, March 30, 1972
My Darling Girl/Boy,

Barbie is very well and the trip has done her good. As I told you last night, they are going to open a Gallery in London and Gino will be traveling to London regularly from now on. He wanted us all to go to London for a month and live in the City, marvelous, but his mother is coming here for at least a month, which he had forgotten all about! My parents are due to arrive on May 19th so we cannot all be in London at that time. Anyway, things are hopping around here! The kids love London and will be very happy to spend time there.

Somewhere you asked me what do my parents know about you? Well, when I went to England in the fall and I had received maybe two or three letters from you, I was playing the "Brel" record and I said to my mother, "You know, Marc's daughter is FAR MORE like me in EVERY way than anyone knows or realizes, including HER, I think" My mother simply put two and two together, she knows. However, I have not mentioned it since or insinuated or confirmed more. I have said little, in fact. Of course, my mother would just love to see me married. She will not discuss anything which she doesn't like. I can explain that to you a lot more easily in the summer.

All my love, Shirley/Bébé

New York   Thursday, March 30, 1972 1:30 p.m.
Dearest Bébé,

About your magic way of taming horses by singing to them, should I EVER be difficult (and I realize that I do get that way sometimes, I can become very stubborn too), sing me a song! Of course, if that doesn't work, back to the old-fashioned way, just hit me over the head!

I haven't the vaguest idea whether Francine knows any other Lesbians! Of course they're intrigued! I don't know what people are saying exactly, except that I'm one! That's easy to gauge, just from when I meet people. Whatever they're saying, I hope it's grossly exaggerated and I'm being depicted as a lecherous fiend—yea, that's really me! I have gotten the treatment about my week in Spain and what an exciting time I'm supposed to have had. (I did, I did!)

March 31   5:00 a.m.

How are you this morning? You know, when you ask me if I'm aware of what I'm saying when I tell you I love you, or is it just habit, that really makes me smile. I'm afraid I'm really a nut on the subject of "love" and have very definite thoughts about it. I think it's the rarest and most precious of all things and yet, treated most of the time in a careless way.

You can die of anguish when you're in love, waiting to see if that love will be returned and yet, once it is, it becomes just another fact and one takes it for granted and it becomes a habit and one thinks if one says "I love you" well, that's sufficient. You fall in love with someone because something, usually indefinable, with a magic element, takes absolute possession of you. And yet, when love is returned, you promptly set about trying to change the other person—and in the process, completely destroy that elusive something that made you fall in love in the first place. It's the most deceptive of emotions because it works from the outward to the inside—you meet someone and the first attraction is physical and you think, "Yes, that's a nice person" or "I like the way she looks" etc. Eventually, if it's love, it works itself into the heart. Yet other emotions such as fear, anger, start off as, exactly that, an emotion that works outwards into a physical expression, whether it's ranting and raving or screaming, with a flow of adrenalin, etc. Love is an emotion, a gift, when offered freely and openly, and yet, too often it is then locked up and not allowed to breathe. I'll continue in a while...

I hope you realize that what I'm saying on the subject of love, doesn't mean that one has to live on a cloud away from reality? Not at all, nor do arguments or even fights, have anything to do with what I'm saying. When you say, "Will you still write me letters and leave me little notes?" Yes, this is exactly what I'm speaking of...it's the little things, the nonsense, the

"Woodstock" and "Snoopy" characteristics one sees in each other, and the feelings they inspire that must be kept, the innocent and childlike aspect of it all, which are so important and should be treasured. They are possibly, in the long run, the most important aspects of the relationship and yet, somehow, always the first to be trampled on and cast away.

At any rate, all this because yes, I AM aware of what I'm saying. I DO love you, I AM in love with you, WANT you—yes, for always. Do I believe that this can or will happen? Well, I believe in love. I haven't seen much of it around, not in straight people or gay people, perhaps Marc, yes, for him it was like that! I'm not so sure about my mother though. Anyway, it's hard to judge when it's one's own parents. But even if I don't see it around, at least not MY idea of what love is or should be—if you and I don't get together, for whatever reason, I can say, yes, love is possible and yes, love does exist! And it's a far greater miracle than birth or creation or walking on the moon!

And that's enough on that subject, *et c'est tout pour aujourdhui!*

I'm glad you miss me—"Can't do without you! What an admission!" ... I just want you to be happy, a stupid way of putting it, and of course, I want to be the one to make you happy. And remember, everything IS possible.

All love, Your Pipsi

New York   Friday March 31, 1972 11:30 a.m. the office

Dearheart, A Happy Good Friday! It's very quiet, so I can write. I have no work to catch up on or to prepare.

Yes, I read the article in *Life* magazine about the woman leaving home. I don't read many articles like that, it's not a question of facing reality, not at all. Perhaps I saw too much ugliness when I was rather young, I don't know. My first experience with death, when I was only eight, was that of my little brother who died at the age of seven months or so. They said that it was "crib death." I've never forgotten it. I was in the house when it happened. We were on holiday in Zout, near to Knokker. I remember my mother screaming and Poppy weeping horribly in the garden. Later on, as I've told you, I had a rough time with Patricia's death and still later, I spent time with Rose, my mother-in-law, who died from cancer. So it's not a question of not facing reality. Besides, yes, I can understand your tears and sadness and anguish, but what about all the rest like Bangladesh, Vietnam, etc.? I know, it's too many, when it concerns hundreds of thousands or millions it's mind boggling, but reading about a single case can make the deep impression. I know, I know. I'm not hard, really I'm not.

Well, now you fall asleep when writing to me! Soon it will be when you're reading my letters! What is this world coming to?

Kisses and very gentle caresses,

All love, Pipsi

Spain, Cortijo de las Yeguas   Friday, March 31, 1972
11:30 a.m.
Querida,

Yesterday, as I mentioned, we all went off to Malaga to watch the "Holy Processions." Of course, it's one of "the" things to see here. At this time in the past, it has always poured with rain and I never went, but I joined the crowd this time. The floats were beautiful, lots of flowers, candles, gold and silver chalices, etc. It was all very impressive and parades of horses, bands and loads of people in sort of Ku Klux Klan outfits. However, hav-

ing seen it now, once is enough for me.

...As for Irene—I have not said anything to her about the situation at all. I told her that you had asked me to "marry you" and that I had answered "Ask me when you're free, and anyway, I'm going to marry your father!" The only other time that you have been mentioned, was the other day when we were riding, she asked me if I still heard from you and I said, "Yes, of course, daily, we write two or three times a day and it is like having a "twin soul"!" Nothing more was said! Frankly, I do not see the point of saying more at this stage.

I have problems that are entirely different from yours. I CARE about these TWO people. I really don't know. I mean, both of them are sweet. One I've known for a long time and the other? The other I feel as if I have known for a LONG time but it's been a short time. The one has nurtured and picked up the pieces and has put them back together again and has been VERY good to me and I love her. And the other one? I love her too! And, well, the thing is...I want them to keep loving me like that, you see, because I feel sort of safe. In some ways, I don't want to be hurt or to hurt, and I know that's unavoidable.

Also, along the way somewhere, there's an understanding, well, I'm not one-hundred percent sure you see, but there's a sort of understanding that if anything happens to Peter, Irene and I might possibly set up house together. It has been mentioned. I don't know if it were to come to that point whether she would want that or not and whether she could actually live openly in a Lesbian relationship? This is the thing that IS important now, to me. I am SICK and TIRED of pretense. I was *open a long time ago. I was open even in the oil community where most everyone knew. Delyn and I were accepted as good people. We were no longer the central topic of conversation once everything was admitted.*

I don't want to live a lie any longer. Now, on one hand I say that but on the other I would never do anything to hurt Marc! I mean I JUST COULD NOT DO IT. I was thinking about it this afternoon, when I was riding. Many of the men I have met in my life—the relationships which I've had with them all, my IDEA of them, what I've built up in my mind, the image that I have of them, has resulted, somewhere along the line in my having been always disappointed in them. Now I AM aware of Poppy's idiosyncrasies and his little pettiness about certain things, which certainly come with age and with living alone and one thing and another, but I have a lot of patience with him. But remember, he is NOT my father so I see him entirely differently. I just don't think that he's going to disappoint me as an individual, as a person. I find it very difficult to explain...

Yes, you are right, I am full of fears I suppose, but those fears are fast disappearing! You know, I was very touched by your words about you making, or rather, wanting to make me happy—that is what love is all about!

Kisses and hugs, love and happiness!
Shirley/Bébé

During April the children and I looked forward to the arrival of Celia Crossley and her three sons. John Crossley soon joined us, having flown in from Turkey. Unfortunately he received a telegram informing him of the unexpected death of his brother. John and Celia returned immediately to England. The boys remained and I organized various activities in which all the children participated with exuberance and enthusiasm. It was a great opportunity for the Hollander children to social- ize with their peers.

April

New York   Sunday, April 2, 1972   5:00 a.m.

Dearest One,

Poppy came yesterday. We discussed the Mexico trip and he told me what he wants. All I can say is, get into shape, you're going to be doing a lot of sightseeing!

There was a VERY sticky hour when Marvin came home from work. (He goes to the office on Saturday mornings.) We told him about the trip and BOOM! He clammed up and disappeared upstairs. Later, he drove Poppy to the station, came back and of course, we had a long discussion. I won't go into it too deeply. I thought he'd faint when I told him that we'd be sharing a room! He said that he was convinced that we'd go to bed and, more interestingly, told me that he wasn't sure that I didn't "swing both ways" or some such expression. When I came back from the Costa, he had asked me if you had made a pass at me and I had said that he had it all wrong and that I'd made a pass at you! We had a long talk and he asked if it would make any difference if he said "You can't go" and I said, "No." I was afraid of only one thing: that he would ask if I had gone to bed with you—afraid because I might have answered "yes" etc. This is, of course, the type of thing that I told you about, a small thing, a question, a wrong word, which might make me respond in such a way that I'll mess things up. At any rate, he called up Marc, his own idea, believe me, I had nothing to do with it, and told him he had been worried about business, etc. and of course he didn't mind my going.

And that's all, at least for now. He accepts the fact, after our conversation, that I'm very firm about doing what I want and of course, that being a travel agent has radically changed not only my way of life, but me. I should also say that I was very detached about the whole thing. Yes, I was sorry for him and I hope you can understand this—I am neither a cruel person or indifferent to feelings. The only thing I was aware of, was that I should blow it. And I guess I didn't, and so much for that!

Oh yes, I discussed further, with Marikasha, about the half-percent override. I imagine that this coming school year, September to September, I'll probably average about $6000 and this is not too bad for a start. I like the business tremendously and I think of perhaps an agency in Europe? (But only vaguely.) I don't know if it would pay or even anything about it. It's hard to get started here. By the way, YOU would make a very good agent.

I've given you a lot of news and chit chat here and no words of love. All is the same. Yes, I really care, some things DON'T change. And don't come back at me with: "But you changed your relationship with Deborah and Alexis." I know how I felt about them and I know how I feel about you! Can I help it if I used to be ignorant?

All love, Pipsi

Cortijo de las Yeguas Sunday, April 2, 1972
My Darling,

I think, just for the Hell of it, I'll go and fix myself a sweet vermouth, mainly because I'm missing you an awful lot today, an awful lot! There, that's better, it tastes good I must admit. I'm just out of the bath, having spent the day sunbathing. My legs are now sporting a healthy tan, I'm pleased to say. Everyone went off after lunch, to a stream to fish, but I decided to read and sunbathe.

You know...the way I'm feeling today, rather low, and missing you very much, feeling a great need for you and wanting reassurance...if it weren't for Poppy, I feel like getting on the next plane and saying, "The Hell with everyone except Pipsi and Bébé! Here I am!" There, I feel better already for having said it! Of course we're talking about two years...my God, the things that could happen in two years! Well, I refuse to think about it. I talk of school years because, as a teacher, that has been the way I think of it.

You ask me if I'm ever going to trust anyone again? Yes, I trust you but even you cannot be so sure that you are going to continue loving me. People's feelings change. You might not love me after you've been with me most of this summer. You have to admit that it's possible? Okay, so what I have to do is to think positive! Here I have someone who loves me, is madly in love with me and is likely to continue loving me. Right? Right!

Oh Pipsi (no, I still prefer Pips), today I have hit my low and if you were here, I would say, "Please take me away and look after me for ever and ever." You can see that I'm all "girl" today and in need of loving, comfort and security. That name, "Bébé," really suits me today. Mind you, I might be feeling entirely different tomorrow. As you keep pointing out, I am a woman and governed by emotions!

All for now, much, much love,
Shirley

Cortijo de las Yeguas   Sunday, April 2, 1972
My Darling,

I'm playing some Vivaldi....Lise is sitting here reading her Time magazine and Siri and Danielle (Herbie Kretzmer's daughter) are taking a bath in my bath water. Unfortunately we're very short of water and my bath water isn't really dirty, so it's better than nothing! I gave them some toilet water and talcum powder at which point Lise said, "My goodness, I'll come and take a bath here every night!"

Do you think that it's going to come as an awful shock to Marvin, you leaving, I mean? Has he ANY idea at all? Will you get divorced do you think? I have not asked you many questions about your marital relationship with Marvin.

You know, part of my problem, I'm sure, is that as a child I never played with myself! (Are your ears red? ... Well mine are!) It had crossed my mind that I should buy some Vaseline and try it out before the summer, after reading The Sensuous Woman but I've decided against it. I would rather that you do the experimenting! And no more nonsense about not making love while we're in Mexico. Mexico City is at a high altitude and so one has to take it easy until one becomes accustomed to it. One can get sloshed easily!

And now my darling, that is all for today. Sunday is almost over, thank goodness. I love you!   Your Bébé

New York   Monday, April 3, 1972   7:00 a.m.

Dear Heart, It's Monday, it's Monday! I love it, I always feel liberated after the weekend. Inspired by your tales of your maid's cleaning of your little Pueblo house, I've started my spring cleaning! I might add that it's probably the first time in five years and I'm now surrounded by drapes and curtains lying all over the floor, window screens soaking in the tub, a throat full of dust and I've joined you with broken nails and roughened hands! Margaret doesn't come EVERY Wednesday, but every two weeks, which ain't much.

6:45 p.m.

Your letter of the 28th reached me today. I'm not wild about owning a bar either. I lived that sort of life at least for two or three years when I was first married and I can do without it. ...You know, you're a funny little thing. You ask me so many questions such as, where will we live, and how, etc., and you get, or at least seem to get, all confused and bothered when I try to answer.

Well don't. We can talk it over, and discuss in detail all of this in the summer. It's simple enough to get the kind of information we need, here in New York. I think that perhaps you're feeling a bit bewildered and tossed about. I know how you feel about city life and noise and about not liking the cold and all that. But don't worry about all this now! I'm more delighted than ever that Celia and her boys are coming, it will be a distraction and very good for you.

Okay, I'll make love to you in Mexico! As a matter of fact, I spent the morning booking our flights and making hotel reservations and they're true "Hollywood Gothic"-style hotels! You can be sure of seeing me in a state of eternal, giggly collapse. Never mind, I'm sure we'll drive everyone insane! They'll all be wondering who the "intriguing trio" is and you'd better be warned in advance—I can get pretty mischievous when in a certain mood! I'm quite likely to lounge in the bar and sort of whisper (a stage whisper), "Oh Wow! Let's do that again, what we did last night, that was SO fantastic!" Yes? No!

What do you mean about managing with Poppy in the next room! We'll be QUIET! That's how! Unless you mean that you'll feel peculiar about it? I don't THINK he'd walk in unannounced!

April 4,   5:15 a.m.

...I think, when I said; "It's another ball game when you're the boss" I was speaking of being in charge while Marikasha was away. Until then, I did my work, and did it well, but I assumed no responsibility, nor did I have to tackle any problems. Then for those few days, I did and that worked out fine too and I enjoyed it! There had been the question in my mind of whether I would be able to cope without getting flustered and tangled up and sidelined? That turned out to be okay too. Since her return, we have been busy and I am assuming a lot of responsibility.

She is blunt and I'm diplomatic. She calls everyone, clients and all, "Honey" and I'm very correct and formal. I'm charming, she is not. She can spot someone who is just passing the time and who has no intention of taking a trip and I cannot. I'm a whiz at handling young couples, older people, and blue-collar workers, whereas she does far better than I with the middle-aged Jewish group. So you see, it's a good combination and we compliment each other. We like each other and work well together.

...Back to the boy's education. I used to worry a bit about the two years when both boys would be in college at the same time. I don't anymore, not since I'm working, I know that I can make a living, even if it's a modest one. And as for myself, my needs are non-existent, I don't care about possessions. For those I love, of course, nothing is good enough, so you see, you're right, I'm a wee bit like Marc. And I love him and Stevie and David—and I love you! These are my horizons and

I have no trouble seeing them clearly.

For you, if you feel cornered, don't! From this end, at least, will you remember that no one is asking for anything or demanding. I'm just TELLING you that you are deeply loved in everyway! And we'll talk, and talk, and talk, all summer long!

> Je t'embrasse très fort,
> Your own Pipsi

Cortijo de las Yeguas   Monday, April 3, 1972
My Darling,

Yes, I have asked you many questions and yes, you have answered and thank you and I can see that we will have LOTS to discuss in the summer!

Yes, I'm in love with you if being "in love" means that you think of someone all day long, night and day, day and night, and if one cannot begin to imagine life without them and one wants to be with them all the time! The thing which confuses me a little is that I feel like that about two people right now...it's my problem. But actually, YOU take up a lot more of my time in both thought and deed....Yes, I love you very much and what's more, of course, you have known it for a long time and so have I!

How are you coping with your house full of teenage boys etc.? I recall mixing with a crowd of students, although the guys were slightly older and from Canada, after I left college. I remained good friends with an Australian guy called Brian. He was doing his Ph.D. at Birmingham University. He fell in love with me and asked me to marry him. I liked him as a friend but that was all. I was also involved with Desiree at that time. Anyway, he went to Italy on holiday and asked me if there was anything that I would like him to buy for me from there? I said, "Yes, there's a book which is not published in England but is published there, and it can be purchased in Italy. It's called The Well of Loneliness. Of course he read it before giving it to me. He had also bought a lovely hand-tooled leather book cover for it. He wrote in the front, "To Dearest Shirley, with love and understanding, Brian." I believe he went off to the States and I know that he married and returned to Australia. He was really a very nice chap and everyone wanted me to marry him, except me, of course.

I'll get back to you later because I'm off on my bicycle and I'll be thinking of you as I pedal along.

Later: My Darling,

My thoughts of you were not interrupted by actively chattering birds, or the wind whistling past my ears, but by Mathew, a seven-year-old who wanted very much to ride with me into the village and who chats a mile a minute! So I had company.

...You asked me about faithfulness...I guess I can be too. During the time that I was with Delyn, I slept one night with an ex-nun. And does this make you smile? She was an American and also a teacher working for the Iranian oil company in Iran. We were on an Independent Schools Educational Conference, held at the Tehran Hilton. We spent a week there. Delyn was back in the Masjid-i-Suliman Hospital (I believe it was when she fell from a horse and fractured some discs in her spine?) She and I were supposed to share a room and I missed her dreadfully. As it worked out, I was together with the only other Lesbian I happened to know. It was not at all successful, we both regretted it bitterly,

I know I did, and it was just a one-night thing. I felt very guilty. I should add that I was also very sloshed, but that's not a good excuse.

I want someone who is going to be MINE ALL MINE and I will be theirs for ever and ever, AMEN.

Wish that you were going into the tub with me, flesh against flesh I mean! I'm not sending any more talc in my letters in case the mail personnel think it might be some form of "dope"!

> With all thoughts and very much love,
> Shirley/Bébé

Cortijo de las Yeguas   April 4, 1972
Dearest Pips,

Cartoons and letters galore, and yes, Vaseline as well as telepathy, because this morning I mailed a letter to you in which I had sprinkled some of my talc. I hope that it spilled all over your black pants and that it made you squirm and wiggle with wanting me! Anyway, I opened the envelope before I opened the letter and Lise saw me with this tube of Vaseline in my hands and absolutely doubled up with laughter! She said, "You're mad, absolutely mad, the pair of you!" I agreed and told her that you were concerned about my splitting nails!

As for the Vaseline—if you have a large jar of it, you do NOT need it and as I NEVER do, as you tell me (at least you say I don't), I'm going to indulge, yes I am, and see if it will work for me. I doubt it because I've never given myself pleasure that way. Well, come to think of it, I've never tried! So I'll give it a try but I wish to God that it was you! According to that book, Sensuous Woman, one should indulge more often!

I don't think that Poppy will leave New York, not at all. Where would he go? Above all, I have a certain loyalty and deep feeling for him and he comes first. How can I explain? I love Marc and did long before I met you...well you know all about that. However, I have offered to be with Marc if he should need or want me. I told him long ago, that as he treated me like one of his own, then I was prepared to do MY share, just as an unmarried daughter might, etc. Oh I wish you were here because you might read me wrong! Yes, it's an unusual trio in many ways! But I love YOU for YOU!

All my love and kisses, Shirley/Bébé

New York, April 5, 1972   3:30 a.m.
Querida,

I KNOW it's early but I really have had enough sleep and want to get back to you and your letters.

Marvin freelances on club dates. He seldom plays them nowadays, although he has three scheduled for this month. It's mostly in private clubs and he enjoys it very much. It's like having a night out with the boys, so to speak. He plays solo and sometimes with small combos. He is highly respected among musicians and really plays marvelously well.

Either Steve or David has been driving me to the office and picking me up, which means that they then have the use of the car. And no, they don't keep me very busy because they are off on their own. Steve wants to find a job in Boston during the summer. He finds Oceanside rather dull and rightly so for someone of his age, and more especially as he's inclined to enjoy big cities. He's aware that the job situation is pretty awful so he will try to get one after the Easter vacation and begin working part time. He stands a better chance, then, of being able to continue working right through the summer. As I told Steve, as long as he feels that he can handle both the studies and the job, it's fine with me. I'm really very pleased with the way he's managing. He has certainly come a long way and seems quite happy. He seems to do extremely well within the field of "Mass Communication." As his friends say, Steve is the "ideas" man. He sees things as situation comedies or cartoon strips. I think that, for him, everything is telescoped within the framework of a film screen. He is also absent-minded!

David is fine. He has been accepted at Hobart, which is a small but excellent college in New York State. He is still waiting to hear from the others, so for now, at least, it's Rochester.

I imagine it's very natural really, about your mother not wanting to discuss certain things, not unlike Poppy really. As a matter of fact, I had a long talk with Deborah. She is anxious to meet you and said that if you and I ever decided to live together, Marc would never think of it as a Lesbian relationship. She thinks that his mind would refuse to accept this and he'd probably regard it as an excellently practical idea. In fact, instead of saying "My Dear, Sweet Child," he would say "My Dear, Sweet Children!" She thinks that he will accept this far better than my leaving Marvin. She may be right? I don't know.

Later: 8:00 a.m.

"Of course I must be in love with you"—that's what you say. I know that I tease you a lot but honestly, I think that you won't really know if you are or not, until this summer. There's this damned realistic streak in me which prompts me to say these things. You've seen me probably at my best and you'll no doubt see me at my worst. Just as "our" week turned out to be important, I think that the summer will be an important time for us too, not only from the point of "you and I," but also of Marc, you and I. In answer to your question—"What do we tell Marc?"—to a degree I think that Deborah is right. If one is objective, we have to admit that the situation IS unusual—by that, I mean the man's unique relationship with you—"unique" in the sense that he's never been like that with anyone, except of course, my mother. And here I'm referring to the physical contact that exists between you, his drying your back after having taken a bath, or the kissing on the lips, or whatever. Yes, I know that for you, this kind of physical contact comes very easily and naturally. The point is, that for him, I don't think that it ever has. And granted, I don't really know. I DON'T want to step on his toes, which is why I hesitated about this trip. I don't know if he'll be the way he is with you with me around? Or, for that matter, how natural will you be with him? I certainly think that we're going to have a fantastic time and no doubt we'll drive him wild with our teasing! You see, just as you are a miracle for me, you are for him too. I don't think you realize just how much you've changed him and how very happy you make him! All of which is TERRIBLE for your ego! You'll become so conceited, you'll be impossible to live with!

> I am filled with you from beginning to end and in every way— Pipsi

New York, April 5, 1972.   12:00 noon
My Darling Bébé,

There were three airmail letters from you and I don't know whether to answer those or continue with yesterday's? Poor darling, you sound awfully unhappy. PLEASE try not to be so sad.

Will you believe that I'm doing EVERYTHING I can, but everything that is possible right now? When I say that my eyes are fixed on September, I KNOW what I'm saying. I don't go into every detail of what goes on because I see no point to it. In fact, I'm trying to hammer facts into both Marvin and Poppy.

Now, everything that I do, ticketing classes, seminars, work-related cocktail parties, etc. everything is building up to what I know has to lead eventually to a blow-up. So that, when you ask me if it will be an awful shock to Marvin when I leave him, of course it will...but not as much as you think, because HE SEES how much I'm changing. Furthermore, I told him that I was practically finished with my responsibilities and intended, quite selfishly, to do as I please. True, he thinks it's mostly my work...though long ago, he started saying in jest, that when the kids left, I would probably leave soon after. As far as sex is concerned, as long as we live under the same roof, I'll act the part of the wife. I cook, I clean, and very occasionally, go to bed. If I didn't, then the thing which I'm trying so hard to forestall, the scenes, etc., would occur and I don't want it.

And as far as Marvin is concerned, YOU are not the problem, I am, which is true and which is good. Yes, of course I want a divorce. I'm leaving and I'm leaving clean. I want NOTHING! I want no part of the house, no money, nothing!

If we're going to project, OK, we'll project in terms of school years and July of 1973. As far as loving you, I know all the arguments. I could change, I can't be sure I'll love you next year or the year after, blah, blah! Well, I'm as sure of my love for you, FOREVER, as I'm sure I'm sitting here writing this! You are everything I ever thought of in my idiot dreams and you're completely real to me. I have no illusions as to what you are or are not. You are you. Period. Entity. I KNOW!

All my love, Pipsi

Thursday, April 6, 1972
My Dearest, Darling Pips,

No mail from you yesterday and none this morning, and then, joy of joys, a letter from you this afternoon. It was a letter just like those first letters, written on cream-colored paper and the same style, etc.

...When referring to your friendship with Deborah, I quite understand what you mean when you say that "No part of that relationship remains." I had friendships like that also. I had affairs, then realized gradually that these affairs would never have worked because the women whom I loved were truly heterosexual. These affairs all sorted themselves out eventually. I remain good friends with these women. And I must admit to having enjoyed a variety of nationalities as far as my affairs were concerned!

FOR PIPSI
The memory of your gentle kiss
Caresses my cheek
Like the brushing of butterflies' wings
As they flutter softly, scarcely touching,
Reminding me of those hours of bliss.
And the touch of your firm hand
Entwined with mine, with fingers interlaced,
Those fingers which have so often traced
Familiar circling patterns over softness
On the white virgin sand.

But it is all my own. Of course you could always play around with it and put it to music, that's your department my love. Now if you were to ask me to ride in a horse race, drive in a car safari or race, sail a boat or captain a powerboat, ski or water ski, then I'm your

girl because I do those things quite well! But this kind of
thing, I'm not so good at.

Pause here, while I kiss you, yes, passionately, and
now for a tender, gentle one....

Your own Bébé

New York   Friday, April 7, 1972   3:40 a.m.
Querida,

You are SO right! Poppy ORDERED me to get cholera shots, etc. We spoke yesterday and I told him that during the Mexico trip he could look forward to having his own Greek chorus of "What can you do? What can you do?"

...About my work and what you say about lasting the two years, strangely enough, I think of it as the opposite of what you say. I don't know if I WILL last the two years and THAT mostly because of the work. When I leave here and go to the office, and I ain't going to explain this well, I walk into complete freedom. There's just me and my work—nothing of me as a wife and mother. There are none of those problems, NOTHING of all of this is with me when I'm at my desk. And I'm aware of this, very much so and it makes the rest of it, this house, this part of my life, a little bit more difficult. True, I don't think that I could function without the job but, by the same token, I cope less well within the four walls of this house. And this is what I meant when I said that things were rushing faster than I would have wished. It's all well and good to make plans and say "Two years"...my job...well that's instant freedom, every day for a few hours, but I may well need instant freedom *period*, meaning before two years are up!

The forsythia is blooming and little buds are sprouting, it's lovely.

All my love. Je t'embrasse très fort, Pipsi

Spain, Sunday, April 9, 1972
My Darling,

Right now I'm sitting outside in the same place as last Sunday, when I felt blue and wrote to you. There is a chilly wind but apart from that it's a wonderful day.

And I'm very pleased that you think that I might make a good travel agent. Open a second office? It sounds like a good idea. The more I see of people on the coast here, the more I think it's a bad scene, I really do. There's a tremendous amount of drug use and misuse of alcohol. I wouldn't want to live here or work with anyone, specifically down on the coast, it's that bad. There is something "evil" about the coast area right now, I'm serious! I feel it in my bones. Sorry, but I can't explain. Do I sound odd?

The sun has disappeared. I'm going indoors and I'll return to you later.

As ever and as always, Bébé.

New York   Monday, April 10, 1972   7:00 p.m.
Querida,

Ah the sound of munching! Actually the kid is a pleasure to feed. Give him a steak, a baked potato oozing with butter, some celery or cold asparagus, and bread and butter and that's it, he's happy!

...I don't remember what I answered about "swinging both ways," if I answered at all? But bear in mind that basically, Marvin worries far more about these cocktail parties to which I'm invited because he thinks I might get swept off my feet by some pilot or steward or something. You're right of course, he hasn't asked because he's afraid of the answer. And cool or not cool, I realized that if he did ask about women or men or both, I would have told him the truth. Stupid and

self-defeating, yes, of course it is, but this is what I'm dealing with now and this is of course, how I feel within me. As
long as I'm not asked point-blank, I can keep my mouth shut.
And this is not just where Marvin is concerned, but for everyone. I've reached the strange point where I don't volunteer the
truth...but I won't lie if I'm asked.

Your lines of poetry or lyrics are wonderful, truly wonderful.
I'm copying them down because, yes, I would like to try and put
those words to music. Thank you, I really thank you and love it!

All thoughts and all love, your Pipsi.

Spain Tuesday, April 11, 1972
My Darling Girl,

*Time, time, time, there's simply not enough of it! No
mail from you today but what a bumper crop yesterday!
Comics for Scott, a letter for Lise, and three, yes, three
letters for me from you and a wonderful little note from
Marikasha.*

*...Yesterday I phoned Irene. She told me that Peter
had gone to Rota and would be gone until Thursday af-
ternoon/evening because he went for a medical check-
up. So I suggested that she make arrangements to have
the animals fed and to come up here so that she could
ride and because I hadn't seen her for such a long time.
We had a marvelous ride and a long talk. We had also
talked a long time the night before. I told her that you
had asked me to live with you, that you were, in fact, going to leave Marvin once the boys were settled in their
respective colleges in September. I told her also that the
pending divorce had nothing to do with me and that
you had already planned to do that anyway. I told her
that I was in love with you and that I was also in love*

with her and that I was somewhat confused. She said that she was in no position to ask me to wait around... that if this is what I would like to do...I had her blessing. I was to tell you that.

Anyway, we had this very long talk and everything is much better now that I've told Irene all. She asked me how it was in bed? She also agrees with what Deborah says about Marc, that he's so pure that he would probably think that our living together would be a great thing. Anyway, we will see.

Darling, I'll get back to you tomorrow. I hate it when there isn't enough time for you, but YOU are ALWAYS there! All love, Shirley/Bébé

New York   Tuesday, April 11, 1972   4:00 a.m.
Darling Bébé,

I've just copied your poem/lyrics onto a working piece of paper so that it's there, waiting for me. I hope that I can get to it fairly soon. I think that what I miss most about not having enough time is not being able to sit quietly with the guitar and fooling around with the chords and music. I can't do it unless I'm alone. I may have told you, that up until last September or so, I had never touched the damned thing for between two and three years. So now you can add "muse" to all the rest of the ways you have affected me!

As for the aching sometimes with wanting "us" Bébé, I feel the same, it can get pretty bad. That's one of the sidelines of falling in love...it's pretty rough going at times. And shall I promise you the moon and the stars? I couldn't deliver! "Veal zingara and Palacsintaks" yes, and all my love and all my thoughts for as long as you want them!

All love, Pipsi.

New York   Thursday April 14, 1972
Bébé,

I had meant to ask you when I wrote from the office earlier today, about Iran and the recent earthquake, etc. Is this far from where you were? And are there any of your friends still working in Iran? I'll gladly go to Persepolis on mule back, or do we go in style in a jeep perhaps?

I did go to the beach and I was buffeted about by the wind and the rain. The ocean was magnificent, all gray and wild with white caps. I looked like a drowned rat by the time I came back. Water-logged is putting it mildly, so I took a boiling hot shower, came out looking beautifully pink.

Continued: Saturday, April 14, 1972 3:30 a.m.

There is an old Chinese proverb which says: "He who walks by ocean in pouring rain wakes up with running nose!"

Your word "evil" as descriptive of the Costa set off a chain reaction. I was reminded of a rather brilliant book I read a few years ago entitled *The Banality of Evil* by Hannah Arendt. It's a study of Eichman and I must go to the library and check it out.

Je t'embrasse très fort, Pipsi

New York   Tuesday, April 18   12:10 p.m.
Dearheart,

What a nice letter from you. You're MY Teddy Bear and what a nice thought, me sitting in your lap. A crushed Bébé would be the result.

As I promised, here is my itinerary: I leave May 29th and return on June 20th. As you can see, I'm not booked everywhere. I wish you COULD write but it's much better if you don't. I don't want to go—but I must get over to Europe again. I'll explain this summer.

I told Marikasha that by September I MUST go on salary. I'm not insisting on that for now because I know just how tough things are for her and also because I want to be as free as possible for the summer. She agrees and I think, is rather upset that I'm not on a salary yet.

For whatever it's worth, I feel more in control again. In control of what I'm doing at any rate, in relationship to what I do and say within the four walls of this house. I'm rather blunt and outspoken. I don't like it very much but at least it's not done out of bad temper, it's rather an expression of how I feel about certain things.

Please understand that this is STRICTLY a me-and-Marvin thing, without the boys being subjected to any of it, although I have let loose twice when they were around. It doesn't seem to have bothered them too much. I don't WANT to bitch, not even with Marvin, and I could, very easily. Yech! That's not like me at all.

...I don't know if you have read any of Andre Gide's books? I like his work as an author very much. Mind you, some of what he writes is confusing and I think somewhat juvenile but he writes that each of us, at one age or another, creates his character, his own character, and to this he remains more or less faithful for the rest of his life. And I agree with that, I think it's very true. Some don't, they don't know how. But I do believe that we definitely create a character for ourselves. Have you?

And I'm not speaking of mannerisms even, I'm speaking of something really deeper than that. Not a skin-deep thing but a bone-deep. Yes, it can be altered perhaps, slightly, but once it has had a chance to solidify, I don't think that it can change very much.

I'll continue to write later, in the morning.

Later: 3:30 a.m.

Dear Bébé,

Et me voila! Of course, I have just sat down and yes, wouldn't you know? It's a golden opportunity for Norton to be let in! He's a very annoying cat!

And there you go, all your thoughts are centered on a "girly" bar on Fire Island! There's no mistake about it, you ARE an *"enfant terrible"* and need careful watching! How should I know what we'll DO on Fire Island? But not to worry, by the summer I will be well informed! There's a most informative book about Fire Island which tells ALL. It is very nice and very *"Boheme"* and we'll have fun.

Regarding your comments about "outgrowing people," yes, it happens. You know someone for years and realize that it's all been said and they have become "fixed" in time some where along the way.

Continued: April 19, 1972   7:15 a.m.
Querida,

...I think that one of the great treats that I have to look forward to is being with you while reading or doing a cross-word and looking up every now and then and seeing you with your book or writing letters. I think of that sometimes and I'm ALWAYS filled with quiet happiness and I ALWAYS smile thinking of us that way. It's not that I don't like excitement and all that, I do. I like to go out now and then, but basically, I guess, I like peace and quiet. Does it sound awfully dull? I much prefer having a few people in for dinner rather than having a large party, though I do sometimes, usually to repay hospitality and mostly in the summer. But a small dinner for eight, maybe, including us, and YOU should decide who should come and where I can fuss a bit. I would prepare the day before, working quietly without rushing madly. THAT, I think is great fun. I also think that I'm nuts telling you all of this! I've just put myself back in the kitchen again!

All, but ALL of my love, Pipsi

Cortijo de las Yeguas   Saturday, April 22, 1972
Darling,

Sorry that I never managed to get back to you again yesterday. I took the Crossley boys to the airport and saw them off safely.

You asked me about Iran. Yes, I read of the earthquake and I do know the area but as far as I know, there are no foreign personnel of oil companies living in that vicinity. It's terribly tragic.

I should like to go with you to Isfahan, Shiraz and Persepolis, I really would. They're the only places of interest I did not go to when I was living in Iran and, of course, I'm very sorry about that now. I like to share beauty and these are supposedly very beautiful and somewhere I had planned to share with Delyn with whom I was in love. We had decided we would visit these places together. But for whatever reason, it never came about. Then, when I was in Tehran waiting to move on, I had many letters from her begging me not to leave with the Hardenberghs and saying that she would like to go with me to Persepolis, etc. and against everyone else's advice I eventually succumbed and said, "Yes, I'll go there and then we'll both travel from there overland to Holland and England." And in fact I received all these wonderful letters in which she was telling me wonderful things and saying "Please, please stay and travel with me." And when I eventually said, "OK, that's fine, I'll do that," I received an express letter from her saying

"No, No, no, don't do that. I think you had better travel out and I'll meet you anywhere you want." So then we made arrangements to meet in Bucharest at the airport, and of course, she never turned up. ...

Thanks for your itinerary, I am somewhat amused, tongue-in-cheek kind of amusement, to see that you state, very definitely, "On no condition, no, not even for you, will I go to Germany or Austria" and yet...you're spending quite some time there with Marvin! WHY?

I am pleased to know that you feel "in control" again. I want it all to go just as YOU want it to go. I'm just glad to know that you have the strength of character and the will to do this. Many people haven't! I think that it takes strength, it is time that you looked to YOU! YOU have done, to the best of your ability, your duties as a mother and as a wife, however, you have not been true to YOUR-SELF, and, as you say, NOW is the time! ...

> *Love, hugs, caresses, anything and everything! Bébé*

New York   April 24, 1972
Bébé,

For me it has to be "In the beginning there was freedom." Do you follow? Do you understand what I'm saying? Then there will be you, if you want it. If there is not you, there will still be freedom. What I do with it is not, right now, very important. The important thing is that it is irrevocable. It has been for a very long time and I know I keep telling you this. I really, really want you to understand this. You once wrote something to me to the effect that "it takes a lot of courage to leave someone unless there is someone else." It does not take courage in the way you mean it. ...I've told you I have a horror, a real horror of hurting anyone at all. But I don't, you see, have a horror of hurting Marvin. ...I don't like doing it. Heavens, I don't like hurting a perfect stranger so of course, I don't like hurting him. And as far as the youngsters are concerned, it is something to which they will adjust. I try to be rational. I try not to deceive myself. I am at fault, to a great degree, because I over-estimate the importance that a divorce plays in young people's minds. I notice this far more with Steve than with David. He is three years older and he has been away from home for nearly two years, coming home for holidays but basically he is no longer living here. I am sure it will come as a shock and something that will take a little getting used to. But in reality they are both too involved in their own lives, which is as it should be. I'm a firm believer in "little bird, you're ready to fly, go ahead, flap your wings and go!" I am not, even with all my "Yiddishe Mama" complexes, possessive in that way. I don't at all believe in the concept that children OWE their parents anything.

But in all of this, the basic thing I have to think about—much more so than the kids—will be how Marc will take it? The kids may feel shocked, somewhat bewildered and pretty awful but this will become a question of a couple of weeks or so. Believe me, I'm not kidding myself. I have thought this out very carefully. I have been looking, and observing and it will be more difficult for Marc, I think. (I'm not talking about you and me now. I'm talking about my leaving Marvin.) I don't know but I venture to say he's going to feel awfully sorry for himself, frankly.

He is ONE of the big concerns that I have. And the other one, frankly, is terribly materialistic and it is simply that I MUST earn a living! This is why I'm doing and learning as much as I can right now. A good example is this United Ticketing Course which I start tomorrow. Anything that I can get under my belt, any knowledge that I can acquire, I want to do because I think it's very important. ...

...The trouble with you, dear Hall, is that you picked the wrong people. It's a funny thing, love and relationships and lies. You see with Deborah and me, it was different, of course, because, past a certain point Deborah was always very honest with me as far as Simon was concerned. I always knew. My God, I knew Simon was there before she and I became involved with each other. I lied to her at the beginning...you know...when I began my relationship with Alexis. As I've told you, it was badly handled on my part. Later, when it was just Deborah and me, things happened... circumstances... life, one might say, interfered.

Today I think that we're fine friends. There is nothing I wouldn't do for her, well practically nothing anyway, and she knows it. She and I have known each other for ten or eleven years now and a good part of that time was as lovers. She certainly had my youth, I must say that for her. And you will like her, by the way. Besides, she's bronchial and she has a low voice, so what can you do?

But I will say this too. "Love" is a very funny thing because it is, to such a degree, an illusion! I have to laugh because you know I am, you're quite right, I am completely a "Woodstock." I am an innocent in so many ways. You know I like to think I am desperately sophisticated and I am, to a great degree. I mean, I can certainly sweep into any room or hotel and be greeted by "Yes Madam" or "No Madam" But basically I'm rather naïve. What can you do? What can you do?

Today, you know, you talk about Persepolis and Shiraz and Bucharest and I still hear the hurt. Whereas, in my case, in my mind, it happened to someone else. It didn't happen to me, and yet, I remember it kindly, without anguish, I really do.

I think of things...flashing thoughts during the day that

I must tell you and then I forget. For instance, that services are notoriously bad in Italy, everyone is always on strike, and not to worry if there's no news from me for a while when I'm away.

And I think of YOUR hectic few weeks ahead! We'd better do a lot of nice, easy relaxing this summer. How nice that we're both lazy!

Je t'embrasse très fort.   Pipsi

Cortijo de las Yeguas,   Thursday, April 27, 1972
My Darling, Darling Girl,

I'm playing the Nana Mouskouri record and it's wonderful and you are very sweet and thank you! I haven't had a chance to play the others yet, but I will...

I am very pleased that David has chosen to go to the University of Rochester, I cannot explain why except that I have a very good feeling about it... and of course, you wanted it!

...I did not know that anyone can take a folk tune and write their own lyrics to it. I mention this because Nana Mouskouri sings an old Jewish folk song and now the words are changed. I'll sing a tune for you on the next tape and ask you to put lyrics to it!

While you are away on holiday, I will write a page to you daily, and at the end of the week, I'll mail it so that when you return, there will be about 30 pages for you to read. That will be something to keep you going until I arrive!

...I'm now going to cycle into Pizarra . I need the exercise, then it will be back to you...now I'm going to think of you...don't I always?
Shirley/Bébé

New York   Thursday, April 27, 1972 4:00 a.m.
Bébé,

Me voila! The Ticketing class was fine but very tough. There were about thirty of us and I think that at least half of them won't go back tomorrow! It certainly was NOT a class for beginners... .

Come sit on my lap! If you're going to ask me reasonable questions, to which I will respond with illogical answers, you might as well sit on my lap! I said I would never LIVE in Austria or Germany. I admit that I loathe the idea of visiting these countries too! Why am I going? I feel a complete indifference to the whole trip. I just couldn't care less, it's just something I have to do. It's probably pure masochism and antagonism on my part.

I heard yet one more story about another person who has just recently returned from Austria and who said the anti-Semitism is absolutely virulent! Now, I am certainly a great believer in believing ONLY what I experience myself. I don't go along too much with listening to gossip of any kind. However, this is the seventh or eighth report that I have gotten about this. So I think that when I arrive in Austria I shall certainly check into my hotel and as I approach the desk, I may very well say in a thick Jewish accent, "I'm Mrs. Paymer. Do you haf my room ready und please, can you tell me vere is the nearest kosher delicatessen, ya?" This I am perfectly liable to do by the way! Maybe I won't but maybe I will!

...Yes, you do go on. I don't know much about strengths of character and all that, and I mistrust drama of any kind. I can only say that any strength of character I possess, I have needed all along and still do, for a while. It's not courage that's needed for me to go. For me, there is NO choice. As for being "true to myself," well, you must understand that children, to me, are very precious things. Any child is. And

I've always felt that, as much as was possible, I would like to do the very best I could for my own, and I don't speak from a financial point of view of course. I don't know if I have done a good job or not, probably middling! I am not deceived by the fact that David and Stevie's friends think I'm great. This is nothing more than being able to see things the way young people do or remembering what it felt like to be young. I've certainly been overprotective, not good, not good at all. In the long run, it's all luck. My job is finished of course. I just don't want the boys around for the messy part.

...And what do you mean "Haven't you learned anything?" What nerve! I have learned to like vermouth better than vodka. I have learned NOT to smoke so much. I have learned to BELIEVE in miracles! I have learned that 37-odd years ago, a little girl was born in Birmingham, England and on that very day, there was another little girl, a four-year-old, playing Cowboys and Indians in Antwerp. Each was growing up, going through the traumas of war, having love affairs, marriage and children for one, the other following a career and traveling the globe, but neither of us knew each other until some months ago, and never met until TWO months ago and look at US NOW! And you ask me if I haven't learned anything? I have learned EVERYTHING I know, or will ever know, in the past few months. There is no need for more knowledge! There is YOU! There is ME! And WE love! It's enough.

All my love,   Pipsi

New York,   Friday, April 29, 1972   3:40 a.m.
Bébé,

...Poppy is coming today. Of course, what you said a long time ago is true, YOU have, somehow, I cannot say brought us closer together, Marc and I, but the relationship is now altered slightly, mostly on my side. I am softer with him, it's hard to explain, nothing more than me putting my hand on his every now and then. Where I would take his arm when walking in the street, or just walk alongside him, I don't mind the contact of hand in hand too much anymore. I wonder if you will ever have such an impact as you've already had on the Neukorns? I'm sure that I often shake my head and say "unbelievable." It is very hard for rigid structures to tumble, *et me voila*! Or look at Marc! I'M smiling at you because you are so open and simple. There is right and there is wrong, that's you, I like this and I don't like that! I'm happy, I'm sad, that's you! And for someone like me, who has always been involved with shadings and "ifs" and "buts"—yes, I can say, "ah, how simple." But when you start perceiving what it means to be completely honest in feelings and emotions AND being honest in airing them, you realize that, no, it's not simple at all, but very complicated. Were you always like this, honest and saying what you meant? Forget about being open as a Lesbian, I mean about everything else? Or is this the end result of whatever you've gone through? I think you've done the impossible, brought me down to earth from my clouds. And I find the reality better than the illusions. More difficult, but better.

All my love, Pipsi

New York   Sunday, April 30, 1972 8:00 p.m.
Querida,

Would you believe I'm in one of my "click click" moods? You see, I received a lot of phone calls from different people (because they were bored!) and I had such clever remarks to make to all of them that they got quite hysterical and hung up on me! There was also an S.O.S. from Deborah, who screamed in her usual *"basso profundo"* voice, "Get over here and DO something!" I dashed over, like a nut, yes, I tripped again and now I have a bloody knee! Her cat was dead in her back yard so I had to take care of THAT! So I did, then I went into her house for a short drink and to sit and chat and sympathize for five minutes because I know what it means to lose a pet and was greeted with "Do me a favor, don't bring me any more cats! [I gave her "Peace" about 10 years ago.] So what did you do with him?" So I told her I had put him in a thick plastic bag, not a transparent one, and put the bag in her garbage can. So she threw me out of the house and told me to take myself off, together with the plastic bag and fast! And she never even said, "Thanks"! So I drove around with Peace and then I passed the house of this woman whom I don't like because she's always yelling at the kids and I put Peace in HER garbage can! Then I came back and practiced some difficult guitar chords and sucked my bloody knee!...

...I'm off to bed to read the paper and think of you. I like it that you've picked up some of my expressions. I love you *et bon soir*! Pipsi

Toward the end of April there was increased tension in the atmosphere at the Cortijo. Gino and I agreed to meet to discuss the future. He told me that I had done a great job with the children, but plans had changed. He had decided to travel with the kids and would teach them himself. (Gino was having financial difficulties at this time.) I asked him if my lifestyle and my relationship with Pipsi had influenced his decision to take over my job as the teacher. I reminded him that I had refused a job with an oil company after he had informed me that I was doing excellent work with his children and wanted me to stay. He assured me that both he and Barbie had no problem at all with the Lesbian issue. We agreed to disagree on the subject of education and peer socialization of his children. After this meeting, on May 4, I sent a cable to Pipsi:

MY SERVICES NO LONGER REQUIRED AFTER
JUNE AT THE CORTIJO. SEPTEMBER JOB
NEEDED. SMILE EVERYONE. LOVE BÉBÉ

May

    May was an extremely busy month for both Pipsi and me. She was trying hard to keep the atmosphere in her household as normal as possible because Marvin was becoming aware of her increasing independence and emotional distance. David was heavily involved in his many activities during his final days in high school. The travel agency office offered respite. Apart from planning for clients, Pipsi began making travel plans for her promised trip to Europe with Marvin as well as for our trip to Mexico with Marc.

    The children and I continued to work well together in our usual school routine. I made plans for my parents' visit in mid May. Irene and Peter had graciously invited the three of us to stay with them in the Torremolinos area from where I could commute daily to the Cortijo. I also began preparations for a move to the USA.

Cortijo de las Yeguas   Tuesday, May 2, 1972
My Darling,

    Gino asked to speak to me today, this afternoon actually and told me that he will not need me after June because he has decided to teach the children himself! He readily admitted to the fact that he wants to be ALL and EVERYTHING to his children. I told him that he was making a big mistake. I would have been much happier if he had said, "Look, I would like to change teachers next school year." That would have been nat-

ural in a child's education and I could understand THAT. He had to admit that I have done a great job as regards teaching them all this school year. His excuse is that he wants to travel with them and teach them himself. He says that he doesn't see enough of them. I pointed out to him that he saw more of his children than most fathers ever did and that he did more with them, in the way of interesting activities, than any father I knew or had met, BUT that it was to the exclusion of everyone else! I told him that I had expected it sooner or later.

I wish that I had a better way with words and could have explained myself more clearly to him. The thing which upsets me, of course, is that the children are the ones who will suffer. We did not row or anything, it was a discussion. So that is that. I KNOW how much these children have learned in the past year and how much they have grown and changed. Scott is a MUCH happier boy and he now shows confidence in the classroom and his work shows improvement, and now? Ah well, there is NOTHING that I can do. And no, my lifestyle has nothing to do with any of the above, both Gino and Barbie have always known and accepted. I also believe, and I've mentioned it before, that Gino is short of money, but that was not mentioned to me.

I have just mailed a letter to Marc and have told him that I can use the open-dated ticket because there is no bloody rush to get back...unless I go looking for a job in September. My God, you say that the future has a way of taking care of itself! It sure does! There's one marvelous thing about this, of course, and it's that you will have me for more than a couple months! Great, great...things seem to be rushing ahead!

In any event, I *DO SO* wish that Gino would leave the schooling of his children to qualified professionals, people who know how to teach and deal with them academically. I know him well enough to realize that the novelty will wear off after a couple of months, for all of them and especially for him. They will miss out scholastically and also from a social point of view because they don't often get a chance to socialize or interact with children of their own age.

One of the things which I have admired about you, right from the beginning of our relationship, is the way you are, and the natural way you have, with children. I'm sure you have done your best, in your way, for your children.

All love and kisses. Right now I *KNOW* that you're thinking about me, because I can sense it! Maybe you know that I am filled with the deepest of love for you?
        All love, Bébé

Cortijo de las Yeguas   Wednesday, May 3, 1972 10:00 p.m.
My Darling Pips
    ...Yes, I have always been open and straightforward! It bothered me for a long time not being honest with my parents as regards being Lesbian because I had always been so honest about other relationships. I suppose that, had I told them when I was younger, it would have worried them even more and I expect that they might have tried to change me. I don't know. Anyway, I was greatly relieved when it was out in the open. My sister had known from the first. So yes, I've always been open and honest, but you know, it's not always a good thing because some people don't appreciate it!

Marc is the one man whose hand I really enjoy holding, I really do. I love walking hand in hand with him or having my arm linked in his. I like sitting on his lap while he tells me that I should not have behaved in such a way...I enjoy listening to him and he fusses over me like an old hen...and from him, I like it! For the first time in my life, I feel as if I'm being "fathered." That is all quite apart from all the other feelings of respect and admiration for him as a person, etc. Of course I see some of his faults too. He is extremely impatient sometimes. He gets into a flap over silly little things, usually quite unimportant things. Sometimes he's sharp, witty, an intellect and bright. I love him dearly. I'm looking forward to holding your hands...one on either side of me, father and daughter...it sounds like a Greek drama!

Circles and soft caresses, Your Bébé

Cortijo de las Yeguas.   Thursday, May 4, 1972   11:30 a.m.
Angel,
...The relationship I have with the children at the moment is better than ever. There are no bad feelings anywhere. I do get the sense that they feel somewhat sorry, but they realize, because we have since discussed it, simply that their father's ideas and mine clash. They are aware of it and THAT is the real reason why I will not be returning next year. Lise and I talked a little about it yesterday. The atmosphere is fine really, so I hope that it stays like that. Gino is much nicer than he's been for ages, probably relieved that I'm going!

I feel as if everything is being taken out of my hands. I feel that my life is about to change, but completely! I wonder WHAT your reaction is to my news? I wonder what Marc's is? Well, I'll know in a few days!

All love. I'll write more endearingly later but the feelings are all there and you KNOW! Bébé

New York   Thursday, May 4, 1972   the office   12:00 noon

My Darling Boy/Girl,

There were two lovely letters from you this morning,, and then your telegram came at about 10 a.m. I would like to be very wise at this point, I mean really wise and say all the right things. I probably won't, however, here goes: I want you to proceed exactly as scheduled. Come, spend the summer, just as we've planned, THAT way, nothing has changed. The Neukorns want you and the Neukorns will take care of you. THAT'S speaking for the Neukorns.

Speaking from me to you, Woodstock/Snoopy/Pipsi/Shirley, just "us," since partly, at least, the summer is going to help you make up your mind if you want to be with me for always. If you decide "yes" then I'll just go. I'm being as honest with you as I'll ever be. I've been thinking in terms of either next April or around October or November of this year, it doesn't make much difference. And again, I repeat, I've been mulling it over for a while, so...it has nothing to do with your telegram. As I've mentioned to you, I told Marikasha that I must make money by September. If she can't afford me, I must look elsewhere. But now, I can at least offer myself as an experienced agent. I'm telling you all this for only one reason: That whatever you decide to do will be fine, whether I leave in April or November is inconsequential. Schedules don't mean a thing. Ah Love, all I'm saying is NOT TO WORRY, I'll take care of you, maybe not so great at first, but I will take care of you! Nothing else really matters, not "timing" or me being cool and calm and collected. Of course I'll rant and rave (with M. I mean). I like to think of myself as calm but I ain't really. I only want you not to worry. Believe me, I won't let you starve! Gotta keep your little curves nice and round! Anyway, whether you decide to be with me or not, I'll take care of you. We are friends TOO after all! Think of it, the bonus for letting me take care of you is that you'll lose a little weight! I love you! I want you. Yes, you asked and OK. I loathe the word but yes, I NEED you! OK? OK! And if things are unbearable, do a "Pipsi"— give them a dazzling smile and leave! Come NOW!

All love, always, Pipsi

New York   May 7, 1972   5:00 a.m.
Bébé,

You know, when I spoke to Marc on the phone, we were speaking of you and my job, etc. and I told him that I planned on having my summer basically free as I wanted a lot of time with you. I mentioned very casually, that you'd probably spend a lot of time here because we have the beach, the garden, blah, blah. And he seemed very agreeable about it all. About Marvin and what his reaction is going to be, you are quite wrong. He is bright and certainly talented, but there is something very basic that's missing. His lack of objectivity is appalling. When I came back from that so-called "cocktail party" held by American Airlines, I was astounded to find him sprawled on the sofa. He has to hand in his term paper tomorrow and I knew how much editing and polishing up he had to do. When I said to him, "You're not working?"—he answered, "You know I can't work when you leave me all alone!" This is, of course, the worst thing he could have said to me. I not only get nauseous, I really do, but enraged as well. THIS is the kind of thing that I've been concerned about as far as the boys' being involved, that he would use this kind of emotional blackmail on them. So I'm very watchful with the kids and VERY objective. As I've told you, I think that Steve is doing very well and of course, I speak here of realizations of self-interest and importance. I think that the fact that he wants to stay in Boston for the summer is a sign of this. And David is also starting to toughen up a bit. He may not have learned much in school this year, but he has learned a lot in other ways. I also think that the little episode with this girl and his unhappiness with the whole thing was very good for him. He is out with a different girl every week. His job as Director for *Tea and Sympathy* has put him in charge. He finds it very hard and challenging, not so much the technical side but having to cajole and threaten and having to be firm with the cast, etc. This is probably the first time he has found himself in the position of not feeling "protected" by his friends. Not that he's "wishy-washy," not a bit, but his gentleness and the slight, delicate look of him, have always led his friends to a feeling of protection and taking care of him, and now, he's taking care of THEM. As Director, he's responsible for everything of course, from the building of sets, lighting, costumes, blah, blah and he has learned to say to actors and crews "I WANT it done this way" rather than "Do you think?" So, without deluding myself as to the impact of the divorce, yes, they should be quite OK after a while. As for Marvin, I'm hoping against hope, he'll finish up his Ph.D. and find some sort of new life in the milieu, and here, I speak of social life too. There are MANY unmarried women (straight) with whom he comes into contact while doing his courses and of course he should remarry. But I can't worry about HIS future, I'm far too concerned with mine! And if that ain't a change, I don't know what is! So you see, from a formulation of plans and priorities that really started a long time ago, with ideas of what was important, the timing of what I would do and when has changed slightly—well, perhaps it's more than that. I now believe that I have overestimated the time needed for my boys to absorb all this, and certainly overestimated my ability to stick around for the next two years!

Marikasha will say to me, "How can you be so calm when everything is so complicated?" and I can only answer, But it isn't, it's all very simple." I think I'm simple, that's what I think!

And you, please watch out and look after yourself and take care and be happy because me, I love you fantastically! It's amazing, you send me sailing through the air just like that and I feel so strong!

Your Own Pipsi

Cortijo de las Yeguas   Sunday, May 7, 1972   9:30 p.m.
Darling Pipsi,

Well, I feel that having received such a wonderful telegram signed PIPSI the least I can do is to use your favorite name once in a while! After writing you a note and then writing another letter, I was walking around my room like a caged tiger, wanting the telegram and feeling frustrated at not getting it. I knew that there were a thousand things which needed my attention but my mood was such that I could not concentrate on any of it. I could stand it no longer, so at 7:45 p.m. I went down to the mail office and was delighted to hear a baby crying. The mailman lives on the premises! I knocked on the door and he came and said, "Yes, there is a telegram for you!"

NOT TO WORRY HOW ABOUT WEDDING BELLS
ALL LOVE
AS EVER   PIPSI.

You always think of the right answer at the right time! I returned home much elated and sang all the way! I ran myself a scalding hot bath, then raided the fridge for my supper and made myself fresh coffee.

Oh what a lovely telegram and it gives me a great idea, a crazy idea but a good one! When we decide to wear rings, and I know that you don't usually wear them, let's pool all the gold rings and earrings which we no longer wear and have them melted down and design two new rings? Are you smiling? I am, from ear to ear!

Continued: Monday, May 8, 1972   1:30 a.m.

Sorry there was an interruption here. The horses were all out on "leading-reins" grazing and Cancionero became entangled and also three cows with calves have escaped from the Bull Ranch and were headed this way. We've herded them back towards their own ranch.

Later: To be honest, I tell you lots of things in the letters of course, but YOU seem to have a great sense of knowing when I haven't been one hundred per cent happy. I suppose that everything changed here after Siri's birthday. Gino simply could not have me here. I find the whole thing somewhat cruel and certainly unfair in many ways because—before that, only at the end of January—I had been offered the first refusal of a good job teaching in Abu Dhabi. I told Gino of this very interesting job offer and I asked him what he would like me to do? He told me that I was doing a great job and that they all wanted me to stay—in fact he assured me that it was a marvelous arrangement and he wanted me to remain.

I know that I have done good work with these kids, damned good work and I've enjoyed it. I know what was done before my arrival and what's been achieved since and I've told you about it. I have no qualms whatsoever about my teaching ability, the work I've done with the children, the extra time I've spent with them, from my choice. It has been a good year and the children have gained from it in every way—scholastically, mentally and emotionally. There was certainly enough work for another year with them and they would have benefited. What can I say?

Continued:
My Darling,

You ask me if I like being loved so much, yes, yes, of course I do! I thrive on it! I hope you will too. You did tend to sweep me off my feet at first, but after meeting you, I realized that you were really sincere. You see, I was somewhat suspicious at first, or rather, I had my doubts. I couldn't understand why or how it was possible? I no longer doubt your sincerity and I really have great trust in you. I believe you.

Maybe we'll take care of each other, yes? These things are meant to happen I suppose...look at the timing! As you say, it's no good making long-term plans...it's all probably planned for us...fate and so far, fate has been really good for us!

I must stop now, I have more letters to write including one to Marc. For you, all my special thoughts, hugs, kisses, nose rubs, and parted lips on parted lips, Your Bébé

New York   Tuesday, May 9, 1972
Bébé,

I had all my little "honeymoon" married and unmarried couples in to see me this afternoon and they are all so excited about their trips. I know teenagers fairly well and I consider them to be a totally irresponsible, careless breed, as nice as they may be. Well I was so involved giving them advice and then Marikasha walked right past me, bent over with her hand across her mouth. I thought, "Oh my God, she's sick" so I excused myself and went into the back room area where she's bent over and absolutely hysterical with laughter! I said, "What is it? What's so funny?" and she said, "It's you! You simply don't hear yourself talk! And I said, "What do you mean? I'm simply explaining a few facts to these kids, who have never been to Europe before." And she said to me, "So why don't you go home with them and pack for them!"

The boys are around twenty-one and the girls around nineteen and they are far, far more innocent, these American children, or should I say naïve, than their European counterparts. I don't care if they are sexually active, they just seem so naïve. Realizing that each couple had booked a double room, I simply and casually asked, "Are you on the pill, because if you are, and the same goes for any prescribed medications, make sure that you take a decent supply because I don't think that you can walk into a corner drugstore and get them, especially the pill! You'll be traveling through Catholic countries and they are simply not available, so make sure that you have enough!"

And Marikasha says "Alright, but you didn't have to tell them to put them into two different jars and to put each jar in separate bags! (It's true, I do tend to exaggerate.) Of course my intentions were good and airline bags can go astray and I wanted them to have at least part of their supply! Well, what can I tell you? So, as you can see, I waste a lot of time but they are special, these youngsters

Your own Pipsi

New York   Wednesday, May 10, 1972   11:00 a.m.
Darling Bébé,

It's May 10th, yes, which brings the dreadful thought that thirty-two years ago, the Nazis attacked Belgium! You see, I remember waking up at about 4:00 in the morning thinking it was a storm. It was a Friday. We did not go to school on Thursday afternoons and my friend, Germaine, had her birthday party that afternoon. However, I also had been given a horrible homework task by one of the Bargasse sisters. My notebook was such a disgusting, vile mess and that Thursday afternoon I was supposed to re-copy everything out neatly. Unless I did, I would get into ghastly, but ghastly trouble! But there you have it! I had the choice of Germaine's party or doing my homework! Of course I didn't even attempt to work on the notebook, no, Germaine's party was far more important to me and of course I went! So I woke up that Friday morning around 4:00 a.m. and there was this most awful noise and I really thought it was a storm with fantastic flashes and rolls of thunder and what-have-you. I remember running to the window and seeing all this and saying, "How fantastic! Maybe there's going to be a terrible storm and the schoolhouse will fall down and I won't get into trouble. Thinking that everything was going to be all right, I went right back to sleep and the next thing I remember, it was about 5:00 a.m. and my poor father came running into the room yelling and shouting "Get up! Get up! It's war! It's war!"

So I sat up in bed and said: "Does that mean that I don't have to go to school?" and I'm sure I was treated to a re-sounding "Idiot!..."

All my love, your own Pipsi

New York   Thursday, May 11, 1972   5:00 p.m.

Angel,

David has just left for his dress rehearsal of *Oklahoma*. I'm going to tomorrow night's performance. His own show, *Tea and Sympathy,* will be put on next week for four days starting Wednesday. I received a letter from the Board of Education today telling me he'll be presented with an award next Thursday. I haven't the foggiest as to what it is and neither does he!

Friday, May 12   1:30 a.m.

Go ahead, ask me! Well, the reason that it's so early is that David came in around one from his rehearsal. They all went out for a bite after it was over and he managed to make quite a lot of noise, well, not a lot really, but I'm a light sleeper, so here am I! However, I'll go back to sleep in a little while, I'd better! I feel light headed.

I also feel that Nixon should be impeached! This awful business with the mining of North Vietnam harbors! There seems to be no end to this idiocy. And the lies, the dreadful lies of this Administration that they present to the public is awful and it's just unbelievable! I'm not going to go on with this subject but when you think every step and escalation of this whole conflict has been taken with the excuse that it was needed to ensure Vietnamization, including the invasions of Laos and Cambodia, which is a myth, one wonders how far self-delusion can go?!

Je t'embrasse très fort.   Your own Pipsi

New York   Saturday, May 13, 1972   6:30 p.m.

Darling Bébé,

...You asked why I didn't bury Deborah's cat? Well, I wasn't about to mess up MY backyard by digging a big hole, and

Deborah almost fainted at the thought of it in hers! Besides, all her silverware is buried there, at least seven knives and some eighteen forks. And you're saying to yourself, "What is the idiot talking about now?" Well, I told you that she is orthodox, and through the years I've often used her cutlery that was meant for meat with dairy dishes, and vice versa. When one does this, one is supposed to bury the utensil or whatever in the dirt and leave it there for a year I think. Of course, she hasn't the vaguest idea where all this cutlery is. I tried telling her to mark off a little square but everything is buried all over the garden, Lord knows where! And you see some day she might decide to dig up the silver and that's why we couldn't bury the cat in her garden! I really didn't think I ought to bury him in some stranger's garden!

... Some day I'll get it straight, I mean all the girls in your life! Obviously they're mostly Anglo-Saxon types! Dutch, English, yes, OK. French, no wonder your ego is built up! You see how easy it is for you, you only have to remember just two names of those with whom I had a relationship, whereas I'll have to make long columns of your conquests!

All love and gentleness, Your Pipsi

Fuengirola, Spain   Sunday, May 14, 1972   Evening
Darling,

I have just returned from spending a lovely evening at Winnifred's, it was most enjoyable and when one gets to know Diane, a friend of LaVeta's who is visiting from New York, she really is a riot! Anyway, I took LaVeta and Diane to the Campo de Tenis. Then we drove to Coin where we had a most enjoyable lunch in a fascinating restaurant, Muy Típico.

...No, you never sound stupid in your letters, I think

you sound very sensible. Yes, we WILL look for an apart-
ment and YES, we will look for a job for me because I
have to live with you, and you with me, we have to try
it anyway, otherwise how will we know if it works?

I think that you're right about staying in the States
for a while. I can understand your possible desire to live
in Europe, after all you're European. I certainly would
give it a try, but quite honestly I have NO idea where
I would LIKE to live. We don't have to face that NOW!
Yes, what you say to me makes sense.

I will get to New York right on your heels darling,
maybe I'll give you time to unpack and that's all!

Much, much love and many, no, ALL my thoughts,
kisses and love,

Shirley/Bébé

New York   May 15, 1972
Darling Bébé,

...I can say that if I love you WELL and DEEPLY enough,
then we're going to be very, very happy! And if I don't love
you well enough, well, you know that's impossible! In other
words, I'm saying that if you and I don't make a go of it, it
will be my fault, I won't have loved you enough! And...I cannot imagine NOT LOVING YOU ENOUGH!, This is not just
a one-sided thing, it is not just physical, you know. But it's
EVERYTHING that you ARE!

It's so silly you know, the chatterbox part of you, the
blabber-mouth, the girl who sings to young foals who are
just born, or who listens to nightingales singing on moonlight walks, or who runs madly around playing games with
children. It's just every side of you that I know well and that I
LOVE! And I think we're going to be MAGNIFICENT together, I

really do! And you know, I don't think of the future filled with
rosy clouds particularly. I have my feet on the ground but I
think that you and I are... I think we're capable of laughing.
Yes, we're capable of laughing at a great many things and
we're capable of crying. We ARE children you know. We are
children. But perhaps we're a couple of tough little kids!

You know, I ask for something which sounds so simple
and I'm asking for the most complicated thing in life—happiness! It is not something which is found often. I must sound
very, very foolish, I'm sure, and very idealistic! But it IS
THERE you know. It is there within the reach of our hands
and I, for one, certainly intend to grab it!

Je t'embrasse très fort.   Pipsi

Cortijo de las Yeguas Monday, May 15, 1972   4:00 p.m.
Dearheart, Sweetie, Angel,

*Some three letters from you today, INCLUDING
THE TICKET! A MILLION thanks for all of the above!
Needless to say, I have just written to Marc to thank
him for the ticket.*

*...Do you know—well, of course you don't—but we
were discussing over the weekend that there is a great
need in the Malaga and coast regions for a Funeral
Parlor. There do not seem to be any "businesses" of that
nature. It could prove to be a goldmine from the use by
expatriates alone! I'm serious, there are no such places
here. I can't imagine that it would be too difficult to
open such a place? It would be marvelous to have a nice
office with sympathetic staff dealing with all those details and problems relating to funerals, cremations, etc.
like they do in England or the States. Winnifred asked
me why I didn't think seriously about opening such a*

business, after all it's a service that's always needed because people are always dying! Actually I don't think I could but in all seriousness, it would be doing the "foreign nationals" here a great service.

You know, you talk glibly of walking out and not taking anything but you need to be practical over some things...and as you say, the house is one of those things! And you will have to have a "place" which has a spare bedroom or something because you have to think of the practicality of where will the boys stay when they want to visit you? They have to have a "home" to return to, particularly David who is only going off on his first year, no? I'm just thinking aloud and jotting it down, that's all....

All thoughts and SO much love, Your
Shirley-Bébé

New York   Tuesday, May 16, 1972   5:00 a.m.
Querida,

I had such a nice letter from you yesterday. ...It's extremely hard to answer your questions about the boys. Are they aware that the situation between Marvin and I isn't a good one? Well, you see, the whole point of my staying around so long, for all these years, was to try and create an atmosphere of pleasantness and ease. I suppose I created an illusion for them in which to grow. Whether, in the long analysis, I did the right thing, I don't know. I only know that I wanted them to grow up with as little discord as possible. There was enough of it between Marvin and Steve until a few years ago, and now it's OK. It's a difficult situation to explain, because anything which I have done, as far as the kids are concerned, has been done by instinct. I don't know if they realize that I'm unhappy. Perhaps they only know that I'm NOT happy and there is a difference. They do realize, and here I speak mainly of David, that things have changed since I started to work. I think that I created an illusion as a background for their formative years, when they were growing up. Whether it worked or not can only be judged later, I imagine, as time will tell. I'm convinced that they won't fall apart on account of this. What IS important, is that they are not hurt too badly. Their whole bringing-up was by my instinct and it's this instinct that continues to tell me that they'll be OK.

    Many kisses, hugs and an awful lot of love!
    Your own Pipsi

New York Tuesday, May 16, 1972 4:10 p.m.
My Darling Bébé,

  I think that one of the reasons I'm so much in love with you is that you delight me so much! I'm delighted by everything, your chatter, your questions, even your doubts, just everything, including your definite dislikes. Next summer, you and I, wherever we are, so perhaps it might not be Fire Island, but wherever it is, we'll spend some time at the beach with sand and sea and gulls and nothing but you and me and that's a promise! My first one, maybe? AND, Bébé, don't make any plans for Christmas and New Year, please don't! No, I'm not inviting you out for evenings of fun—I'm saying that I hope that you're good at Christmas tree decorating, especially a wee one! I CAN cook a goose, I can, really, and you're thinking of giving marriage a try? Good! Move in with me, oh I don't know, October, November, but let's be on our own by then! Will you think about it, or am I pushing too fast once again? I AM being logical and my head is NOT in the clouds! I KNOW that a goose is too big for the two of us to eat so we'll invite Poppy! No problem! No problem at all! (Except for taking care of your visa!)

Wednesday, May 17   3:15 a.m.

...Having spoken to Poppy last night, I know now that his latest advice was something to do with you looking for a job at one of the American military bases in Spain. He wants you married I think! Marc Neukorn, my Yiddishe Papa! Of course, he means well you know, he really does!

Continued: the office   Wednesday, May 17, 1972   2:00 p.m.

Angel,

MY GOD! YOU SAID YES! You did, you really did! "Yes, we will look for an apartment." That's it, great, just great! I adore you and I'll do everything, but everything I can to make you happy.

Continued: Thursday, May 18, 1972   3:00 a.m.

I'm glad that you understand about living in the States for a while. You are right though, I am European. But this country has changed so, or maybe I have, but the past ten years or so it seems to have gone downhill all the way, from every aspect. This latest with Governor Wallace is more of the same! And I still maintain that a country of this size and population cannot exist on a constitution which was written 200 years ago. I think that this country is bank-rupt all the way, economically, intellectually, socially and politically and I don't think that it can be saved. Too much technology and going to the moon is a magnificent achievement but not when libraries have to close down for lack of funds and not when there is no government support of theatre, music, the arts, or of the Olympics for that matter. One day this summer, we'll drive around New York and I'll show you sections which have literally been abandoned, not by people, but by government. There are no sanitation trucks, no garbage trucks, no police force, no firemen, nothing! Have some of these people brought it upon themselves? Probably, yes but there must be an answer?

Okay, I'll be quiet and stop raving! I love you, I'm so glad that you want to give "US" a try! I want to make you so happy that you'll forget there ever was a time when you were not!

Je t'embrasse très fort,   Pipsi

Hotel Las Pyramides, beauty salon   Friday, May 19, 1972   11:30 a.m.

Angel,

Such a lovely, lovely letter from you yesterday! Such a lovely, lovely letter from Marc too! He really is sweet and you have inherited all his good points!

Well, now, I'm sitting waiting for Irene. My hair has had a good washing and it's dry.

My parents are due in today, in fact soon we'll be off to meet them. Thank God the weather has improved tremendously and the sun is shining.

You know, your letter really was such a nice one and I roared with laughter at the story of Deborah and her silverware buried in the garden. Can we go on a treasure hunt?

Oh, and about the girls, or women in my life—I'll make you a list which should make it easier and then feel free to ask. OK? OK!

YOU ARE PRECIOUS! And not only to me!

Anyway, enjoy. All love, your Shirley/ Bébé

New York   Friday, May 19, 1972   11:00 a.m.
Bébé,

    Sweetheart, Angel, Love of my Life and Delight of my Soul (that's pretty good!) a FUNERAL PARLOR is NOT the salon of Madame de Stael! It's a front for a MORTUARY, and I don't know anything about such things! I certainly don't relish the thought of bodies all over the place! Furthermore, you KNOW I'm clumsy! Would we have to live on the premises? A "pleasant, sympathetic staff and a nice office" indeed! My God, you're NOT really serious are you? ARE YOU? ...

                I adore you. Your own Pipsi

New York   Saturday, May 20, 1972
Dear Bébé,

    Yah! Well, sometimes "Woodstock" ain't so brilliant! Marvin came home last night in a ghastly mood, waited until David had left the house (thank God!) and then badgered me with, you know, "What's wrong with you? Why are you so different?" I told him that I didn't want to talk about it now, but of course, that was no good, so I told him that I want a divorce, that I'm set on it and that nothing will change my mind. I also said that I wanted to keep up appearances for David's sake, etc. until the kid had a foothold in college and that meant about the end of October or so. I'm sorry, I guess that I blew it in one way but I feel very relieved in another. He realizes that this is IT. His reaction, of course, is pretty bad. I'm quite sure that he'll go along with what I asked, namely to keep up appearances. He asked me if there had been lovers and I told him that I didn't have to answer that. He asked about you, Alexis, Deborah and Suzanne—WOW! Here I told him that we were good friends and that's all. Angel, I hope you understand that I could NOT tell him the truth about that, and since that ain't the reason that I'm leaving, I want to keep "US" out of it! I did not behave like a fishwife and I was very quiet and gentle but also immoveable. He asked, and I told him that it had been years and years that I had felt this way and that the only reason I had stayed, was because of the kids. I told him that Poppy didn't know and that I would tell him when I thought the time was right.

I also told Marvin that no one knew of my decision. Bébé, this makes very little difference to the summer, except that I'll probably have more freedom to move around. I don't think that the atmosphere will be too bad.

I really would have preferred waiting until the fall for all of this but it just didn't work out that way, which makes me smile. The Captain in the King's Guard has countermanded his own orders!

The thought of you is a terrific comfort, it makes me feel, oh I don't know, calm I guess. Anyway, I'll write from the office later on. It's pouring with rain and Norton has disappeared!

Je t'embrasse très fort, Pipsi

New York   Sunday, May 21   4:00 a.m.
My Darling Girl,

...And I don't know what happened but I told you that Norton had disappeared? Well, when I returned from work yesterday, he was lying under a tree in front of the house, then he crawled in and five minutes later, he was dead. It's pathetic really. My vet is away or I would have taken him in to find out the cause. I have a feeling that he might have been hit by a car and perhaps he bled internally? I don't know. He was a very dumb cat but I liked him very much.

And the trip is still on, we're leaving as scheduled. So far, things are not too bad. I just hope that all is well and quiet today because Poppy is coming.

I wonder if your reaction to my asking Marvin for the divorce was a feeling of being scared? We're sort of out of the realm of fantasy and into reality, all this between us, our relationship I mean?

The enclosed flower, the name of which I couldn't remember, is called Daphne. Now that's a very nice English name and you, besides being a great, sexual nut, and cute besides, are also a very nice English girl.

All love and gentle kisses,   Your own Pipsi

Cortijo de las Yeguas,   Monday, May 22, 1972   10:30 a.m.
My Dearest, Darling girl,

Summer has arrived at last, and over the week-end my parents and I sunbathed.

I received two letters from Poppy and, yes, he thinks that I should try to get a job at the U.S. Naval Base. One has to be a U.S. citizen or a Spaniard for that and retired U.S. Army Generals do not have THAT much say in a NAVY Base! Dear Poppy wants to see me married. My mother is just the same! She thinks that if Marc gets used to having me around and enjoys my company so much, he might want to make the arrangement permanent! I've told her, she doesn't know Marc! I have told her that Marc made a promise to Regine (and I believe that he has mentioned this to me but I truly cannot remember) that he would NOT re-marry!

I'm not letting my mother NEAR my closets! I'm sorting them out and saying "Here, do you want this or that" sort of thing. She is a great "hoarder" and collector of things, plus she is one of the untidiest people I know! She stuffs things in drawers and closets and when one opens them and everything comes tumbling out— it's just terrible!

The American visa I have runs out in August but NOT to worry, I've been through all this type of thing before, it is a "multi-entry" visa which means that I can travel in and out of the USA until August and then stay six months, then renew the thing.. Now I have to dash off to Pizarra and mail this. I want you to get this before you leave. For now, hope you have a good, safe flight and I'll be thinking of you, I always am, so that's NOT new! My thoughts, my feelings, my love, all go with you. Shirley/Bébé

New York   Monday, May 22, 1972   4:45 a.m.
Bébé,

Good morning, kiss, kiss, kiss. Consider yourself hugged and squeezed! You should have seen Marc yesterday! Dashing ain't the word! He wore a navy-blue blazer, pale grey pants, a white shirt and gorgeous tie! He ALWAYS looks just so, but this was too much! I think he should wear a monocle! He's in a fine mood and looking forward tremendously to the Mexican trip. The day was quite OK, he only found Marvin to be somewhat subdued and I simply told him that he was a bit tired. (Marvin behaved very decently.) Steve called and yes, he has two jobs, one at Jordan Marsh in the stockroom and a part-time one as a cashier in a movie theatre. He's VERY happy and I must say that I'm delighted! It's good experience for him and of course it will give him a great feeling of independence.

David, who had been rehearsing all day, walked in with three of his friends at 3:00 p.m. I think that Poppy was shocked at how they ALL looked. I told them to look in the fridge and help themselves to a bite to eat. Oi! Locusts couldn't have done a better job! Well, this is the last few days of rehearsals and then they can all collapse quietly in a corner after that!

...And in case you're worrying about me, Poppy looked me up and down yesterday, in his usual Prussian General way, and said, "You look better than usual, not bad at all! And THAT, on his part, was a GREAT compliment indeed!

Je t'embrasse très fort, Pipsi

Benalmadena Costa, Tuesday, May 23, 1972   12:35 a.m.
Querida,

I think that you should know that I'm probably better at decorating a Christmas tree than I am at flower arranging!

I took my parents up to the Cortijo and they spent the morning chatting with Mrs. Hollander. She was glad to have someone to chat to!

...Yes, of course, we'll work something out and we'll live together, we have to now, anyway, because time is short and precious, but we mustn't rush. We'll just take it easy and we'll decorate a Christmas tree. What's a good Jewish kid like you doing—cooking a goose and decorating a Christmas tree? The next thing you'll be telling me is that on Christmas Eve, we'll be celebrating mass in St. Patrick's!

...Yes, Poppy wants me married and he mentions some 10,000 men at the Base and thinks that I might find at least one to my taste! Dear, sweet man, he just doesn't understand! And it's not surprising I suppose because he sees me as someone who is warm, kind, affectionate and I've tried more than once to explain! Ah

well, what can you do? What can you do?

I hope that this reaches you before you leave! I miss you, yes, I do! Hope you have a safe and pleasant flight. I'm very much with you, and you know that.

All love, Shirley/Bébé

New York   May 25, 1972   3:30 a.m.

Querida,

I'm going to stop by and see Deborah after work this afternoon. I don't know what's going on but she seems very troubled. I think that, partly, it's exhaustion. These last few weeks at the end of the school year are hard, not only for the kids, but on the school staff also, especially the teachers. I'll let you know what's what!

As far as Marvin is concerned, for the past two days he's been in a great mood as opposed to the previous four days during which he just sat and stared into space. I don't know how long it will last but I'm grateful for it. He does know that I'm adamant about the divorce and won't change my mind. He's also being very good about David, no innuendos or anything like that to the boy. I told him that you were arriving on the 26th etc. and all is well as far as that's concerned too.

A month from tomorrow you'll be here, it's all fantastic! I think I would be quite happy right now, just holding your hand in mine! Very soft kisses all over and I'm rubbing noses with you.

All love and thoughts, Your own Pipsi

Cortijo de las Yeguas, Wednesday, May 24, 1972   1:00 p.m.

My Dearest, Darling, Little Big Man,

I have just returned from the mail office and I received your letter of the 20th in which you tell me that you have told Marvin that you wanted a divorce. I'm not at all surprised! I want very much to be with you right now and hold you and sit you on my lap.. I don't know, of course, if you're going away as planned, or not. I expect you will feel relieved? I hope that Marvin is not being too horrid about the whole thing.

Of course, NOT A WORD to Marc. This is something that you, and you alone, can handle. If at any time you feel that I can help, please let me know what you would like me to do or say. I want to help you in every way possible. ...I must admit that I'm anxious about you. ...Like I said in one of my letters recently, everything is moving so fast lately, like events and things, that I feel as if we are like puppets on a string.

All love, Bébé

Benalmadena Costa, Wednesday, May 24, 1972 midnight
My Dearest, Darling Girl,

You know, these are the times when letters are not enough. I want to know if all is well with you and how are you coping? How is Marvin behaving? I don't mind at all that you tell me about it, in fact I want to know and you certainly don't have to apologize to me about it. It had to surface sooner or later and I was wondering just how long it would be before it all came out. Did you tell him that you didn't like men or what? Do you think that he suspects you? I suppose he must if he's asking all those questions?

You know...I realize that it's time for me to join you and deep down I know it. Yes, Pipsi, there MUST be a reason for the timing of all these events!

All love, Shirley/Bébé

New York   Thursday, May 26, 1972   5:00 a.m.
Bébé,

I really wanted to get up earlier but I just slept on and on! Really, many thanks for the cable. I had no letters in the past two days and was glad that my "news" didn't upset you.

And it was a "FIRST" for David! Oceanside has never had a "Drama Award" before and it was presented last night for the first time. Of course David wasn't there because he didn't want to leave his cast, so I collected it for him. There was a wonderful ovation from kids and parents! I was swamped afterwards with compliments about *Tea and Sympathy*. I'm going tonight and from what I hear, he has done a superb job. Even Deborah, who is notoriously critical, told me it was quite a feat. Of course I never got to see her yesterday and today is also impossible. I just want to calm her down a little and also tell her that I asked Marvin for a divorce. Certainly she's entitled to know it. You see, I want to assure her that there will be no messiness as far as she's concerned. I've told Marvin that no one knows, so I would like to advise her and keep her up to date and to be prepared. I owe her that much.

You know, it's a funny thing, here I am, really believing that "love" is something that you nurture, like a baby, feed it often, with words, with nonsense, with anything and everything that one can think of...and there's not time to write you the kind of letters that I like to write, not time for music and silly jokes and all those things and they're SO important and there's no time for it. It's not right, it really isn't! And one month from today, you'll be here! I'll feed you SO much love, you'll probably be glad to see me go to the office every now and then! And that's where I'm heading soon.

I love you.   All thoughts, Pipsi

Cortijo de las Yeguas   Thursday, May 25, 1972   1:15 p.m.
My Darling,

No mail today, but then again it's Thursday.

....Are we wise or foolish? Happiness is so very important and I want to give you that and certainly I have great love for you! I think that the whole situation, from its beginning, is truly fantastic and almost ethereal, or "out of this world." And all this timing is SO significant, don't you think?

I'm so very glad, and thankful, that you came to Spain in February although I would still have met you in the States this summer ...but now we are ahead of ourselves! The letters and tapes have been truly magnificent, wonderfully exciting, and timely in both of our lives and that part is drawing to a close. If the "living and loving" will be as good as those letters promise, then it will be "Great, just great!" as you would say, and a marvelous adventure!

Much, much love, kisses, caresses, movements, tongues entwined with arms and legs clasped around each other. Bébé

New York   Friday, May 26   3:00 p.m.   the office
My Darling Girl,

Three lovely letters from you today! And of course, you make me jealous with your sunbathing and chicken barbecue!

...Yes, Poppy told me he thinks that you should get married! Of course I ventured to say that you might not be interested but I was treated to HIS left raised eyebrow! And of course, I can see your mother looking at the whole relationship (you and Poppy) a certain way. It makes her, to me, seem very sweet and very, very human. I gather that you haven't said anything to your Mama? She'll probably say, "But Shirley, it's the father I want you to marry, not the daughter!"

Tonight I go and see *Tea and Sympathy*. I AM looking forward to it. Have a lovely time Bébé and I will try to get a bit of a tan while I'm away. Picture me thus: sitting at some outdoor café, looking at all the girls, and not really seeing them at all, because all my thoughts are with you! Your own Pipsi

Continued: Friday, May 26   6:15 p.m.

MOMENTS IN MY LIFE: Today's conversation between David and me.

Pipsi: Did you get my tickets for *Tea and Sympathy*? Are the seats   reserved?

David: Well, you can sit next to me.

Pipsi: Okay.

David: But don't speak to me!

Pipsi: Okay.

David: And don't tell me if you really like a scene.

Pipsi: Okay.

David: And also, don't tell me if you don't like a scene.

Pipsi: Okay. David?

David: What?

Pipsi: Do you mind if I sit by myself and enjoy the show?

David: Yes, I mind. You should sit next to me.

Pipsi: Okay.

This was the real conversation!

Je t'embrasse très fort, Your own Pipsi

New York   Saturday, May 27, 1972   8:30 p.m.
Bébé,

You know, I don't understand women! I really don't! Deborah just left and we've been talking for over one and a half hours. She says that she cried because of premenstrual tension! I told her about the divorce, etc. etc. I don't know, maybe there must be something that's wrong with me? Her reaction was "Jeeezus!" and then there was a whole rigmarole about taking it slowly! And THEN she says, "But nothing can stop you and nothing will and you've never looked better but you look like a mouse!" and she became hysterical with laughter!

Continued: Sunday, May 28, 1972   4:00 a.m.

I DON'T want to go on this trip with Marvin! MERDE!

And I can think of nothing nicer than you and me being together in each other's arms and loving each other and learning and discovering about each other. I still think it's funny because my "masculinity" is evident more than ever according to Deborah and yet I've never felt so soft in my life! But that's with you and it's true, I often feel very Boy and soft at the same time..

You will never know how very happy you have made me all these months. The problems? Not to worry! If we can't handle them, nobody can!

Je t'embrasse très fort. Your own Pipsi.

Cortijo de las Yeguas   *May 31, 1972*
My Darling,
We have just arrived home. We have been to LaVeta's and Margaret's in Fuengirola, for cocktails, not a party though. It was most enjoyable. We enjoyed our visit and Winnifred came along and joined us also. I invited them all to join us at Casa Kicki. This is a tiny, typical Spanish restaurant where LaVeta and Margaret eat quite frequently and it's within very easy walking distance. So I said, "Casa Kicki I can afford so you're all invited to dinner!" So I took the seven of us and we ate soup, a main meal, bread, wine and some had deserts and cof-

fee and the cost? $15! Can you imagine? I think that in the States I'll probably live on hamburgers!...

I wonder how you have enjoyed your holiday? I received a letter from you today dated May 26th, so I have no idea, at this very moment, as to where you are? And today, on the Spanish Radio News Broadcast, I caught the fact that there was a plane in Rome and that there were terrorists belonging to the Palestinian Liberation Front who had opened fire at the airport! Oh my God, my heart skipped a beat! And then I realized that it was either an El Al flight or an Air France flight going from Rome to Tel Aviv and that all these horrible acts had taken place in the Tel Aviv Airport. WHAT ARE PEOPLE THINKING OF? It's all so shocking. All those poor people just standing there being slaughtered! But I must say that when I hear about a hijacking, and it seems to be the fashion, my heart goes into my mouth when I know that so many people are traveling at this time by air. I just keep my fingers crossed.

Much, much love, Bébé

My parents and I enjoyed our wonderful vacation together with Irene and Peter. I explained to my parents why my job with the Hollanders would end in mid June. I emphasized that Pipsi had decided, long ago, to leave Marvin and had told him she wanted a divorce. I also emphasized that I had played no part in her decision to divorce him. They returned home during the first week of June, happy in the knowledge that I would spend a week with them prior to my departure for the States.

At the end of May Pipsi left for Europe. (Marvin followed a day later—they always flew separately.) She sent cards to the

Hollander children and a few letters to me.

Before my departure from Spain, I was busy from morning to night organizing the many personal details involved in planning to relocate from one country to another. I rented my house. My car, some furniture, and personal effects were stored in Irene's garage. Other items had to be packed and mailed. I DID find time to write to Pipsi, which was always a priority.

June

Cortijo de las Yeguas   Thursday, June 1, 1972   10:30 a.m.
My Darling,

I would have loved to have seen the performance of Tea and Sympathy. David seems to be a very talented boy.

My mother has heard your record and she enjoyed it. I have also told my parents that you will probably get a divorce and that you have only stayed with Marvin until the boys are settled in at college, etc. I don't want her to be surprised at this news when she finally hears it. I think that she realizes. She knows that I'm extremely fond of you and that I'll probably live with you but we haven't discussed it further than that! She has an idea that I will be in the States for quite some time.

My parents leave tomorrow. They have thoroughly enjoyed their visit and Irene and Peter have been wonderful hosts, they all got on very well, so the whole thing has worked out well.

There is no school today because it's another religious holiday celebrating "Corpus Christi." I haven't a clue what it's all about but I saw that all the streets in Pizarra were lined with palm branches and tree branches were against the walls and there is to be a procession of sorts.

... And you can say that again, about me changing my life...I know it, gosh, how I know it! People say,

"How long will you be away?" and I reply, "I don't know but maybe forever!"

All love, wiggly thoughts, caresses and kisses, Your Bébé.

Cortiijo de las Yeguas   Thursday, June 1, 1972   1:00 p.m.
My Darling,

At last, confirmation that you made it as far as Geneva! Thank goodness I got that letter, together with one mailed on 29th May from the States. ...

No...I have never been searched but do remind me to tell you of the occasion when Delyn and I returned from one of our marathon overland drives from Holland to Iran. We were almost in Abadan, on the actual border between Iraq and Iran and were virtually held captive by the Iranian border guards! We were kept in "quarantine" and left incommunicado for at least ten hours! I made a fuss about calling the Dutch and English Consulates and eventually the guards used a field-type telephone and contacted the personnel at the oil refinery. They were only doing their job because there had, indeed, been an outbreak of cholera in Iraq! The Iranian head of the personnel department came out and rescued us but only by giving his solemn word that we would be quarantined in the Oil Company Hospital in Abadan for a week! He kept his word!

I see that the FBI is going to employ women now that J. Edgar Hoover is dead? Did you know that he was gay? I read that his second-in-command is dying from a broken heart?!

Much love, as ever, love, love and then some! Love Shirley/Bébé

Postcard: Liechtenstein   June 3, 1972
Dear Hall,

You deserve this card! You're always bragging about weird places you've been to like Iran, Qatar, Guatemala, and Rumania (shades of Elvire Popesco). Anyway, I bet you have never been here! Yes? No! I'm off to Austria in the morning. I'm eating like a pig and sleeping like a log! Yes, and burping a lot too. Not to worry, you'll hear from me from Vienna. I'll let you know if the Danube is really blue, or have you been there too?

Love, Pipsi

Post card: Venice   June 6, 1972
Dear Shirley,

Yes, well the Danube ain't blue at all! Neither is the Grand Canal I might add! And this is just to let you know that I'll be waiting for you at Kennedy airport. Of course me, being me, I'll be on time, not like some people! Right? Right! And please give your parents my regards.

Take care, much love, Pipsi

Benalmadena Costa   Monday, June 5, 1972
My Dearest One,

No mail from you today but a lovely letter from Marc mailed to this address. Now he suggests that I see what is available in Gibraltar as the climate is most agreeable and it's near the Costa, etc. and there are plenty of army and navy personnel there, etc. ... So I have just replied, thanking him for his concern and suggestions but saying that he should give up any ideas of seeing me married and that the only MAN

I have ever had "tender" feelings towards has been him! I also added that I was not joining this get-mar-ried-at-all-costs campaign so that there would now be more males available for those male-hungry women! I told him that I was happy enough in my own way. (I did not tell him what that was) and that the days of women marrying for financial security were long over. He is a dear and I thanked him again for his concern but said that if he wouldn't marry me then he should not think of foisting me off onto some other fellow!

All love, Bébé

Hotel Astoria   Thursday, June 8, 1972   6:30 a.m. (Thank God!)

Bébé,

Did you get my cards and letters? I hope so, it's awful not getting letters. The days seem to be crawling though I'm on the go constantly. I'm doing a lot of sightseeing and walking and I am sleeping well and Marvin is being rather decent but it's all very idiotic and stupid! I'm sure you must have wondered WHY I went ahead with this trip? One reason, of course, is to keep up appearances since I'M the one who asked Marvin to do this for the next three or four months. And the other reason, well that's one of those things which I'll explain once we are together.

If you're having doubts about how much I love you, don't! I love you and that's all there is to it!

Je t'embrasse très fort, Your own Pipsi

Benalmadena-Costa,   Saturday, June 10, 1972   11:45 p.m.
My Dearest Pipsi,

This evening I packed a box full of your letters. Of course all these boxes will arrive and I have only the vaguest idea of their contents! However, I remember the shape of this special box containing the letters and the box containing the vibrator!

...My God, only one week to go and I leave for England. I can hardly believe it! There is still a lot to do and I would love to be finished by mid-week so that I can relax for a couple of days.

My Angel, I'm going to read a while. Sixteen days and less by the time you read this and my lips will be brushing yours for real! Je t'embrasse très fort!

Benalmadena-Costa   Saturday, June 17, 1972   11:45 p.m.
Darling Girl/Boy,

I drove up to the Cortijo this afternoon to collect schoolbooks, saddles, bridles and other paraphernalia and the car is still full and it all has to be sorted and repacked! It will be a miracle if I ever get on that plane tomorrow! I have sent off yet another package, this time, my typewriter! Well, it has played a big part in this relationship so I just had to make sure that it goes with me!

The transportation arrangements for Cancionero have been arranged and he will be trucked down to Fuengirola on July 1st and housed in the stable there. I will pay for half of his keep, some $25 per month but I'm going to suggest to Irene that maybe we should sell him after Christmas...I just don't know and it's not an immediate problem.

I know that my life is about to change...right now, I would like to curl up close and have your arms around me...I want to be protected...Mind you, I might feel like the protector when we meet on the 26th.

Love, kisses, love and all my thoughts and then some! Bébé

Sutton Coldfield, England   Monday, June 19, 1972
My Darling,

Well, welcome back to Oceanside! How are you? I am fine apart from a stiff arm and the feeling that there is going to be a definite reaction to the cholera, typhoid and para-typhoid shot I got this morning!

Darling, I simply can't believe it, that I'm on my way to the States and that I'm leaving a week from to-day! I do so hope that all went well for you and that you had a good flight? Oh, will I be glad when we are there, both of us, together where we belong!

Do you think that I could get a job as a courier, es-corting all these helpless Americans on their first trips abroad—anywhere? People tell me that I would be good at that.

My thoughts are with you and I think that for "US" we have to be together NOW. Maybe the Gods are on our side?

All love, as ever, Bébé

Milan Airport   Tuesday, June 20, 1972   9:15 a.m.
Darling Bébé,

How good it was to speak to you with a clear phone con-nection! I think that I never was so scared as I was yesterday morning. There were only Italian newspapers and there was that awful headline about the BEA crash. I can't describe what I felt during the moments in which I was trying to decipher what it meant exactly and then discovered that it was a London/Brussels flight! My God, I can well appreciate what your poor parents must have gone through too! Anyway, thank God you're OK.

Thank you for being home when I called. Have a good flight on Monday and don't get confused when we meet, or do, it doesn't matter! I mean I'm pretty shaken up just from hearing your voice, so you can well imagine how confused I'll be! Plus you'll be taking note of my driving! Oi!

You know I think that ESP will ALWAYS work for us!

Je t'embrasse très fort, Your own Pipsi

Sutton Coldfield, UK Wednesday, June 21 1:00 p.m.
My Darling,

I sent you a brief note yesterday while I was in town shopping. I simply had to sit down and write a few words to you now and hope that it might reach you before I do!

The weather here has been really very cold, and I mean COLD. There have been very heavy showers and cold winds. Last night I went with my sister and Ivan to hear some local jazz band which was pleasant and the jazz was good. This week will not go quickly enough and yet I wouldn't have missed it.

...My mother knows now. I told her yesterday. She could see that I was very happy and she knows that come what may, we will not hurt Marc. That was one of her concerns.

...Take great care, you are more than precious. You

have promised to take care of me, love me, and cherish me, remember? I'm looking forward to that! Will Mon-day ever come?

All love, Bébé

Oceanside   Thursday, June 22, 1972   4:30 a.m.
Cheri/Cherie

I finally landed at 11:00 p.m. Tuesday! WOW! I'm referring to my joy when I saw my desk drawer full of letters! I took half of them to read on the train and when I came back to the office after meeting Poppy, I took the rest!

Everything was shipshape here. David quit his job and together with Don has rented an ice-cream truck. (My son the entrepreneur!) This truck is now parked in my driveway and plugged into the garage so that the ice cream doesn't melt overnight!

You ask, "Was your mother gentle?" because of Poppy's reference to her. No, she wasn't, at least I didn't find her so. I don't think she liked me very much. She herself had a miserable mother. I'm past the age of passing judgment on people because there are too many things involved. In my father's eyes, she was a saint and that's the way he sees her. For me, she remains a foolish, spoiled woman, very much a snob impressed with her family name and all that. Yet she suffered, having had two children who died and two who lived who never understood her. That's the regret, you see, that if she were alive, I would be so much nicer to her.

June 23, 1972   4:15 a.m.

...Yes, vibrators, let's discuss vibrators...what do you mean, you've swapped? I think that's awful! You do the most outrageous things, yes, you really do! I think it only fair to tell you that before you use that vibrator on ME, I'll do my proverbial Jewish trick. I'M BURYING IT IN THE BACK YARD!

All my love and gentle kisses and yes, little, soft circles and arms and legs all intertwined. And sleep well my love,

Your own Pipsi,

Oceanside   Saturday, June 24, 1972   5:00 a.m.
Bébé,

I think that if I could, I would tiptoe around for the next two days and speak very, very softly. I feel so...I don't know how to put it but I have a light-headed, heavy-chest sort of feeling and I do not feel in control. I feel frightened, I want you here now! I know it's an anxiety about the plane and the flight. You know, I won't feel easy until you've landed.

Continued: June 24, 1972   10:00 a.m.   the office
Angel,

I am VERY glad that you told your mother about us. I wish that I could do the same—and I hope she will like me. You know, except for Poppy, and the kids, and this ONLY because of their age, I don't give a damn who knows I'm a Lesbian. As far as Marvin is concerned (except that I'm uneasy about his reaction, again, in regards to the boys and Poppy), I have no qualms about telling him. I have told him, or rather, repeated, that I will NOT answer questions now. He IS pushing hard but I told him that after David leaves, I'll answer anything he wants to know. I do think that it will come to that, but we'll talk about it, you and I. The only thing that I would lie about to him would be about Deborah, out of respect for her. I don't THINK he would tell Marc, David or Steve, and I can get pretty tough if pushed hard enough and he KNOWS this. He really hates Deborah and I won't do anything to leave her vulnerable to whatever he might do. I'm seeing her tonight at my house and she will probably pop over here to the office with coffee and a sandwich. I have told her to be careful because anyone who sees us together, I mean you and me, will know. She also maintains that she's quite capable of handling people like Jewel and Francine, etc.

Yes, I do know that you love me but will you after this summer? Yes, you will!. And you know, about my promise to love and cherish and take care of you, this is not a promise that you must EVER worry about! You're part of me, you're my life I guess, it's the only way I can put it! Except to say that perhaps as much as I need my heart beating to live, my brain working to think and my hand to hold this pen, yes, I NEED you like that too!

Yes, we'll both be shy and yes, we'll stare and stare! Not to worry about your confusion, you think YOU have problems? I'll be afraid to smoke for at least three hours before you arrive! I feel faint at the thought! I think I'll take my toothbrush along and smoke like a fiend beforehand! Then I'll dash into the loo and brush like crazy!

And there's so much love, so much love and tender feelings.

Always you own Pipsi

JUNE 26! 7:00 a.m.   WOW! WOW! WOW!

Are you curled up in your seat and sucking your thumb? I'm mentally sucking mine! Bébé, I'll see you in a few hours. My heart is going thump, thump! Will you remember that all my feelings, and all my love are real, and that it's you I'm in love with and NOT an illusion and that everything is going to be fine! And I don't just believe this, I KNOW it!

Thank you for "US" until now and for the "US" that is about to begin!

Je t'embrasse très fort.

All love as ever and for always, Your own Pipsi

After spending the week with my parents in England, I traveled to London where on June 26 I boarded BOAC flight 501bound for New York. The culmination of all our correspondence left me exhilarated, excited and exhausted. I collapsed into my window seat.

As promised, Pipsi was at JFK to meet me. We hugged each other with relief and happiness. One journey had ended. A new Journey was about to begin.

Epilogue

Marc, Pipsi, and I enjoyed a wonderful vacation in Mexico. During the last week of the holiday, Pipsi told her father of her intention to divorce Marvin. Marc was taken aback and irritated by the news, but Pipsi explained she had decided on this long ago, and that nothing he said would change her mind. She said nothing about her sexual orientation at this time.

In late July, when Pipsi, Marc, and I flew back to New York, an obviously angry Marvin confronted us at the airport. He took Pipsi aside and informed her that he had been to Marikasha's office and had taken two suitcases containing all of the letters and tapes I had sent from Spain. After we dropped Marc off at his apartment, we drove to Rockville Center where I checked into a hotel. Pipsi contacted a lawyer on the following day and filed for a divorce. She insisted that Marvin immediately return all the letters and tapes.

In August I moved into a small apartment in Manhattan. After David left for college in September, Pipsi, with letter-filled suitcases in hand, joined me there. Her anticipated period of transition, during which she would live alone, never materialized. She soon found a job as a travel agent on Wall Street. I was hired as an office manager for a small company on 55th Street and shortly thereafter obtained my Resident's Permit.

Marc was pleased that we had both found jobs and could manage financially. One evening, he invited Pipsi to his apartment. To her father's direct inquiry, "Are you a lesbian?" she replied that she was and that she had recognized it long ago. She went on to explain that once she was married, she felt a strong responsibility to her two boys and wanted them to grow up with their father. She also explained that it was she who initiated the relationship through correspondence and in no way was I responsible for the breakup of her marriage. Furthermore, she explained that as both boys were now in college, she would have divorced Marvin in any case. Within a few weeks, Marc gradually came to understand that our relationship was one of love and commitment. It also helped that other family members living in Manhattan had accepted our relationship.

During this time, we maintained an easygoing relationship with Steve and David, who felt free to bring their friends over to stay with us for the occasional weekend. Our relationship with the boys has remained mutually loving and caring to this day.

After Pipsi's divorce was finalized in the summer of 1973, we went on vacation to Europe to visit family and friends.

In August of 1974 we purchased a Ford Pinto station wagon and set off across country to San Diego where I had been accepted at the United States International University. Pipsi soon found employment as a travel agent, which she enjoyed. After attaining my Master's Degree, I returned to the field of education, initially as a Resource Teacher for a Migrant Education Program and later as an elementary school teacher. I retired in 1993. Pipsi retired in 1995.

We continue to live happily together in our home in La Jolla, California.

As for:
MARC NEUKORN
Marc visited Pipsi and me quite often in Southern California. He had a close, happy relationship with us and enjoyed

meeting our many friends. He remained in communication with my parents and with the Hardenberghs. In 1978 he succumbed to lymphoma and was buried next to his beloved Regine in Westchester, NY.

MARVIN PAYMER

Marvin took my advice and went on a cruise where he met Edie, whom he married in 1973. He died of lung cancer in 2002.

DEBORAH ROSEN

Pipsi introduced me to Deborah and her husband Simon (who never learned of Deborah's extramarital relationships) in July, 1972. Deborah continued teaching until her untimely death from melanoma in 1977 at the age of 52. (After Deborah died, Simon retired and moved to Florida. Pipsi remained in touch with him until his death.)

ALEXIS BLUMBERG

Alexis and Michael Blumberg moved away from Oceanside in the mid-sixties. Alexis died in the mid-seventies from pancreatic cancer.

PETER HARDENBERGH

In 1973, Peter was diagnosed with terminal cancer. He and Irene traveled by military transport to Washington, D.C., where he was admitted to Walter Reed Army Medical Center. I went to Washington every weekend to give Irene moral support until Pipsi and I left on our European vacation. Shortly after our departure, Peter died. He was buried in Arlington National Cemetery. Marc Neukorn attended the funeral.

IRENE HARDENBERGH

Upon learning of Peter's death and of Irene's plans to return to Spain, Pipsi and I arranged to drive to Madrid where Pipsi and Irene met for the first time. Pipsi and I then drove Irene to her home in Torremolinos. The three of us remained close friends and visited each other frequently in Spain and California. Irene died from metastasized cancer in 2001. She was buried next to her husband Peter in Arlington National Cemetery.

IRENE AND ERNEST HALL

Pipsi and I arranged to meet my parents in Switzerland for a vacation in 1973. Both Rene and Ernie accepted Pipsi and loved her right from that first meeting. During the 70s and 80s, we regularly visited one another's homes. Ernie died from cancer of the liver in 1987, at the age of 72.

After Rene began showing definite signs of dementia and was diagnosed with Alzheimer's, I began making regular twice-yearly trips to England to help her and to relieve other family members. Each winter we arranged to have Rene brought to the warmer climes of California. She thoroughly enjoyed basking in the sunshine and the hospitality shown by our large circle of friends.

Despite the family's goal of trying to keep Rene in her own home for as long as possible, her deteriorating physical and mental condition necessitated a move to a small care facility. She passed away peacefully in 2004 at the age of 88.

GINO AND BARBIE HOLLANDER

Pipsi and I had no contact with the Hollanders for quite a number of years. We met briefly during the 80s when Gino and Barbie attended an exhibition of his paintings at a gallery in San Diego. We then renewed contact as a result of an

Internet search I initiated. Gino and Barbie reside in Aspen, Colorado. Both are in their eighties and still active. Gino continues to paint and Barbie continues to write. They maintain close ties with their children and grandchildren.

The Cortijo de Las Yeguas, the Hollanders' home in Andalucia where I lived and taught from 1971 until June 1972, is now owned and operated by the Municipality of Pizarra as a public museum. Exhibited there are antiquities collected by the Hollanders as well as a few of Gino's paintings.

JIM HOLLANDER
Jim is a successful photographic journalist who has lived in Israel since 1983.

LISE HOLLANDER
Lise recently married for the second time and lives near her parents in Colorado.

SIRI HOLLANDER
Siri lives outside Taos, New Mexico where she rides daily. She is a successful sculptor who specializes in large equine pieces. One of her first works stands outside the Malaga Airport in Spain.

SCOTT HOLLANDER
Scott works in Hollywood in the film industry as a key grip and cameraman. He is a keen sportsman who enjoys rock climbing and skiing. Scott's photography reflects his passion for the wilderness. He got married in 2007.

CELIA AND JOHN CROSSLEY AND FAMILY
Pipsi and I have remained good friends with the family I have known since I taught at the Oil Company School in Ah-

waz, Iran in 1964. Celia and John live in Surrey, England and enjoy frequent visits with their sons and grandchildren. The Crossley boys remain in contact with us.

MARIKASHA

Pipsi and I regret that we lost contact with Marikasha.

STEPHEN PAYMER

Steve graduated from Emerson College in Boston with a degree in Communications. After working for NBC in New York, he moved to Los Angeles where he became a successful sitcom writer and actor.

DAVID PAYMER

David attended the University of Rochester for two years. He then transferred to the University of Michigan at Ann Arbor, from which he graduated with a major in Theatre Arts and Psychology. He lives near Los Angeles where he has built a successful career as a film and television actor and also as a television director. He is happily married and has two daughters.

We are in very close contact with both Steve and David and his family, and exchange visits frequently.

And time still passing...passing like a leaf...time passing,
fading like a flower...time passing like a river flowing...time
passing...
and remembered suddenly, like the forgotten hoof and wheel....
Time passing as men who never will come back again...
and leaving us, Great god, with only this...
knowing that this earth, this time, this life are stranger than
a dream.

—Thomas Wolfe
The Hills Beyond

ISBN 142516518-4